ONE LIFE

ONE LIFE

———

TOM LAMPERT

Harcourt, Inc.

Orlando   Austin   New York   San Diego   Toronto   London

© Carl Hanser Verlag München Wien 2001
English translation copyright © 2004 by Tom Lampert

www.HarcourtBooks.com

This is a translation of *Ein einziges Leben*.

Library of Congress Cataloging-in-Publication Data
Lampert, Tom, 1962–
[Einziges Leben. English]
One life/Tom Lampert.
p. cm.
Includes bibliographical references.
ISBN 0-15-100716-0
1. World War II, 1939–1945—Atrocities.   2. Holocaust, Jewish (1939–1945)
3. War criminals—Germany—Biography.   I. Title.
D805.A2L2613   2004
943.086'092'2—dc22   2004009223

Text set in Sabon
Designed by Cathy Riggs

Printed in the United States of America

First U.S. edition
A C E G I K J H F D B

CONTENTS

FOREWORD

An old man is led to the guillotine—a seventy-four-year-old
pensioner with a chronic hip ailment, advanced arteriosclerosis, and high blood pressure. Six months earlier, in the late
summer of 1942, he wrote the following inscription on the interior wall of the public toilets at Mariannenplatz in Berlin: "Hitler,
you mass murderer, you must be murdered, then the war will be
over." He is condemned to death for high treason. Is he an elderly
man with diminished mental faculties? The victim of an unjust
and arbitrary legal system? A resistance fighter?

The accounts in this volume reconstruct the lives of a disparate
group of individuals who lived during the Nationalist Socialist era
in Germany. The book is based on extensive research, in particular unpublished materials from institutes, archives, and government agencies in the United States, Israel, Germany, Poland, the
Czech Republic, Switzerland, the Netherlands, and Austria. Although I have organized the materials for these eight accounts into
narratives, they have a strictly documentary character, containing
neither invented dialogue nor subjective forms of narration that
are not based on evidence such as personal correspondence or the
statements of the people involved. Even terms and expressions,
along with chapter and section headings, have been drawn in

nearly every case from existing evidence (when longer passages are cited completely, I mark them as quotations; when passages are slightly abridged, I do not). As far as possible, the material has been presented to the reader without explicit commentary; I have tried to limit my own judgments to the structuring of the material into narratives. In some cases it was possible to reconstruct relatively complete life histories; in other cases, the reader is presented only with the circumstances and interpretations of a person's final act.

Although the protagonists of the stories have been known to scholars of National Socialism for some time, they have received little attention to date, remaining marginal figures. Various reasons could be given for this. Some individuals are too "insignificant," their lives not measuring up to the standards of heroic resistance or historical infamy. After the war, for example, records of a theft and fraud trial conducted against Mirjam P., the young Jewish woman in "White Lies," were destroyed because authorities deemed that they were not "worthy of archiving." The relatively prominent figures have remained marginal in large part because their actions do not fit cleanly into the accepted categories used to interpret the National Socialist era. The longtime Nazi and anti-Semite Wilhelm K. was deeply involved in the extermination of Jews in White Ruthenia, but at the same time he fought—in vain—to rescue of a number of German Jews deported to Minsk. Karl L., the one person K. was able to save, headed the Jewish Ghetto Police in Theresienstadt and conducted a relentless battle against theft and corruption in the camp community. To this day L. remains a controversial figure. Fifty-nine years after the liberation of Theresienstadt, there is still no scholarly investigation of his activities in the ghetto.

My decision to write these accounts as narratives rather than as conventional scholarly analyses or documentary reportage requires some explanation. In the course of researching the book, I sensed that the narrative form would be more appropriate to the subject matter, allowing the complexity and ambiguity I found latent in the documentary materials "greater space to unfold." And this, I hoped, might in turn alleviate some of the moralizing pressure, which almost inevitably arises when dealing with such issues, to "speak out" or to "take a stand"—imperatives that make it difficult if not impossible to think concretely about National Socialism or the Holocaust. Formulaic abstractions that identify individuals as evil perpetrators or innocent victims—as if victims of Nazi persecution are less victims if we find in them moral transgressions or human weaknesses—may ensure that readers reach the "right" conclusion, but they can also suppress uncomfortable or inconvenient facts and thereby prevent us from learning anything significant about the past. In these stories, I have sought to avoid didacticism of this kind. The opportunity to think independently—a book can offer its readers no more than this.

ACKNOWLEDGMENTS

I would like to thank the following people for their support: Arthur Strum, Isaac Kramnick, Karen Kenkel, William David Weinberg, Rebecca Egger, Jo Anna Butler, Pamela Selwyn, Volker Strümpe, Reinnhard Pauls, Andrea Kunkel, Petra Eggers, Annette Wunschel, and, above all, Steffie Schulze.

Arthur Strum assisted me in translating this book into English.

Material from Karl L.'s Compensation and Restitution files is used with the permission of his sons.

ONE LIFE

———

WHITE LIES

In September 1933, Mirjam P. emigrates from Germany to Palestine.

Earlier in the summer, her mother, sensing the impending threat of the new era, sent for the fifteen-year-old, requesting that she return home to Berlin from the city of Jena. P., banished to a reformatory school and youth sanatorium on the outskirts of Jena for the previous year and a half, has long been considered a "difficult child." After her parents' divorce in the early 1920s, she was raised by her doting grandparents. When her mother remarried in 1929, P. returned to live with her. The stepfather, a lawyer, proved to be a strict disciplinarian. P. was convinced that he didn't like her, although the stepfather refused to admit it. She wasn't fond of him either and made no effort to hide it. After a fight with her mother in February 1932, P. wanted to run away. She took money from her mother's purse, then decided not to leave after all, giving part of the money to her friends and spending the rest foolishly. Afterward, she was sent to the Trüper'sche Home on the Sophien Heights near Jena. When P. returns to Berlin eighteen months later, preparations to leave the country have already begun. Shortly thereafter, daughter, mother, and stepfather travel to Tel Aviv.

Promised Land

P. has difficulty adjusting to her new home. She finds the heat (not infrequently over one hundred degrees in the shade) inhuman—only early in the morning and late at night is it somewhat bearable. Instead of forests and trees, there is brown desert steppe as far as the eye can see. The roads are different as well: one doesn't so much drive them as careen from one pothole to the next. There are new languages to learn, Hebrew and Arabic. In spite of this, P. is determined to make a new start and not to cause any more trouble.

False Start.   P. lives with her mother and works in the kitchen of a children's home. Everything goes well at first. After a while she begins to neglect her job, which isn't really very interesting. She's dismissed and finds a new job working in a private household, which she soon loses as well. The mother divorces the lawyer; her relationship to P., however, does not improve. In the fall of 1934, P. takes money and clothes from her mother and travels to Haifa to her biological father, who has also emigrated to Palestine. After a few days, she returns to Tel Aviv, rents a hotel room, and commits a series of petty crimes, buying expensive clothing in a number of stores under her mother's name. The debts that P. incurs are discovered, but the case never comes to trial. Her mother requests assistance from Child Welfare Services in Tel Aviv, which arranges for a detailed examination of P., including evaluations by two medical specialists.

The specialists take the case very seriously.

First medical evaluation (Dr. Ernst K., Tel Aviv): "The 16-year-old pubescent P. presents an advanced case of a serious psychopathy with pronounced ethical defects. She lies, incurs debts, and has stolen repeatedly from her mother and from her friends. She has run away from home a number of times, most recently with money and clothes from her mother's locked dresser. She roams the streets and is in danger of becoming morally depraved as a result of her strong sexual drives. In order to avoid further violations of the law, she must be admitted to a mental institution as quickly as possible. Since such an institution does not exist here, it is absolutely essential that she be sent back to Germany immediately. I recommend that she be required to report with this evaluation to Professor Seligmann, Director of Public Health for the Jewish Community, upon her arrival in Berlin."

Second medical evaluation (Dr. H. H., Medical Director of the Psychiatric Hospital Esrath Nachim, Jerusalem): "P. is a psychopath with severe ethical defects and insufficiently developed powers of judgment. She tends to thievery and vagabonding, incurs debts, and has already developed the character traits of a swindler. On the other hand, she is very agile intellectually, knows how to present herself well, and is at times very trusting and receptive to instruction in the best sense. According to both her mother and herself, she sometimes works very diligently. In order to avoid the threat of moral depravity, it is urgent that she be admitted to a remedial educational home. On the basis of my 10½ years of experience here, I know that no such institution exists in Palestine or in the neighboring countries. It is therefore *absolutely necessary* that the patient be sent back to Europe without delay for the purposes stated above. Otherwise, serious damage to the patient herself, to her family, and to society as a whole will be unavoidable."

Second Chance.   Child Welfare Services in Tel Aviv is able to place P. with a private remedial educator in Jerusalem. Later she is transferred to a home for girls, where she is under constant supervision and receives special instruction and treatment. P. struggles to fit in, without success. The director of the home sends her back to her mother. In Tel Aviv, P. finds another job in a private household but after a few weeks she begins to roam the streets, live in hotels, and incur debts. She is arrested, put on trial, given probation, arrested again, put on trial again, and finally expelled from the country. Her father tries in vain to stop the deportation order. In October 1936, P. is sent back to Germany. Her mother cries at her departure. P. doesn't believe her tears.

Alone and On the Move

Homecoming.   In Berlin, P. stays with her grandmother. There are plans to travel with relatives to London, but these come to nothing. After three weeks, P. leaves Berlin, fearing the Gestapo will put her in an education camp.

On the Road.   From Berlin P. travels to Luxembourg, where she looks for work. She finds a job through the Jewish welfare services. After three months, she is forced to quit. As a German citizen, she can't get either a residency visa or a work permit. P. leaves Luxembourg for Belgium. While looking for work in Antwerp, she meets a young man and becomes involved with him. The relationship quickly sours. P. travels from Belgium to Holland, where she looks for work for three weeks but finds nothing. From Holland, P. sets out for Switzerland, where she doesn't look for work at all.

By Other Means.   At the end of March 1937, P. arrives destitute in Zurich. She manages to rent a room in a modest hotel and borrow 10 Swiss francs from the owner. She tells him that an acquaintance has stolen 100 francs from her and promises to pay the money back when her husband arrives. As collateral, she offers a worthless ring. Four days later, P. leaves the hotel without having paid her bill. She goes to a pension, where she rents a room under the name Frau Bühlmann and persuades the manager's husband to lend her 15 francs. She tells him she's in Zurich with her eight-cylinder Ford automobile and wants to buy gasoline with the money. She promises to pay him back soon; she is expecting her husband, an actor, any day now. In passing she mentions that she has an engagement in mid-April in a new revue at the Corso Theater. After a few days, P. leaves the pension with a debt of 53 francs. She is reported to the police and arrested the next morning. For twelve days she sits in the Zurich District Jail. On April 28, 1937, she is expelled from Switzerland. A policeman drives her to the German border. Two months later, the Juvenile Court in Zurich convicts P. in absentia of repeated petty larceny and sentences her to the twelve days she has already served in prison.

Conflicting Accounts

A German policeman picks P. up at the Swiss border and drives her to the train station in the German town of Singen. He releases her there. In the vicinity of the station, she encounters Wilhelm R., twenty-eight years old, from Stuttgart, who is on business in the area. P. asks him about hotels. He offers to drive her to Constance. Since P. seems to have no plans for the immediate future, R. takes her along on his business trips and lets her do promotional work for him. Their personal relations become intimate. Ten days later, the two arrive in the town of Schwenningen, where they stay in the Hotel Kurhaus for a week. P. tells R. that she doesn't want to remain in Germany, that she would like to go to Hungary or France. R. promises to accompany her abroad. They continue on to Stuttgart, return briefly to Schwenningen, then travel to Munich. In Munich, R. gives P. money and leaves her in a hotel. She is supposed to wait for him, but he doesn't return. Soon the money he has given her is gone. P. travels to Stuttgart to look for R., committing a series of petty crimes along the way. In Stuttgart she finds not R. but his wife, whom she robs as well. In Baden-Baden, still looking for R., P. rents a hotel room under a false name and leaves the next day without paying the bill. In Karlsruhe she finally meets up again with R., who more or less promises to accompany her to France. Shortly thereafter, P. is arrested.

In August 1937, the Regional Court in Karlsruhe finds P. guilty of theft and repeated fraud in Munich, Baden-Baden, and other localities and sentences her to eight months in prison, which includes her three months of pretrial detention. She serves the remaining five months of her sentence in the Aichach Women's Penitentiary in Upper Bavaria.

During her trial in Karlsruhe, P. claims to have had sexual relations with R., which he emphatically denies. The senior district attorney in Rottweil initiates an investigation of R. on charges of *Rassenschande* (defiling the race). At the end of September, R. is arrested. Interrogated again, he denies having engaged in sexual intercourse with P. but does admit to a number of indecent sexual acts, which in themselves constitute sexual relations as defined by the Law for the Protection of German Blood and German Honor.* Only the subjective dimension of the case remains to be clarified; that is, the question of whether R. knew that P. was a Jew when he had sexual relations with her. P. claims that she informed R. of this fact before the indecent acts and that R. saw her birth certificate and passport as well. R. vehemently denies this account. However, the senior district attorney has reason to doubt R.'s credibility. R. assured his wife there was nothing between P. and himself, while at the same time he told P. that he was not married. Furthermore, the district attorney finds it suspicious that R. drove P. to Munich and gave her money even after he dis-

---

*The Greater Legal Panel for Criminal Matters (12/9/1936): "The term 'sexual intercourse' as used in the Law for the Protection of German Blood and German Honor does not include every indecent act but is also not limited to coitus. It includes all natural and unnatural forms of sexual relations, therefore in addition to coitus, all sexual activities with a member of the opposite sex, which are intended to satisfy, in place of coitus, the sexual drives of at least one of the persons involved."

covered that she was a Jew. "He [R.] really had no reason to do this if he felt that P.'s claim to be an Aryan was a lie. Had R. known there was a possibility that P. was a Jew and nevertheless entered into sexual relations with her—this alone would constitute a crime."

The trial against R. is held before the Regional Court of Rottweil in December 1937. On the witness stand, R. finally admits to having engaged in sexual intercourse with P., who appears as a principal witness during the trial. She testifies that on the day they met she informed R. that she was a Jew. This occurred, she explains, in the following way. The German policeman who had picked her up at the Swiss border happened to be sitting in the restaurant where R. was staying. He greeted her, and R., curious about their acquaintance, asked her how she knew him. P. then told him of her expulsion from Switzerland. As they continued to talk about her plans for the future, P. mentioned that as a Jew it was difficult for her to find work in Germany. That same day, she showed R. her passport, and he said he didn't see how her religious or racial affiliation was indicated on the document. P. explained that this was evident from the double underlining of her family name. R. disputes this story. He claims that he became aware of P.'s religious affiliation only during their second brief stay in Schwenningen; that is, after he had already engaged in sexual intercourse with her. By chance, he saw her birth certificate and noticed the entry "Religion: Mosaic." P. told him that this wasn't correct, that she had it added to the document in order to get a job in Palestine as an actress. Then she tore up the birth certificate. The whole thing seemed suspicious to him, and later he related his suspicions to several acquaintances, who verify this in court. Following this, he gradually ended his relationship with P. He drove her to Munich only because he wanted to get rid of her.

The court finds P.'s version of events plausible. Her claim that R. was aware of her racial affiliation seems to be supported by the fact that, on their arrival in Schwenningen, he paid to have her dark blond hair died light blond. During the trial, the judges determine that P.'s racial features make her easily recognizable as a Jew. R. himself concedes that during encounters with acquaintances, they pointed out to him that his companion was Jewish. In spite of these suspicions, the court cannot bring itself to believe P. completely. The judges are not convinced that this very intelligent and crafty young woman—who was completely dependent on the assistance of others at the time in question and who was ready to join up with the next available person—would have told a complete stranger the extremely compromising fact that she was a Jew. The court cannot find sufficient evidence that R. acquired knowledge of P.'s true identity before engaging in sexual intercourse with her. Two days before Christmas, he is acquitted of all charges.

Between Colleagues

The Israelite Bavarian Welfare Office in Munich is assigned by the court to supervise P. following her release from prison in Aichach. At the beginning of December 1937, while she is still serving her sentence, the Jewish welfare office in Munich requests information about P. from Child Welfare Services in Tel Aviv. On December 27, 1937, the caseworker in Tel Aviv files a detailed report. Closing paragraph: "In the course of our supervision here, we came to know the young woman. It was our impression that she is a mildly debilitated, psychopathic, and unrestrained person. She lags far behind in intellectual development. Over the years here, she acquired only an inadequate knowledge of the language. However, she is manually very dexterous and quite good at housework. Her mother and extended family here went to great lengths to exert a positive influence on her and took various measures to try to alter her life. But all these attempts failed. The mother, who is gainfully employed and with whom P. lived intermittently, was unable to provide adequate support. As a supplement to our report, we include the medical evaluations made at the time by Dr. H. and Dr. K."

The caseworker at the Jewish welfare office in Munich, Dr. Anne R., arranges for P. to be admitted to the Heckscher Psychiatric Hospital and Research Institute in Munich for observation after serving her prison sentence. Following a psychiatric evaluation, a decision is to be made about the young woman's future. The day before P.'s release from Aichach Prison, Dr. R. sends a copy of the report from Child Welfare Services in Tel Aviv, including the two medical evaluations, to the Heckscher Clinic.

On February 18, 1938, P. is transferred to the Heckscher Psychiatric Hospital and Research Institute. On admission, she is given a medical examination. Physical findings: a large young woman in good nutritional and physical condition. Psychological findings: P. is friendly, talkative, and articulate. Speaks rather uninhibitedly about intimate relations. Adequate emotional state. In the course of the conversation, no intellectual deficiencies were evident.

One week later, P. is given an intelligence test. She doesn't score very well. Excerpts:

BASIC KNOWLEDGE

Who was Luther? Answer: Reformer of the Christian Church.
Who was Bismarck? Answer: German prince.
What form of government do we currently have? No answer given.

ARITHMETIC

1. 7×9 = Answer: 63.
2. $51 - 16$ = Answer: 32.
3. $x - 3 = 14$ Answer: $x = 17$.

GENERAL PRACTICAL KNOWLEDGE (PART I)

Why are houses built higher in the city than in the countryside? Answer: Due to lack of space.

Why do children go to school? Answer: In order to learn.

Why do courts exist? Answer: So that people obey the laws.

GENERAL PRACTICAL KNOWLEDGE (PART II)

The difference between:

A mistake and a lie? Answer: Unconscious—conscious.

Borrowing and giving? Answer: In borrowing I get it back, in giving the other person keeps it.

GENERAL ETHICS

Why does one study? Answer: To get ahead in life.

Why is one not permitted to burn down one's own house? Answer: Because it's arson.

What is one supposed to do when one finds 5, or 20, or 500 marks? Answer: Keep 5 marks, return 500 marks.

How do you see your future? Answer: First study, then pursue a career.

What would you do if you won the lottery? Answer: Go to Brazil.

DICTATION

"The eagle and the turtle. A turtle complained to the birds that no one would teach him how to fly. Well then, said the eagle, I will teach you to fly. And he took the turtle up with him almost to the clouds and then suddenly let him go. The turtle smashed down on the rocks." Retelling: adequate. P. cannot give a satisfactory definition of a fable. She is, however, able to interpret the dictation from the perspective of the animals.

On the basis of the intelligence test, Countess Frau Dr. von J. produces the following psychological evaluation: "P. possesses an average, not particularly well-developed general ability and an average memory for theoretical, new, and unusual facts. Higher, logical, and combinatory theoretical tasks are not completed independently. The scope of her psychological capacities is limited, although there is no debility. Her physical and impulsive drives predominate. Her desires and life goals are determined emotionally and exceed realistic possibilities. Any planning of future activities is shaped by her impulses; desired successes are assumed to be already accomplished realities. During the examination, P. placed a great emphasis on external correctness. However, any insight into her own lack of restraint appears to be limited, superficial, and not entirely clear."

Case History

Week 1.　P. attempts to follow the rules in the clinic. However, since the nurses find her rather demanding, they keep her on a tight rein. She wants to listen to the radio downstairs with the children and spends long stretches of time on the telephone with the Jewish welfare office. She is talkative and friendly and tries hard to make a good impression.

Week 2.　P. does some sewing, mending her underwear and clothes. She begins to grow impatient and seeks permission to leave the clinic. She says she would like to learn a profession, to take courses in typewriting, stenography, and languages. She wants to become a foreign correspondent. But if they don't provide her with an education, she certainly won't let herself be placed in a home. She is convinced that within a few days she could find a well-paid position in a Jewish household. The only problem is that she's not too keen on housework.

Countess Frau Dr. von J. submits her psychological evaluation: "P. is an unrestrained psychopath who is essentially ruled by her drives. Her powers of judgment are limited, although she is not feebleminded. As the prognosis is very unfavorable, I recommend that she be placed in a secure institution and be declared legally incapacitated as quickly as possible."

Week 3.   P. doesn't want to stay in the clinic any longer. She tries to borrow money from the nurses and from other patients to buy writing implements and fruit and to make telephone calls. The nurses complain that she often expresses herself indelicately and becomes indignant when she doesn't get what she wants. One nurse continues: P. always talks about how much she yearns to work but is quite lazy here in the clinic. Her room is in complete disarray, and she spends most of her time applying cosmetics or lying in the sun for hours in order to get nice and brown. While she does admit her mistakes, she attempts to place the blame on her relatives and circumstances. In spite of bad experiences, she judges her situation in life very optimistically, overestimates her own abilities, and makes highly imaginative plans for the future.

The Heckscher Clinic sends a report on P. to the Jewish welfare office in Munich: "In our judgment, P. is a mediocre but normally endowed, weak-willed, unrestrained, and asocial psychopath. Predominant are her physical urges, her limited powers of judgment and insight, and above all her lack of ethical and moral inhibitions. She is incapable of leading a responsible and purposeful life. It is therefore almost certain that P. will succumb to her aversion to work if left to her own devices, that she will not be able to resist her disorderly urges and desires, that she will break the law, and that she has the potential to be a bad influence on other young people as well. In order to prevent this, it is urgently necessary that she be placed in a secure institution with appropriate work opportunities. Through such strict measures, it might still be possible to reach this young woman and make her realize how serious her situation is. External compulsion might gradually teach her the value of regular, long-term work and an orderly, honest life. We recommend that she be placed in the work unit at the State Mental Institution and Nursing Home in Taufkirchen on the Vils."

Week 4. P. urgently requests permission to leave the clinic. She would like to go to the Jewish welfare office and to the Jewish employment agency. Since the welfare office has no interest in helping her, she wants to look for a job herself. She says that she's sick and tired of being locked up. If they don't let her out, how can she ever prove that she won't do anything stupid again? And she certainly won't do anything stupid, because she's had too many bad experiences. A nurse advises her to take the matter up with the head of the clinic, the non-Aryan Professor Dr. Isserlin. Dr. Isserlin gives P. permission to leave the hospital, with the justification that the Heckscher Clinic is an open institution and cannot keep a patient locked up against her will for an extended period of time. Directly after lunch, P. leaves for the Jewish welfare office. The welfare office, learning of her plans, informs the Heckscher Clinic that it is neither ready nor willing to meet with P. at this point in time. P., however, is already on the way. The welfare office notifies the police and requests that P. be arrested, but withdraws the request after speaking again with the Heckscher Clinic. That evening, P. returns to the clinic in great excitement. She says that she has been to the employment agency, where she was offered a job working in a Jewish lawyer's home. She is to report there the next day. P. is overjoyed, has the best intentions.

Week 5. P. doesn't get the job. The Jewish welfare office—without going into details—has warned the lawyer's family about her. P. is crushed, but quickly regains her composure and says that she intends to look for a new position. She suspects that the welfare office is behind the matter and is incensed that the very people who demand honesty from her would go behind her back like that. Over the next two days, P. is hardly in the clinic at all, not even returning for lunch. On the first evening, she claims that she has found a job as a cook in a Jewish pension and must report there the following day for an interview. She returns the next afternoon in a state of great excitement, telling another patient about a young man she has met. She says he left for Frankfurt that morning; she would like to join him but doesn't have enough money. However, she does have a plan: the patient should write a letter claiming to be P.'s mother. When the patient refuses, P. becomes angry: "Are you really so stupid, or just infantile?" Early the next morning, she attempts to leave the clinic but is stopped by the station nurse, who insists that she wait for the doctors' rounds. Shortly before lunch, P. is granted permission to check the mailboxes. She leaves the clinic and does not return.

On the Run

P.'s final days in the clinic are hectic. She has realized for some time that life in an institution would be impossible for her. From the beginning, she regards the job as a housemaid as merely provisional. Even on the day that she receives the offer, she continues to look for something better. Her alternatives, however, are limited. In the newspaper she sees an advertisement from a marriage broker. At night, alone in her room, she secretly composes a letter (March 27, 1938): "Dear Madam, I noticed your announcement in the paper and would like to get married as quickly as possible. I am from Berlin but currently live in Munich. I would prefer to marry out of the country and am looking for a man who is well situated and relatively intelligent as well. He can be up to 30 years old and must be relatively good-looking. I myself am 20 years old, 5 feet 6 inches tall, tan, slender, and stylish. I love music and sports, am intelligent and practical, speak English and French and am proficient in Hebrew and Arabic. I would like a husband I can make happy and for whom I can be a good life companion and housewife in these difficult times. I am a German Jew but would also happily marry a foreigner. I think, Madam, that you now have a good idea of who I am and what my wishes are. Unfortunately, there is one thing that I don't have, and that's 'wealth,' but I believe that mutual affection is what really counts. If you should think it necessary to have a photograph of me, I will have one taken. Please answer me in detail as quickly as possible, as I can be reached at my current address only for the next week. I hope very much that you will be able to find something for me, and remain respectfully yours, Mirjam P."

After losing the housemaid job through the intervention of the Jewish welfare office, P. knows that she can't remain in the clinic and that she is on her own. In a nearby cafe she meets an Egyptian medical student. She speaks Arabic with him. He wants to improve his German. P. promises to tutor him. She tells him she is a neurologist at the Heckscher Clinic. She claims to be Catholic, her father is German Consul in Palestine. Next month, she is to be married in Frankfurt. The medical student is taken with her, gives her his telephone number. A few days later, P. calls him up and visits him in his room on Theresien Strasse. After two hours, the student leaves the room to ask his landlady if the mail has arrived. In his absence, P. finds a money purse in a drawer of the night table. When the student returns, she tells him she has to report back to the clinic. On the street, she discovers that the purse contains 120 reichsmarks. She decides to leave Munich immediately. At the central railway station she boards a train to Mannheim. On route she stops briefly in Stuttgart to buy a small suitcase and the necessary toiletries.

That afternoon, the medical student's landlady calls the Heckscher Clinic and learns that P. is not a doctor there but a patient. The caseworker at the Jewish welfare office is notified and reports the incident to the police: P., who was to be admitted to the work unit of a mental institution in the near future, has left the Heckscher Clinic without permission and is strongly suspected of

tance and apologizes. They begin to converse. He tells her that he's a salesman. She tells him that she is an employee at I. G. Farben and sells paint. She has a company car for the job, a Ford Eiffel, which is currently being repaired at the Haas and Bernhardt Garage. H. invites P. to have a cup of coffee. They spend the evening together in a number of bars in Darmstadt. On entering the locales, P. raises her arm in the German salute. She calls herself Maria Schneider. She is a widow, her husband having been fatally injured in a car accident. P. spends the night with H. in his apartment. The next day, he invites her to lunch. Then they drive together to Frankfurt am Main. In Frankfurt, P. suggests they go to the Café Esplanade. Here, H. notices that there are Jews sitting at a number of tables. He becomes uneasy and asks P. why she chose this particular establishment. P. responds that there are Aryans here as well and that one doesn't have to look at the Jews. Only after the waiter assures H. that the Esplanade is in fact an Aryan café does he relax. On leaving, P. gives the German salute.

P. spends a second night with H. Around 10:00 the next morning she gets up and prepares to leave while H. remains in bed. She requests that H. check the stairwell so that she can leave the apartment unseen. While H. is on the stairs, P. takes his wallet, which is lying on a bookcase. When he returns, she makes a date with him for the afternoon: they agree to drive in P.'s car to Cologne, where she has to take care of some business. H. immediately notices that his wallet is missing, but he can't follow P. because he's not completely dressed. On the street, P. realizes that there is no money in the wallet. She speaks to a little girl on the street corner and asks her to return the wallet to its owner. Dressed and in possession of his wallet again, H. hurries to Rhein Strasse, where he first met P. two days earlier. By coincidence he discovers her on a side street. He waves to her. She runs away, disappearing into an office building. H. catches up with her in the hallway of the building and reproaches her about the wallet. P. tells him that she is in desperate straits and will explain the details to him later. He asks her if she is actually an Aryan. She affirms this but can produce no identification. Instead, she gives him two notebooks in her possession. In the notebooks, H. discovers a number of Jewish names and addresses. He again suggests that P. is not an Aryan, which she again disputes. He pressures her until she admits that she is a Jew. She begs him not to report her to the police.

At the police station, P. confesses to everything. She admits that she lied to the medical student and stole his money purse. She still has the purse but has already spent the money. P. also confesses that she was broke when she rented the hotel room in Darmstadt. She claims that she wanted to borrow money from acquaintances (whom she doesn't want to name) and insists that she never intended to defraud the hotel owner. She also admits to deceiving H. and taking his wallet. She says that on the evening they met, she had actually planned to go to the central train station in Darmstadt and telephone her acquaintances to discuss whether they should pick her up or send her money. H. finally persuaded her to stay with him. She had also intended to remain in Frankfurt on the following day, but H. convinced her to return to Darmstadt with him.

During his interrogation by the police, H. reports that he was in possession of a large sum of money—600 to 700 reichsmarks—which he then gave to a colleague for safekeeping. He suspects that P. was after this money and didn't know that he no longer had it—something P. vehemently denies. H. claims it was only that morning that he suspected Maria Schneider might actually be a Jew. In his apartment, she had shown him a number of photographs, including several of her deceased husband and of a friend she claimed was an Arab. In addition to this, she had a small picture of her mother, which she didn't want to let him see. H. noticed that all the people in these photographs had a certain Jewish appearance and began to suspect that he might be dealing with a Jew. Upon further questioning, H. claims that he could not reconcile it with his conscience that a Jew—with whom he had engaged in sexual intercourse—had pulled the wool over the eyes of German comrades and damaged them so despicably. In response to reproaches by the police: H. affirms that he knew Germans are not permitted to engage in sexual intercourse with Jews. He insists that he would never have had anything to do with this Maria Schneider, let alone have sex with her, had he known she was Jewish. Unsolicited remarks: H. explains that although he suffered no financial damage from this Maria Schneider, he held it to be his duty to protect fellow Germans from such a hussy. That is why he notified the police and turned this swindler over to them.

Convicted

In pretrial detention, P. is ordered to write a brief summary of her life. Excerpt (May 22, 1938): I am a person who has always needed someone around to give me advice as well as emotional support. Because there was no one in my life to do this, things have gone downhill for me. If asked to envisage my future, I know only one thing: I cannot and do not want to remain in Germany, because as a Jew it is impossible for me to amount to anything here. I would be very *thankful* if the German state would expel me. After serving my sentence, I absolutely want to leave Germany. I do not, of course, *want* to be pushed around again from one country to the next. Rather, I want to go home to my father in Palestine. I am currently corresponding with him about this. My last offense was more the result of desperation than anything else. As I had been free for only two months, I certainly had no desire to end up behind bars again. I really should have pulled myself together more. But if one puts oneself in my position, then what I did certainly cannot be excused, but it can perhaps be understood.

P.'s lawyer informs the court in Darmstadt that her father has obtained a visa to Palestine for her. He asks the court if his client, who has exhibited symptoms of psychological illness since childhood and is still legally a minor, might be granted amnesty. He adds that the visa is valid only for a brief period of time and cannot be renewed after it expires.

The district attorney's office in Darmstadt commissions an evaluation of P.'s mental condition from the public health department. The examining physician, Senior Medical Officer Dr. V. (June 1, 1938): During the examination, P. answered questions smoothly and clearly. However, she also passed over inconvenient facts and did not stick to the truth. Over the course of our discussion, I noted no deficiencies in intelligence other than a conspicuous lack of judgment and self-criticism. P. places the blame for everything on unfavorable circumstances. Her plans for the future are vague. She says she will have her father arrange for her to travel back to Palestine. It is clear to her that she cannot avoid a prison sentence. She wants to have nothing more to do with the Jewish welfare office. She would like to travel to another European country, and is convinced that she will be able to find work somewhere.

Psychological results: In general, P. has adapted well to prison, although she tends to be rather demanding. Her attitude is one of indifference and could even be described as carefree. A certain smugness is often unmistakable. No signs of any existing mental illness could be found.

Physical results: Nothing unusual other than a superficial injury to her left wrist. P. admits that she inflicted this wound herself in a suicide attempt. When questioned, she claimed to have attempted suicide earlier through an overdose of Veronal.

Expert opinion: P. is an unrestrained psychopath. While she is not feebleminded, her powers of judgment are limited. Given her status as a minor, she must be considered of limited accountability in the sense of Paragraph 51, Section 2, of the Penal Code. We concur with the medical expert at the Heckscher Clinic in recommending that she be admitted to a secure mental institution.

Three days later, the district attorney's office issues its own findings: "The accused is a danger to the public. Not only is she an unrestrained thief and swindler, she has intentionally sabotaged the racial laws of National Socialist Germany in every possible way and has caused credulous Aryans to be suspected of the crime of *Rassenschande*. Given these facts, it is imperative not only that she be punished as an example to others but also that she be placed in a secure mental institution so that she will not be able to continue her criminal activities."

On July 7, 1938, the Regional Court in Darmstadt sentences P. to a prison term of fourteen months. Since P. has confessed to her crimes, the ten weeks she has spent in pretrial detention are subtracted from her sentence. The court rules that she is a danger to public safety (Paragraph 42b of the Penal Code)* and that following her sentence it is therefore necessary to keep her under surveillance in an institution for an indeterminate amount of time. Closing words of the judgment: "Given her unrestrained and extremely careless nature, P. will in all probability take to prostitution if she is released and thus will continue to break the law. Even after serving the sentence she has received today, she will not be in a position to earn a living through regular work; rather, she will continue to abuse her freedom and to commit further crimes. She will continue to pose a significant threat to public safety for years to come, at least until that point in time when, in the opinion of experts, she presumably attains a certain spiritual maturity. We must confront this danger to Germany by placing her in an institution."

---

*The Law Against Dangerous Habitual Criminals, and Measures for Security and Improvement: "If a person commits a punishable act while in a state of incapacitation (Paragraph 51, Section 1, of the Penal Code) or while in a state of reduced legal capacity (Paragraph 51, Section 2), the court may order the confinement of that person in a mental institution if public safety requires it."

Behind Bars

P. serves the rest of her sentence in the Hessian Regional Penitentiary in Mainz (division 4, cell 463). Life in prison is monotonous.
P.'s only comfort is that she works with six women gluing paper
bags together—in itself monotonous as well but in any case better than nothing.

Written Contact.   Each prisoner is permitted to send and to receive a letter once every four weeks. Only paper issued by the
penitentiary is to be used for correspondence. In writing letters,
prisoners must keep to the preprinted lines. Letters containing improper contents and letters that otherwise give rise to objections
by the prison authorities will not be sent from the prison or distributed to prisoners. Prisoners who write such letters and who
do not keep to the preprinted lines will be subject to disciplinary
punishment. Letters addressed to prisoners must also be written
neatly and in pen and ink.

Human Contact.   Visits from relatives are allowed once every
month. Visiting hours: Fridays 8:00–11:00 A.M. and 3:00–4:00 P.M.
Children under fourteen will not be admitted. All donations of
food and similar items are forbidden on the grounds of equality.
Visitors are urgently warned not to believe the stories told by
prisoners.

Conduct.   In prison, P. is punished three times for breaches of
penitentiary rules.
    First offense: In December 1938, P. is discovered in possession
of several onions "with intent to consume." Punishment: one day
without food.
    Second offense: In February 1939, a prison guard observes P.
climbing up to the window of her cell and looking out. Punishment: three days solitary confinement.

Third offense: In May 1939, P. is again caught climbing up to the window of her cell. When questioned, she claims that she had to climb up on the table because the metal rod that opens the window is not long enough. She admits that while doing this she did look out the window briefly. An inspection of the window reveals, however, that it can be opened by means of the metal rod without having to climb up on the table. Punishment: P. is issued a warning.

Obstinate.   The second decree concerning the enforcement of the Law on Family and First Names requires that as of January 13, 1939, P. use the name Sara in order to identify herself clearly as a Jew. ("If this additional name is omitted, a prison sentence of up to six months can be expected—or in the case of negligence, a sentence of up to one month.") In signing the document acknowledging this decree, P. leaves out her new name and has to add it to her signature after the fact.

Letter 1 (February 5, 1939).   My dear Papa! I received your letter. Since I have such important things to tell you, I have not written to Tel Aviv this time. Why don't you ever tell me, in spite of my repeated questions, what you think will happen after my release from prison? I have no peace of mind about this. I don't think you have any idea what will happen to me if you don't really get going. Things aren't so rosy here for Jews—you must know that yourself. What will become of my Papa, what have you been able to accomplish at the consulate in Jerusalem? I am tortured day and night by worries about this, and will have no peace until I receive a positive answer. Please deal with the matter more thoroughly and answer all of my questions and do not avoid them again. As you can see, soon I will no longer be able to write a neat and orderly letter. My nerves are completely shot. Tell Mama that I can't write her on her birthday because I have such important things to discuss with you. Congratulate her for me, tell her to write me. Please write sooner next time. I was very concerned. Please put a reply coupon in your next letter. And answer every question. Affectionate kisses, be well! Your Mirjam.

By order of the prison authorities, the letter is not sent.

Letter 2 (April 18, 1939). P.'s father writes from Haifa to the senior district attorney in Darmstadt: "Dear Sir, Mirjam Sara P. is my daughter. She is currently serving a prison sentence in Mainz, which will be completed at the end of June this year. I wish to inform you that I am currently making arrangements for my daughter to emigrate to Palestine, and that I plan to have a lawyer or consul submit a petition to repeal the court order that she be placed in a mental institution following her prison term. Sincerely, Erich Israel P."

In mid-June of 1939, the Regional Court in Darmstadt orders that P., after serving her prison sentence, be placed in the Philippshospital (State Mental Institution and Nursing Home) in Goddelau.

Last Chance

In the Philippshospital, P. continues to try to arrange for her emigration to Palestine. On October 3, 1939, she writes to the district attorney's office in Darmstadt: "Since my release from prison three months ago, I have been in a mental institution in Goddelau. As you may be aware, I am seeking to emigrate from Germany as quickly as possible. Since I no longer have any relatives in Germany, there is no one to assist me in the process. Everything I can undertake here through written correspondence is practically useless. If one isn't able to deal with these things in person, nothing ever gets done. Furthermore, there is no one here, such as a lawyer, who is really interested in the matter and who could take care of things for me. As a result, my plans to emigrate have come to a complete standstill. In spite of the serious political situation today, there is still a possibility that I might be able to travel to a neutral country. From there I would be able to contact my parents, who are ready to assist me. For some time now, all contact with my parents—who live in Palestine—has been cut off here. My request to you is the following: now that I have been locked up for a year and a half, I ask that you set me free. I can find board and lodging at the Jewish Home for Girls in Frankfurt. In addition to this, I have been in contact with the Jewish Relief Association there for some time now. I believe I can say with certainty that I will be out of Germany within four weeks if I am given an opportunity to deal aggressively with my situation. You can rest assured that there is no risk of further offenses. My punishment was too long and I have experienced too much hardship and difficulty firsthand to ever even think of violating the laws of the Reich in any way again. I beg you to set me free, that is, to let me go to the Jewish community in Frankfurt so that I can finally arrange for my emigration and begin a new and orderly life. In the hopes of a prompt response, I sign respectfully, Mirjam Sara P."

At the end of October 1939, the Reich's Association of Jews in Germany sends an inquiry to police headquarters in Frankfurt am Main regarding the possibility of P.'s emigration. The police forward the inquiry to Dr. S., the medical director of the Philippshospital in Goddelau, and request his opinion on the matter. Dr. S.'s response (November 1, 1939): "P. was sentenced by the Second Criminal Division of the Regional Court in Darmstadt to a prison term of fourteen months. In addition to this, the court ordered that she be institutionalized. P. was admitted to my hospital July 1 of this year. Since that time, she has sought to be released from here, in particular through the Reich's Association of Jews in Germany (Emigration Division), with the aim of leaving Germany. If it would be possible for P. to be expelled directly to a foreign country, I would support repealing the court order, which calls for her institutionalization on the basis of Paragraph

42 of the Penal Code. Otherwise, such a repeal would, in my opinion, be out of the question for the foreseeable future, as the grounds for her admission here (danger to the public safety) have not, of course, been addressed in such a short time. I believe I am justified in assuming that the senior district attorney would also welcome the possibility of P.'s emigration and would in this case suspend the institutionalization order. According to a statement from the aforementioned Reich's Association, emigration to Belgium requires the payment of several hundred dollars in foreign currency, an amount P. will have great difficulty procuring. If a government authority does not take up the matter, there is little chance that P. will be able to emigrate."

One year later, the Reich's Association of Jews in Germany is still searching for a better alternative for P. In December 1940, the association's regional office in Mainz (Welfare Division, Horst Wessel Strasse No. 2) informs the director of the Philippshospital, Dr. S., that they are currently working on a concrete possibility. Dr. S. recommends that they first contact the senior district attorney in Darmstadt. On January 24, 1941, the association's regional office in Mainz writes again to Dr. S.: "We intend to speak with the senior district attorney only after we have actually found a place for P. in another institution. We believe that the Reich's Association's Home for Young Women in Neu-Isenburg would be an appropriate place for her. This institution is prepared to admit P. as soon as the state of her mental health has been assessed in a psychiatric evaluation. We therefore request that you fill out the enclosed admission form and the other questionnaire. As soon as the director of the home has approved P.'s admission, we will send an inquiry to the senior district attorney in Darmstadt, as you suggested in your correspondence of December 12, 1940."

Dr. S.'s response (February 3, 1941): "I cannot comply with your request that I submit a psychiatric evaluation of P. before the senior district attorney has stated his position regarding the repeal of her institutionalization order. In the meantime, Fräulein P. was transferred from here on February 1 to an institution designated for Jewish patients."

Conscious Duplicity

Euthanasia.   In October 1939, Hitler signs the secret Führer Decree, backdated to September 1, 1939, ordering the "mercy killing of incurably ill patients." The decree serves as the official basis for the extermination of "life unworthy of living," a project that has been in preparation for some time. The systematic murder of institutionalized patients (code name Operation T4) is organized in a villa on Tiergarten Strasse No. 4 in Berlin. Officials disguise the transfer of patients to death institutions as "a measure taken in the context of a planned economy." Senior civil servants and physicians participating in the operation themselves use assumed names.

The central headquarters on Tiergarten Strasse is in charge of the following cover organizations:

The Reich's Association for Mental Institutions and Nursing Homes, responsible for the distribution of patient registration forms as well as the pro forma evaluation of patients (evaluations are not required for Jewish patients).

The Charitable Foundation for the Maintenance of Mental Institutions and Nursing Homes, the official employer of T4 personnel; in dealing with other authorities, the Charitable Foundation acts as the organization responsible for Operation T4.

The Charitable Ambulance Service, responsible for the transportation of institutionalized patients.

The six T4 death institutions—Grafeneck, Brandenburg, Hartheim, Sonnenstein, Bernberg, and Hadamar—are equipped with gas chambers and called state nursing homes. Patients are killed with carbon monoxide shortly after their arrival. Death certificates are issued later. The reported cause of death is falsified in order to keep relatives from becoming suspicious; the reported date of death is pushed forward in order to continue charging nursing fees.

At the end of the first phase of murdering "mentally ill" patients in August 1941, many employees of Operation T4 are assigned to the extermination of Jews in Sobibor, Treblinka, and Belzec (code name Operation Reinhardt).

Jewish Patients. In January 1940, the first Jewish mental patients are murdered in Germany. Beginning in the summer of that year, Jewish patients are concentrated in certain mental institutions and then transported to unnamed destinations. That fall, a number of them are deported to the T4 death institution in Brandenburg, where they are immediately murdered in gas chambers. Several months later, falsified death certificates are produced in Berlin under the cover address "Insane Asylum Cholm, Post Lublin" and are sent to relatives and to the responsible authorities.

Hessia. On January 10, 1941, the Reich's Minister for Internal Affairs orders that Jewish patients be sent from mental institutions in Hessia to the Heppenheim State Mental Institution and Nursing Home, so that "they can be transferred by means of mass transport to an institution designated for Jews." On February 1, 1941, the twenty-nine Jewish patients at the Philippshospital in Goddelau are picked up by a bus from the Charitable Ambulance Service and transported along with their administrative and medical files to Heppenheim. In the Philippshospital, they are officially listed as "discharged." Three days later, on February 4, 1941, sixty-seven Jewish patients—including the twenty-nine patients from Goddelau—are transported from the Heppenheim State Mental Institution and Nursing Home to an unnamed destination. On that same day, sixty-seven newly arrived patients from Heppenheim are registered in a logbook at the T4 death institution Hadamar. Their names are not recorded.

Three months later, the district attorney's office in Darmstadt addresses a written inquiry to the Philippshospital in Goddelau, requesting information about the institution to which the patient P. has been transferred. The director of the Philippshospital, Dr. S., replies (May 6, 1941): "In response to your correspondence from May 3, I recommend that you contact the Charitable Ambulance Service in Berlin W9, Potsdamerplatz 1." One month later, the district attorney's office receives the following notification from the Insane Asylum Cholm: "We herewith confirm the receipt of your letter, which was forwarded to us by the Charitable Ambulance Service. We wish to inform you that the patient Mirjam Sara P. died here on May 27, 1941. Heil Hitler!"

Coming to Terms with the Past

On July 10, 1946, P.'s father writes from Haifa to the State Mental Institution and Nursing Home in Goddelau: Dear Sirs, My daughter Mirjam P., born on June 28, 1918, was interned in the Philippshospital by judicial decree at the outbreak of the war. I would be very grateful if you could tell me something about her fate. Sincerely, Erich P.

One week later, Dr. B., the temporary director of the Philippshospital, responds. Although Dr. B. worked at the mental institution in Goddelau between 1939 and 1942, he does not appear to be familiar with the Charitable Ambulance Service (July 18, 1946): "Dear Mr. P., In response to your inquiry from July 10, we wish to inform you that your daughter Mirjam P. was transferred to the State Mental Institution and Nursing Home in Heppenheim in accordance with an order by the Reich's Minister for Internal Affairs, which stipulated that Jewish patients be sent to a collective institution. Here in Goddelau, we know nothing more about her fate. However, it appears as if she was transferred from Heppenheim to an unnamed institution in the so-called Government General in Poland. According to a memorandum from May 19, 1941, in the files here in Goddelau, a letter that arrived at our hospital addressed to a Charitable Ambulance Service (Berlin W9, Potsdamerplatz 1) was forwarded with the request that it be sent to the patient at the appropriate institution."

The memorandum mentioned above, along with the entire written correspondence from the Charitable Ambulance Service—with only a single exception—can no longer be found today in the files of the Philippshospital.

ONE LIFE

Wilhelm K. is born in a barracks in Silesia on November 13, 1887, the son of Richard K., sergeant and administrator of the Fifty-eighth Infantry Regiment's store in Glogau, and his wife Ida K. (née Kad.), of unclear descent, rumored to have been a Czech who never really mastered the German language—something that Wilhelm K. will later heatedly dispute.

K. embarks on a humanistic rather than a military career. Beginning in 1899, he attends To the Gray Cloister, the oldest secondary school in Berlin, where the Iron Chancellor himself once studied. In 1908, K. graduates thirteenth in his class of thirty-one students, enrolling in the same year at the Royal Friedrich Wilhelm University of Berlin. Here he studies history, political science, philosophy, and theology. His professors include Dietrich Schäfer, Eduard Meyer, Otto Hintze, and Adolf von Harnack.

An Activist by Nature

Knowledge for its own sake, however, is not enough for K. His entire being yearns for practical life. Even at a young age, K. has strong political views. Spurred by the elections of the Berlin Free

Students at the end of November 1909, a number of likeminded students, among them K., come together and form, in conscious opposition to the cosmopolitan Free Students, the German Völkisch Student Alliance. The alliance promotes and cultivates the national awareness of German university students and—not unimportantly for the status-conscious K.—seeks an understanding between fraternity students (uniformed and nonuniformed, dueling and nondueling) and nonfraternity students. The goal of their members is to become authentic German personalities rather than formula men. K. is elected vice chairman, then chairman of the alliance.

In 1910, K. is awarded a scholarship of 650 marks from the Moses Mendelssohn Foundation. The foundation, established by Privy Councilor of Commerce Franz Mendelssohn in honor of his great-grandfather, supports needy, worthy, and diligent students in the humanities at the University of Berlin (limited to citizens of the German Reich, without consideration of their religious affiliation).* During the summer semester of that year, K. becomes an active member of the Association of German Students, the first programmatically anti-Semitic fraternity in Germany. In 1911, he is awarded a Moses Mendelssohn Scholarship for a second year. That same year, he cofounds the *German Völkisch University Newspaper,* a publication of the German Völkisch Student Alliance, which is now active in a number of German cities, including Breslau, Greifswald, Leipzig, and Königsberg. The paper makes a stand against anti-German parties (Poles, Social Democrats), promotes the value and importance of German colonies, investigates the heritage and race question, and opposes the influence of foreigners at German universities as well as the excessive and corruptive role of Jews in public and political life in Ger-

---

*In 1938, the foundation is renamed the Study Foundation for the Humanities, and scholarships are awarded only to "German-blooded" students.

many. Wilhelm K., history major, writes articles and reviews and is responsible for subscriptions.

In 1912, K. is cofounder of the Association Against the Presumptuousness of Jews.

Rhetorical Achievements

After eight semesters at the university, K. breaks off his studies, bids farewell to his parental home, and sets off on his own. Initially he accepts a position as a private tutor in the Upper Lausitz (Petershain Castle near Mücka), before following his true inclinations and turning to journalism. K. settles in Breslau and works at the *Silesian Morning Post* as an editor and at the *Silesian Herald* as the editor responsible for newspaper correspondence. Through arrangements by the central office of Albrecht von Graefe's German Conservative Party, he is also hired as the editor of Graefe's newspaper in Wismar, the *Mecklenburg Vantage Point*. In addition to this, K. remains politically active. He founds and directs the Silesian Association of German Völkisch Academics, the goals of which are similar to those of the German Völkisch Student Alliance (main areas of activity: the race question and the battle for the German people), and he works his way up the hierarchy of the German Conservative Party. During this time, K. settles down and starts a family. On November 8, 1913, he marries Margarethe (Hansi) Schm., the daughter of a civil servant at the local district attorney's office. A year later, their first son, Horst, is born; five years later, the second, Wulf-Dieter.

Brother-in-Arms.   Initially K.'s life is little affected by the Great War. Only in July 1917 is he drafted into the First Replacement Battalion of the Fifty-first Infantry Regiment as a Home Guard recruit with no prior military service. Although judged at his medical examination to be fit for active duty, he is released the same month—after a complaint by the German Conservative Union because of his duties as their general secretary—and his military service is deferred until September 30, 1917. Later, K. will ascribe the deferral to a heart defect that he contracted as a schoolboy from overzealousness during a field trip in the Erzgebirge, and complain with bitter disappointment that he was not permitted to serve on the front. With only twenty-one days of garrison duty during the war, K. makes it to the rank of private. After the war, he appears in public in a sergeant's uniform.

Shaken but Undaunted.   Following the German defeat, K. returns to civilian life and dedicates himself entirely to politics. He joins the newly established German National People's Party (GNPP) and is appointed general secretary of the party's regional division in Silesia. K. also continues to cultivate his close ties to the German youth movement. In 1919, he founds an organization for young people, the Bismarck Association, which he also leads.

A Lightning-Fast Tongue and the Voice of a Rhinoceros.   K. distinguishes himself as a quick-witted speaker, appearing at countless events and rallies. With hammer blows and rapier parries, he rails against the Treaty of Versailles, against the Weimar Republic, against the Poles, and against the Left, which is not without its dangers. K. is said to have taken part in the Great Breslau Chairleg Battle of 1919.

Literary Inclinations.   In 1920, as a poetic rejoinder to the German decline, K. composes a historical drama, *Totila*. Totila, leader of the Gothic youth, marries the beautiful Schwanhilde and is chosen King of the Goths. Duke Alarach (the Balt), angered by the loss of throne and maiden, plans Totila's downfall with his sister Mechtildis (Schwanhilde's mother). The two avenge themselves by committing treason against their own people, conspiring with the enemy of the Goths, the Byzantines ("a state without a people"—a mixture of Greeks, Persians, Thracians, Lydians, Syrians, Macedonians, Jews, and Galacians). Narses, the Byzantine general, has 20,000 Franconian soldiers ("all of them treacherous, lying dogs") prepare the bloody groundwork by luring the Germanic people into a trap, where the Byzantines can eradicate them. Schwanhilde, Totila, and the entire Gothic people—including women, children, and the elderly—are killed. Surrounded by the enemy, the last Goths march heroically to their death.

The tragedy is performed for enthusiastic friends in Breslau.

A Politically Turbulent Career

Change of Location.   Life in the Silesian provinces proves increasingly difficult for K. In addition to troubles with Poles and Social Democrats, interparty conflicts develop. In September 1920, K. decides to leave Breslau and continue his battle in the Reich's capital city. He becomes general secretary of the GNPP's Regional Division in Berlin and a Berlin city councilman and organizes the Bismarck Youth of the German National People's Party.

Change of Party.   After three years of hard work, the membership of the GNPP's Regional Division in Berlin has doubled. The friction in the party, however, has not abated. K. complains of excessive moderation: the people's party is not populist enough. On the other hand, there are rumors that K. himself has engaged in corruption and deceit. He is ordered to relinquish the leadership of his beloved Bismarck Youth. He resigns from the party and founds a new youth organization, the German Bismarck Order, designating himself as the group's supreme master. K. would like to join the German Völkisch Freedom Party (GVFP), but the group has been temporarily banned. Instead he joins the *völkisch* organization German Herold, becoming a member of the German

Völkisch Freedom Party shortly after the repeal of its ban. K. is appointed Reich's party whip and leader of the GVFP's Berlin District, but remains the same intrepid warrior.

Völkisch Politics.   The members of the banned National Socialist German Workers' Party (Nazis) and the German Völkisch Freedom Party merge as the National Socialist Freedom Movement. In 1924, K. is elected to both chambers of the Reichstag, becoming one of fourteen members of Parliament from the National Socialist Freedom Movement. As a member of the Reichstag, he makes devastating speeches against the system and is named Expert for Youth Welfare. The alliance, however, is short-lived, dissolving in 1925. With Adolf Hitler's early release from prison in Landsberg, the Nazi Party is founded anew. The German Völkisch Freedom Party changes its name to the German Völkisch Freedom Movement (GVFM).

Blows of Fate.   K. is attacked from all sides.
First Blow. From the ruling system, which accuses K. of being involved in plans to assassinate the Prussian minister of the interior, as well as in the murder of Dammers. The district attorney files charges against K. and requests that his immunity as a member of Parliament be revoked. In 1927, criminal proceedings against K. are abandoned because the Reichstag refuses to permit prosecution.
Second Blow. From the police, whose informants follow K. everywhere. (1) Undercover investigations at public rallies. Police Division IA reports that K. has publicly attacked the Weimar Republic ("It is nothing but a fraud.") and railed "in a most hateful way" against Social Democrats, Democrats, and the center. K. is also reported to have spoken disparagingly about police officers from Division IA. At a rally, he ordered his audience to watch for people taking notes, adding, "I will settle accounts with those louts and informants and throw them all down the stairs." (2) Undercover investigations of K.'s private life. Excerpt from a con-

fidential police report: discreet inquiries have unearthed nothing disadvantageous about K.'s personal behavior. His private life in the greater Berlin area offers no points of attack. However, K. is frequently on the road.

Third Blow. From the Nazis, who no longer regard K. as a comrade-in-arms. In the summer of 1926, a series of rallies by the German Völkisch Freedom Movement are broken up by organized Nazis groups. These gangs are particularly keen on attending meetings at which K. is scheduled to speak. There are brief clashes. Once, as K. is leaving a beer hall, he is greeted by a number of National Socialists, who taunt him by shouting out "Hangman!" and follow him to another locale. K. is rescued by the police. During the encounter, the Nazis yell, "We'll beat K. to death."

K.: I have no intention of allowing my constitutionally guaranteed freedom of speech to be restricted by young, immature *louts.*

In early September 1926, K. requests that the police initiate criminal proceedings against the Nazi Party leadership in Berlin. The disruptions and threats, however, continue unabated. Police officers on duty at the rallies do not intervene with any particular zeal, nor do they appear interested in questions of constitutionality. Once again, K. writes to the police chief:

Your Honor!

I hereby submit the following complaint on the basis of the Law for the Protection of the Freedom of Assembly (passed May 23, 1923):

For several weeks now, young men wearing the Nazi insignia have repeatedly attempted to disrupt German Völkisch rallies—probably on instructions from the Berlin District Leadership of the National Socialist German Workers' Party. On Friday, September 10, there was a public rally of the German Völkisch Freedom Movement in the War Association House (concert hall) at Chaussee Strasse No. 94.

During the organizer's opening remarks, approximately two hundred young members of the Nazi Party began to disrupt the rally with their howls. The speaker was repeatedly interrupted by prearranged shouting.

At this point, I, the undersigned, assumed control of the rally and demanded that the supervising police officer ensure (on the basis of the Law for the Protection of the Freedom of Assembly, see the *Reich's Law Gazette* from 1923, No. 37) that law and order be maintained and that the troublemakers be removed from the hall. Despite being approached six times, the police officer refused, claiming that the only possible infraction here was trespassing and that heckling was allowed. When I responded that approximately two hundred people shouting such things as "swindler" or "louse" could no longer be regarded as heckling, he smiled and said that that was not his responsibility. In any case, I must point out that the officer on duty was not familiar with the Law for the Protection of the Freedom of Assembly. I therefore request that police headquarters undertake the following measures:

1. A criminal investigation of the district leadership of the National Socialist German Workers' Party. I request that the police determine who has ordered the systematic disruptions of German Völkisch rallies.

2. Disciplinary action (on the basis of the Prussian minister of the interior's decrees for the implementation of the law from May 23, 1923) against the police officer who neither knew the law nor enforced it.

Respectfully yours,
Wilhelm K.
Chairman of the Berlin Constituency of the German Völkisch Freedom Movement, Member of the German Reichstag

Given the lack of police protection, K. decides to take matters into his own hands. He orders that the following signs be posted at his rallies: "No Admittance for Nazis and Jews!" This only provokes the Nazi storm troopers, however, and they offer K. an unambiguous demonstration of their position on the matter. The signs are changed accordingly: "No Admittance for Social Democrats, Communists, and Jews!"

Fourth Blow. K. is attacked even within his own party. Extremely serious accusations, which are not made public, are leveled against him. K. himself describes the charges as troublemaking and gossip. He is summoned three times to appear before the disciplinary court of the German Völkisch Freedom Movement but fails to show up at any of the appointments. At the beginning of February 1927, he is expelled from the party. The majority of members in the Federation of Völkisch Freedom Fighters take K.'s side in the dispute. They leave the German Völkisch Freedom Movement and found the Reich's Federation of Völkisch Freedom Fighters.

Attention!

The Reich's Federation of Völkisch Freedom Fighters is, unfortunately, frequently confused with the Federation of Völkisch Freedom Fighters. We therefore inform you that the Reich's Federation is not identical with the Federation of Völkisch Freedom Fighters, which has only a few paying members. The latter organization consists merely of members of the German Völkisch Freedom Movement, whereas the Reich's Federation is a political organization with members from all *völkisch* orientations and is currently striving to create a unified *völkisch* party.

Reich's Federation of Völkisch Freedom Fighters
The Federation Leadership
F., Schu., Schm.

Change of Party. K. contacts Gregor Strasser in order to discuss the possibility of merging their parties or of joining up with the Nazis. Instead he joins up with "Cudgel" Kunze's German Social Party. After disputes with Kunze, the merger is dissolved. K. calls his newly founded party the Völkisch Social Workers' Community of Greater Berlin and appoints himself district leader. Shortly thereafter, he transforms the Berlin District into a Regional Association Berlin-Brandenburg, without undertaking any organizational changes.

Imperialism as the Highest Stage of Finance Capitalism

In November 1926, K. founds his own newspaper, the *Märkische Eagle,* in which he rails against international finance capital and the exploitation and enslavement of the German worker. He describes Germany as a colony of international capital. The enemy is on the left! The *Märkische Eagle* fights against Jews, Jesuits, and Jacobins.

The *Märkische Eagle* demands: the union of all ethnic Germans into a Greater Germany on the basis of the right of a people to self-determination; the end of interest-rate slavery; profit sharing for the employees of all large-scale enterprises; the establishment of a comprehensive retirement plan; the creation of a healthy middle class; the immediate communalization of large department stores and the nationalization of banks; the introduction of German law in place of Roman law; the establishment of a people's army; the repeal of all peace treaties under which German national comrades suffer.

Conditions: Only national comrades can be citizens. Only people of German blood, regardless of their religion, can be national comrades. Jews can never be national comrades. All Jewish participation in newspapers, theaters, and the arts must be forbidden. All people of foreign blood who entered the country after August 1, 1914, must be expelled from Germany.

Merger

In 1928, K. joins the Nazi Party after other political organizations have rejected his approaches. Excerpt from a private correspondence: "I heard that you were particularly angered by my switch to the National Socialists. As you know, I have searched for months for another satisfactory solution. Given the obstinacy of those nationalist circles led by particular feudal classes—something that you, my dear comrade, have experienced yourself with the *Stahlhelm*—my attempts, unfortunately, were unsuccessful. Even the leadership of the GNPP has failed. They attach no importance whatsoever to attracting activists, but prefer instead to splash around contentedly in the wake of Dr. Gustav Stresemann. The most important thing for these feudal lords is that they can participate in the government—nothing else matters to these dimwits. If I'm right about you, my dear comrade, I am certain that you will now approve of my decision. With heartfelt German greetings!"

"Moveable Mouthpiece."   Not all National Socialists welcome K. with open arms. The revolutionary wing regards him with extreme mistrust. They consider "the beautiful Wilhelm" to be a party bigwig and a "slimy petty *bourgeois*" with excellent connections to court councilors, Reich's Bank directors, down-at-heel Hohenzollern princes, and general agents.

Man of the People

May 1928: K. is elected to the Reichstag as a representative of the Nazi Party, but refuses his seat at Adolf Hitler's request. June 1928: K. is elected to the Prussian State Parliament as a representative of the Nazi Party. September 1928: K. is appointed Nazi Party leader for Ostmark (the administrative district Frankfurt/Oder and the Province Grenzmark Posen–West Preußen). The newly established

Ostmark district lacks any Nazi Party organization and consists of a mere sixty-six paying members. K. embarks on a protracted political battle. At the end of 1930, party membership has grown to 5,000.

"Prussian Führer." After nearly five years of work, there are 43,000 paying members of the Nazi Party in the Ostmark district, including 20,000 storm troopers and SS men. Following elections in April 1932, the Nazis are the most powerful party in the Prussian State Parliament, and Wilhelm K. is their leader. They boast that they are not a debating club of arrogant statesmen but an intellectual combat troop that can, if need be, resort to brute force.

On the Eve of the National Revolution. The Ostmark district has the highest percentage in the entire Reich of both Nazi Party members and election votes. On March 5, 1933, fifty-five percent of all voters in the district cast their ballot for Adolf Hitler. The Brandenburg district (administrative district Potsdam) is unified with the Ostmark district to make the Kurmark district. K. is appointed party leader of the largest Nazi district in Germany.

Sieg Heil and Rich Pickings

Victor. By April 1933, K. has been named an honorary citizen of nineteen cities and towns. These honors are bestowed in part before the Nazis' assumption of power, when K. is merely a district leader of the Party, for example, in the cities of Brätz, Fürstenburg on the Oder, Frankfurt on the Oder, Sorau, Cottbus, Buckow, and (something that causes quite a sensation) the Bavarian community Unterwössen im Chiemgau. Honors are bestowed after the Nazis' assumption of power in Spremberg, Altbeelitz, Züllischau, Lübben, Müllrose, and Arnwalde. In other cities—including Borkum—streets and squares are named in K.'s honor.

Impediments.   Now that he's in the driver's seat, K. experiences firsthand the inertia of established political structures. As a National Socialist official, he would of course like to appoint Nazi Party comrades to administrative positions, but this is not always immediately possible. K.: "It is simply ridiculous how we, the actual victors of the National Revolution, still allow ourselves to be given orders by the bureaucracy and its statutes."

Domestic Politics (1933).   There are disputes between K. and his landlady, who does not, in his mind, treat him with proper respect. K. seeks recourse through political channels. He writes to his friend Kurt Daluege, a Nazi comrade and member of State Parliament: My dear Kurt, I would like to request that you investigate whether my so-called landlady—a Frau H. who resides at Martin Luther Strasse No. 42 and is owner of the building on Stubben Strasse No. 3 in Berlin-Schöneberg—is a citizen of the German Reich. If she is not a citizen, the removal of this Jew from Germany would be a welcome measure. With a heartfelt *Heil* greeting, Your K.

Three days later, Daluege writes back: My dear K., In response to your question, I was able to obtain the following information from the local police station. Frau H. is married to an Oskar H. (born 9/25/1882). Oskar H. is Prussian and thus a citizen of the German Reich. Frau H. used to be Russian, but through her marriage is now a German citizen. We will therefore have to learn to live with her.

Stage Politics.   At last, a political climate has been created in Germany which allows K.'s artistic achievements to be recognized. *Totila* is performed in numerous theaters throughout Prussia to the wide acclaim of German audiences and critics. Only in the capital does a staging of the drama meet with difficulties. Following a complaint by K., the Prussian minister of culture intervenes at the beginning of 1934: "The old Nazi fighter and current President of Prussia K. has written the play *Totila*, which has already been staged with great success for the umpteenth time. However, it has not yet been possible to perform the drama in Berlin. I request that the necessary steps be taken immediately to assure that K.'s play is performed there as well. Deadline: three days."

As an author, K. would like to join various writers' associations in Germany. However, he runs into difficulties with the Association of German Playwrights, even though he is indisputably Aryan and can provide two impeccable witnesses to vouch for his political views (A. Hitler and Dr. J. Goebbels). He again seeks redress through political channels. K. writes to the Führer, only to be informed by his deputy, Martin Bormann, that the Führer has decided not to intervene in the matter. Bormann requests that K. investigate whether admission to this organization is necessary and customary for the author of a single dramatic work.

Pedagogical Work.   K., who is still active as a journalist, emphasizes (in contrast to Josef Goebbels and Julius Streicher) the pedagogical aims of the press, fighting "in a respectable tone" against all the enemies of the German people, in particular the Jews. Example (1934): "What the plague, consumption, and syphilis mean for the human race in terms of health, that is what Jews mean for the morality of white people. The carriers of this plague must be isolated and eradicated."

Full Steam Ahead

Peaks and Valleys.   Peak: K. gives the funeral oration for Field Marshal Göring's first wife. Valley: an article by K. in the *Völkischer Beobachter* in early June 1934 (three weeks before the ostensible "putsch attempt"), in which he praises Erich Röhm as the Führer's most loyal warrior.

There are more peaks than valleys. K.'s official posts include: leader of the Nazi Kurmark district, Prussian councilor of state, president of the Brandenburg and the Grenzmark Posen–West Preußen Provinces, Reich's commissioner and state commissioner for the Corridor, member of the Reichstag. Main areas of activity: culture, education, administration, domestic politics.

On the Road.   K. orders that he be greeted by church bells when he travels through his district.

Parade Through the Town of Nauen (1935).   Their faces flush with excitement, the schoolchildren form an honor guard. A trained waiter in an SS uniform accompanies K. (and receives in return a signed copy of K.'s book).

Private Telephone Number (Top Secret!).   Hunter A 1 4584. Even before the Revolution, rumors abound about corruption ("a filthy den of nepotism") and womanizing ("skirt chaser"). Nadir: K. is suspected of helping Elli B. (his private secretary) obtain an abortion. The Gestapo begins an investigation in Cottbus.

Pinnacle.   K. meets the beautiful twenty-two-year-old actress Anita Li. from Hamburg. They fall in love. In October 1935, she gives birth to a son.

"In-Laws."   The fact that Anita Li.'s father was a member of the Social Democratic Party and the Peace Society during the Weimar Republic doesn't disturb K. in the least. Nor does the fact that her brother is married to a Jew. On the contrary, his relations with the family are excellent. K. feels an artistic bond with his "brother-in-law" Friedrich Li., who is himself a writer (pen name: Johann Lu.). And although his wife, Leonore (née L.), is a Jew, she is also a dancer and comes from a well-situated family in Paderborn. K.'s "father-in-law," a former employee at the city archive in Hamburg, was forced into early retirement by the Nazis because of his political past, but not before declaring his unreserved willingness to serve the new regime.

K. advises his "brother-in-law" to emigrate from Germany as quickly as possible with his non-Aryan wife and their three small children. In May 1936, the family sets sail for Argentina on the South American steamer *General San Martin*. In Paderborn, it is said that the necessary arrangements for the emigration were made by a relative.

Crossroads.   After the birth of his son in 1935, K. decides to leave his aging and ailing wife. He files for divorce, declaring her to be the guilty party.

Grounds for divorce (excerpts):

(1) For years his wife has refused to bear more children, something which is irreconcilable with K.'s worldview and his position in the Nazi Party.

(3) She has neglected her duties as housewife and mother.

(4–7) She has engaged in adulterous affairs with various men.

Frau K. emphatically denies every accusation and insists that, in spite of her advanced age and ailing health, she is prepared to bear more children. K.'s financially dependent son, the twenty-one-year-old Horst K.—a law student, Nazi comrade, SS man, and budding author—takes his father's side. With unusual sharpness and formal bluntness, he testifies about the adulterous affairs of his mother. The court doesn't believe him. K.'s petition is rejected.

A Dressing-Down

"Shortly before taking office, the Führer said to me: Most revolutions that were suppressed or suffocated by reactionaries were thwarted because they could not be restrained. You are Supreme Party Judge. Your job is to restrain the revolution."

A Moralist.   Walter Buch, supreme judge of the Nazi Party. Born in 1883, a Nazi Reichsleiter and an SS-Obergruppenführer, a military officer by profession, *gottgläubig*. His daughter is married to Reichsleiter Martin Bormann.

Walter Buch: strict and incorruptible; an ardent but provincial National Socialist. Buch exercises his duties as supreme Party judge with the thoroughness and relentlessness of a Prussian officer, which is not always appreciated by his superiors and his Party comrades.

Responsibilities: the suppression and eradication of internal enemies of the Movement. As the leading force in the National Socialist state, members of the Nazi Party have higher duties to the Führer, to the people, and to the nation. If these duties are not fulfilled, then a special Party authority intervenes—in concrete terms: Walter Buch.

Restraining the Revolution.   Supreme Party Judge Buch dedicates himself to the improvement of marital morality within the Nazi movement and among the German people in general. Buch's fear: if the current lax conception of marriage is adopted by the younger generation, there will be serious consequences in both ideal and material terms. He embarks on a campaign against "the Jewish subversion of German marriages and families." District Leader and Prussian President K. has long been the subject of rumors and gossip. His divorce trial is the last straw. Buch feels that a vital nerve of the German people has been touched. He decides to make an example of the district leader. He addresses a letter to K., which he also distributes to a number of senior Party officials.

Munich, December 10, 1935
To:
Leader of the Kurmark District of the Nazi Party,
Herr President Wilhelm K.,
[...] In addition to this I declare:

Whoever adopts the position that adultery—and this includes all extramarital sexual intercourse with a married person—is something that can be reconciled with the Nazi Party's morality and ideological views,

Whoever seeks the protection of the Führer for his adulterous relationship and proudly boasts about the child that has resulted from this adulterous affair,

Whoever is aware that his subordinates have engaged in adulterous affairs with women who are their employees and thus financially dependent upon them, and whoever approves of and thus fosters such relationships,

And finally, whoever, after a marriage of twenty-two years, permits his adult son, who is also financially dependent on him, to testify in a public divorce trial against his own wife and that son's mother,

That person has adopted a stance toward women that has nothing in common with the National Socialist views of the subject. As supreme Party judge, I must therefore deny him the right to speak on these matters.

Heil Hitler!

Results: Disappointing. The letter finds little resonance. Reichsführer-SS Heinrich Himmler, who himself has little use for monogamy, officially approves of the letter but takes no action.

K., on the contrary, is furious. Fortunately, the Führer appears willing to cover for him. In a private conversation: "K., I will not demand that you leave the woman you love."

Cornered

The Gestapo investigates K. for various irregularities in the Kurmark district. In the course of these investigations, SS-Gruppenführer Reinhardt Heydrich orders that the apartment of

K.'s beloved Anita Li. be searched—despite repeated attempts by K. to prevent this. The SS suspects that files from a theft-and-burglary trial have been hidden in the rooms. K. regards this as a serious blow to his honor.

K. Strikes Back

K. cannot sit around and do nothing. He decides to defend himself.

With respect to the SS: in a friendly ("My dear Heinrich") but resolute tone, he writes to Himmler, announcing his resignation as an "honorary leader" of the SS. The Reichsführer-SS, somewhat taken aback, accepts the resignation.

With respect to Supreme Party Judge Walter Buch: K. does not dare make an open attack. He writes an anonymous letter to Buch, whose wife is rumored to be of impure racial descent.

Berlin, April 26, 1936

Dear Major Buch!

You are the supreme judge of a political party that fights and defames every honest Jew. As our relative, you shouldn't do this. Did you know that your wife has Jewish blood? Did you know that your wife's family (Bilernesti, see her family tree!) still lived in the ghetto in Frankfurt am Main from 1820 to 1825? Did you know that you have fathered children who have Jewish blood? Your son-in-law—who, like you, is a Reichsleiter of the Nazi Party—knows that his wife and mother-in-law are not of pure Aryan descent. The Reich's Office for Genealogical Research knows this as well! You are the only one who doesn't know? You have condemned hundreds of people because they happened to share the same tragic fate as your wife, when you, too, are incriminated. What consequences do you draw from this, wise and impartial judge? We are pleased to be able to count you as one of us.

Several Berlin Jews

The Fall

During the course of investigations by the Gestapo, it is determined that K. is the author of the anonymous letter to Supreme Party Judge Buch. Confronted with indisputable evidence, K. confesses.

The accusations contained in the letter are regarded as extraordinarily serious. Through the work of independent researchers—including the Reich's Office for Genealogical Research—the claims regarding Frau Buch's racially impure heritage are officially dismissed as false. Although her mother was adopted as a child by Frau Buch's grandfather under circumstances that could not be entirely clarified, evidence of non-Aryan paternity cannot be found. The case is considered closed.

Supreme Party Judge Buch would like to take stern measures against K. He pushes for K.'s expulsion from the Party. The Führer, however, is opposed to this: Even if K.'s behavior was intolerable, he, the Führer, cannot forget the great contributions this old Nazi fighter made to the Movement. To his great regret, he feels compelled to remove K. from office. He regards this as sufficient punishment.

Buch, for his part, is dissatisfied with the Führer's decision. Soon afterward he suffers a loss of power himself. He remains supreme judge but is excluded from the Party's inner circles and is even snubbed by his own son-in-law. Evidently he misunderstood what the Führer meant by restraining the revolution.

Several months later, the Führer decides to restore K.'s honor, to absolve him from the suspicion of disloyalty, to reinstate his pension as president of Prussia, and to allow him to wear the uniform of a Nazi district leader. The proposed punishment, which would have stripped him of all official titles, is reduced to a warning. There is even talk of K.'s being appointed to a new position.

On Ice

In spite of all promises, K. is not offered a new post. His access to the Führer is cut off. His letters are intercepted before Hitler can see them, and thus remain unanswered.

Out of Commission. For the first time in thirty years, K. leads a completely private life. In September 1936, Anita Li. gives birth to a second son. K. is granted a divorce from his wife, with K. as the guilty party. In 1938, he is finally permitted to marry Anita Li.

Financial Difficulties. K. does have his pension as former Prussian president and Nazi district leader but must provide monthly support of fifty marks to his mother (happily) and 255 marks to his ex-wife (very unhappily). In addition to this, he has a new wife and a total now of five (!) sons—the oldest has just passed the bar but is still financially dependent on him.

Near Miss. In 1938, K. narrowly avoids disaster. He intends to finance a trip to Italy through the sale of forty-four letters from leading Nazi functionaries—mostly personal correspondence (including a postcard with greetings from the Führer). The Gestapo, however, still has K. under surveillance and learns of the plan. Reichsleiter Bormann demonstrates little sympathy for K.'s plight: he forbids the sale of letters from leading Party comrades without explicit approval. The trip has to be canceled.

Hope and Despair. K. continues to send birthday cards and New Year's wishes to the Führer and other senior Party officials. The waiting brings his nerves to the breaking point.

In 1939, for the second time in his life, K. must watch as Germany goes to war without him. He can't bear to sit around and do nothing. In the fall of 1940, he volunteers for the Waffen-SS. At the end of February 1941, he is ordered to report as an SS volunteer for guard duty at the Dachau Concentration Camp. On the same day, his wife writes in desperation to K.'s old friend, Reich's Minister Dr. Lammers, and begs him for help.

In Dachau.   The fifty-three-year-old K. finds his duties as a concentration camp guard exhausting physically and emotionally. After six weeks, there's a minor promotion: K. is named SS-Rottenführer.

In the meantime, Reich's Minister Dr. Lammers searches for alternatives for K. There is talk of his assuming a post as district administrator. K. has reservations about the pay, does not want to give up his pension or return to Prussia. Nothing comes of the district administrator's post. New possibilities, which also come to nothing: administrator in a public works department, mayor of a larger city, diplomat in France, a position in the colonies. Another possibility: registrar at the Technical College and Medical Academy in Danzig. Nothing comes of this position either, as it has already been promised to someone else. A better possibility: registrar at the University of Königsberg. The current office holder is already over sixty-five years old and can therefore be pensioned at any time on the pretext of official interests. K. is immediately prepared to accept the position: as a humanist and scholar, he would not have felt comfortable at a technical college; he has much more intimate ties to the university. Nothing comes of this post either. The Führer insists that K. assume a prominent position in the planned occupation of the Soviet Union. He proposes K. as Reich's commissioner in Moscow. Göring and Rosenberg, who have their own favorites in mind for the post, raise objections. K. is given White Ruthenia.

On Probation

On July 17, 1941, K. is officially appointed general commissioner of White Ruthenia, without ever having been there or even knowing exactly where it is located. What counts is that it's an important position. K. cannot disguise his pride. He calls old friends and Party comrades and offers them posts in his new civil administration.

In Ruins.   At the end of August 1941, K. drives to White Ruthenia with his father-in-law, who, despite his sixty-four years, still wants to serve. On August 31, they arrive in Minsk. It's not what they expected: eighty percent of the city has been destroyed by the systematic bombing of the German Luftwaffe. On their first night, K. and his father-in-law are forced to take up quarters with K.'s old comrade, the current senior SS and police leader for Russia-Center, SS-Gruppenführer Erich von dem Bach. Bach assigns them rooms in the former Lenin House, a multistory building currently without windows. The next day, K. assumes control of the western part of White Ruthenia from the Wehrmacht.

Under the prevailing conditions, the difficult task of establishing a civil administration in Minsk requires individuals with particularly hearty constitutions. After two months of duty, K.'s father-in-law has seen enough. He is granted leave and does not return.

Despite equipment deficiencies and the laborious search for accommodations, K. remains enthusiastic. He continues to plan for the future.

1. In K.'s opinion, there is no point in rebuilding the demolished city of Minsk. He proposes that a new German city be erected to the south. His name for the city: Asgard. It is of Gothic origin and has yet to be used as a city name.

2. According to official ideology, White Ruthenians are Slavic and therefore subhuman. K., however, classifies them differently.

Upon his arrival, he discovers that the population is in large part blue eyed and blond haired. He decides to regard them as Aryan. The confluence between K.'s interests and those of his "stepchildren," however, is limited. There is sabotage and Jewish-Bolshevist activities in the surrounding area and even in Minsk itself. Reprisals are harsh. At K.'s request, the Security Police and the Security Service engage in "mop-up operations" in Marina Gorki and other localities. Over 2,000 White Ruthenian Jews are executed.

Unresolved Issues

Goals.   Apart from crushing the Soviet Union and providing food for the Wehrmacht at the expense of the local population, the official aims of the Eastern Ministry are contradictory with regard to White Ruthenia.* On the one hand, White Ruthenians are viewed mistrustfully as Russians. There are plans to resettle undesirable population groups (including Poles) in White Ruthenia in order to erect a buffer zone. On the other hand, there are also plans to reeducate the White Ruthenian people to oppose Moscow and thus to grant the region at least some semblance of autonomy. K. himself finds the second alternative more promising. He orders that a White Ruthenian Self-Help Organization be established and appoints Dr. Ivan Ermachenko, a former Czarist officer married to a Bessarabian German woman, as its director. Dr. Ermachenko's nickname among the local population: Herr Jawohl.

Borders.   K. is prepared to assume control of the entire White Ruthenian territory at any time. The Wehrmacht, however, shows little interest in surrendering the eastern part of the country.

---

* "Ruthenia," which is simply an antiquated Roman word for "Russia," is employed by the Germans to suppress any connection or commonality between White Russians and Russians.

Sovereignty.   Officially, K. is subordinate to the Reich's commissioner for the East, Hinrich Lohse, and equal in rank with the general commissioners of Latvia, Lithuania, and Estonia. However, White Ruthenia, which is significantly poorer than the Baltic countries and has practically no industry, is granted greater independence. K. strives for further autonomy, regards himself as equal in rank with Reich's Commissioner Lohse and General Commissioner Koch in the Ukraine.

According to the Führer's Decree on Police Security in the Newly Occupied Eastern Territories, regional SS leaders are subordinate to civil administrators. The SS, however, refuses on principle to accept this hierarchy. The SS police leader for White Ruthenia, SS-Brigadeführer Carl Zenner, informs K. that while he is prepared to receive circular letters and the like, he will neither carry out any official instructions from K. nor report to him.

Culture Wars

The Minsk Opera, designed by the former municipal architect in Frankfurt am Main and completed shortly before the German invasion, becomes an object of contention among the various German authorities. K. regards the building as an important cultural asset of the White Ruthenian people, entrusted to him. The SS and the Wehrmacht maintain, on the contrary, a purely materialist perspective: they regard the building as spoils or as raw material for war. There are heated disputes, in particular between K. and a general from the Luftwaffe. Since K. lacks the necessary authority to enforce his views on the matter, the opera is for all intents and purposes turned over to plunderers. Each day, a Latvian police battalion—which is quartered in the vicinity of the opera and distinguishes itself in the extermination of White Ruthenian Jews—burns a row of opera seats.

The battle among the various German authorities expands. An extensive and quite valuable collection of art is almost completely removed from the city. On orders from Reichsführer-SS Himmler, the majority of paintings are packed up and sent to Germany. General Stubenrauch of the Wehrmacht has part of the Minsk collection transported eastward toward the front. Several Wehrmacht officers, whose names cannot be reported to K., drive off in three trucks loaded with furniture, paintings, and art objects (without a receipt!). K. files a written complaint about the theft with his superior, Reich's Minister Alfred Rosenberg, requesting that the valuable collection be returned to White Ruthenia or that, at the very least, its material equivalent be placed at the disposal of the Ministry for the Occupied Eastern Territories. In a conversation with Rosenberg, Himmler calls K.'s complaints ridiculous and announces that in the future he will not deign to respond to them. Rosenberg is sympathetic to this position.

"Penal Colony of the East"

From the beginning, rumors abound about K. and his civil administration. The SS complains, among other things, about three of K.'s old friends from the Kurmark district.

(1) The current city commissioner in Minsk, Wilhelm Jan. The Security Police reports: Jan is a weak-willed man and an alcoholic. His administration of office is shockingly slipshod and corrupt. His wife, who also drinks too much, has committed food embezzlement of the most serious nature. She was also involved in a brawl with the city commissioner's chauffeur. During a "celebration," she undressed a drunken participant in the presence of her husband and blackened several of his body parts with shoe polish.
(2) The director of the Provisions Office, District Administrator Schröt. (the title of District Administrator was revoked by the Eastern Ministry). The Security Police reports:

that in the course of the operation, ethnic White Ruthenians are also driven out into the streets. They, too, are beaten openly with rubber truncheons and rifle butts. There is wild gunfire throughout the city. Even members of the German civil administration are forced to flee in order to avoid being shot. Piles of corpses line the streets. In addition to this, members of the Eleventh Police Battalion systematically plunder the city. Carl intends to lodge a complaint. The battalion commander, however, has already continued on to the city of Baranovichi. When Carl requests that the operation be halted, the deputy battalion commander is astounded. He reports that he has orders from the battalion commander to exterminate all Jews in the city, as they have done in other localities— the liquidations are politically motivated; economic concerns have never been a factor. In response to Carl's vigorous objections, the deputy commander agrees to stop the operation that evening.

The next day, Territorial Commissioner Carl files a report with General Commissioner K. He informs K. that it is not possible to carry out further operations against Jews in Slutsk at this point in time. Peace and order must first be reestablished. He requests that he be spared from working with this police battalion in the future.

A day later, members of the Eleventh Police Battalion deposit money, valuables, and other objects from Slutsk at the cashier's office of the civil administration in Minsk. During this transaction, Reserve Police Lieutenant B. attempts to purchase gold for use in a personal matter. When K. learns of this, he is outraged. He immediately reports the case to the responsible field commander in Minsk and demands that the police officer involved be arrested. However, Reserve Lieutenant B. is released following an interrogation by a military judge. K.'s legal representatives have a completely different interpretation of the law: all private transactions of gold are strictly forbidden in the German Reich. To compound matters, the officer involved is a member of the troop that liquidated the previous owner. K. files a complaint with the Reich's commissioner for the East, his old friend Hinrich Lohse.

In addition to this, K. criticizes the operation itself. Three weeks earlier, he had discussed the matter with SS-Brigadeführer Zenner and they had agreed that Jewish craftsmen were to be exempted from the executions. However, the Eleventh Police Battalion—which is directly subordinate to the Wehrmacht—ignored this directive. K. expresses grave concern about the reputation of the German Reich among the White Ruthenian population, a reputation that has been seriously damaged by the incident.

K.: It is impossible to maintain peace and order in White Ruthenia using such methods. Furthermore, it is an unbelievable *Schweinerei* to have buried alive seriously wounded people, who are then able to dig their way back out of their graves. The civil administration has gone to enormous lengths to win over the local population for Germany, and this goal cannot be reconciled with such methods!

K. submits a petition that criminal charges be brought against all the officers of the Eleventh Police Battalion.

K. has a copy of the petition forwarded to SS-Obergruppenführer Heydrich, requesting that Heydrich review the matter and comment on it. Heydrich doesn't respond. No charges are ever filed against the officers.

"Difference of Opinion"
The SS insists on an immediate resolution of the Jewish Question for political reasons. The Wehrmacht regards such a resolution as absolutely necessary for reasons of general security. The civil administration, in contrast, regards such a solution as impractical for economic reasons.

Reich's Commissioner Lohse—who has also received complaints from other officials about the liquidation of indispensable Jewish skilled laborers—files a request with his superiors that the executions be stopped, at least until suitable non-Jewish replacements can be trained. The response from the Eastern Ministry, however, is unambiguous: "After discussing the matter extensively, we have now attained clarity with regard to the Jewish Question. In addressing the problem, economic considerations are to be strictly disregarded. Any further questions arising in the matter should be resolved directly with the senior SS and police leader."

II.

In Slonim, cooperation among the various German authorities proceeds smoothly. K.'s Territorial Commissioner Gerhard Erren decides to take matters into his own hands. Excerpt from his situation report (January 25, 1942): Slonim was heavily overpopulated and the living conditions were catastrophic. The Jewish operation on November 14, 1941, improved matters perceptibly. It was now possible to completely clear a street in order to set up offices and apartments for German authorities. This street, along with the surrounding neighborhood, will continue to be cleansed in preparation for a future SS base. When I arrived here, the territory of Slonim contained approximately 25,000 Jews—16,000 in the city of Slonim alone, which constituted over two-thirds of the entire urban population. It was impossible to establish a ghetto, as the necessary barbed wire and security personnel were lacking. For this reason, preparations were made for a major operation. First, the Jewish population was expropriated, and the resulting household items and tools were used to furnish all the offices and quarters of the various German authorities, including the Wehrmacht. Those objects that were unusable for Germans were released for sale to the local population and the proceeds were turned over to the cashier's office. Then there was a precise registration of Jews according to number, age, and profession. All craftsmen and skilled laborers were sorted out, issued identification cards, and lodged in separate quarters. The operation carried out by the Security Service on November 14 freed me of many useless eaters. The approximately 7,000 Jews remaining in the city have all been integrated into the labor process and work obediently as a result of their constant fear of death. In the spring, the inspections and selections will continue in order to further reduce their numbers.

Powers of Discernment

In the middle of November 1941, the first trains loaded with German Jews arrive in Minsk. German officials initially plan to deport 25,000 Jews from Germany to White Ruthenia. Over the next weeks, approximately 7,000 Jews are sent from Hamburg, Düsseldorf, Frankfurt, Bremen, Berlin, Vienna, and Brünn. In order to make room for them, the SS executes more than 6,600 White Ruthenian and Polish Jews.

K., curious about the new arrivals, insists on inspecting the German-Jewish ghetto. A tour with SS officers is arranged at the end of November. Present at the inspection: SS-Brigadeführer Zenner, Police General Herf, and several political leaders. Dr. Frank from Hamburg, a lawyer appointed Jewish Elder by the SS shortly after his arrival in Minsk, accompanies the group. In contrast to SS-Brigadeführer Zenner (short and fat, with an "Eastern skull" and an inclination to drink and brawl), Dr. Frank makes an extremely favorable impression despite the unfavorable circumstances. In the course of the conversation, he mentions that a number of the deportees have brothers currently fighting for Germany. K. is outraged by this injustice, declares that he intends to report the matter immediately to the Führer. He requests that Dr. Frank compile a list of the persons involved. In the Berlin section of the ghetto, K. sees two girls who, in his opinion, are Aryan in appearance. He stops them, asks them questions, and records their names and personal details.

K. is strangely affected by the inspection. Over the next weeks, he makes repeated requests for information from the Council of

Elders in the German-Jewish ghetto: lists of Jewish war veterans, military pensioners, German Jews with military decorations, former officers, former members of the Freikorps (irregular soldiers), civil servants, pensioners, German Jews with civilian decorations, *Mischlinge ersten Grades* ("half-Jews"), *Mischlinge zweiten Grades* ("quarter-Jews"). He compiles a list of persons incorrectly resettled to Minsk and forwards it to SS-Obergruppenführer Heydrich in Berlin. One of the names on the list catches K.'s eye: a Dr. Karl Loewenstein from Berlin—according to his own account, a former Navy officer and half-Jew converted to Protestantism, with military and civilian decorations. K. believes that Loewenstein is not only a fellow student from his days at the University of Berlin but also a relative. K.'s brother-in-law is married to a woman with the same last name and from the same part of Germany, the dancer from Paderborn. During his next inspection of the Ghetto, K. requests that Dr. Loewenstein report to him. Loewenstein—appointed by the SS as head of the Jewish Ghetto Police—is cultivated, polite, punctilious, and rigorously military: in other words, the perfect German. K. promises to get him out of Minsk.

In the middle of December 1941, K. writes again to Reich's Commissioner Lohse:

[Top secret matter of state]
My dear Hinrich!

I personally request that you provide official instructions to the civil administration for its actions regarding those Jews deported from Germany to White Ruthenia. Among these Jews, one finds soldiers who fought on the front during the Great War and who are decorated with Iron Crosses both First and Second Class; there are also disabled war veterans, half-Aryans, and even a three-quarter Aryan. Of the twenty-five thousand Jews who are supposed to be sent here, only six to seven thousand have as yet arrived. I do not know where the others are. Through repeated official visits to the ghetto, I have been able to establish that among these Jews—who are distinguished from the Russian Jews by their personal cleanliness—there are skilled laborers who can achieve in one day approximately five times what a Russian Jew can.

These Jews will probably freeze to death or die of hunger in the coming weeks. They represent an incredible health threat to us since they are, of course, just as exposed as we are to the twenty-two epidemics currently present in White Ruthenia. Vaccines are not available for them.

On my own authority, I cannot give the Security Service instructions about the treatment of these people, although certain Wehrmacht units and police units are already very keen on the German Jews' belongings. The Security Service simply removed four hundred mattresses from the German Jewish ghetto—without asking anyone—and has also confiscated many other objects. I am certainly resolute and ready to assist in resolving the Jewish Question, but people who come from our own cultural milieu are quite different than the animalistic hordes here. Should we entrust Lithuanians and Latvians—who are also disapproved of by the population here—with the slaughter? I could not do this. Bearing in mind the reputation of the German Reich and the Nazi Party, I ask you to provide clear orders so that what is necessary can be done in the most humane form.

With a heartfelt greeting and *Heil Hitler*

Your

K.

Preliminary Results.   At K.'s request, the German-Jewish Sonder-ghetto (special ghetto) is separated from the Russian-Jewish ghetto with barbed wire.

Technical Difficulties

The "Expert on the Jewish Question" in Minsk, SS-Obersturmführer Kurt Burkhardt, has his hands full. Almost no other area in Russia is so densely populated with Jews as White Ruthenia. This problem is exacerbated by the not insignificant numbers of camouflaged (i.e., converted) Jews and racial mongrels. At the beginning of January 1942, SS-Obersturmführer Burkhardt estimates that approximately 41,000 White Ruthenian Jews have been executed. Not taken into account in this figure: the Jews executed by earlier *Einsatzkommandos* (mobile police units) and the approximately 19,000 people shot by the Wehrmacht as partisans and criminals, approximately half of whom were Jews. The following significant obstacles currently prevent a definitive and fundamental resolution of the Jewish Question in White Ruthenia: (1) in this territory, Jews make up a very high percentage of indispensable skilled laborers; (2) liquidation operations of a greater scope cannot be carried out in the current weather conditions, since—as a result of the extraordinarily severe winter—the frozen ground has made the excavation of mass graves extremely difficult. In all probability, mass executions can be resumed only in February 1942.

Short Circuit

Skilled workers from Poland, who are sent to Minsk at the beginning of 1942 in order to alleviate the increasing lack of skilled laborers there, are put up in a prison because no other accommodations are available. Shortly thereafter, the Security Service rounds up 280 civilian prisoners in the jail and transports them to a routine execution. Since this does not exhaust the capacity of the mass graves, the Polish workers are also included in the execution.

Special Status

I.

Despite the special attention K. devotes to the Sonderghetto, conditions there remain extraordinarily poor. Of the approximately 7,000 German Jews in the Sonderghetto in January 1942, there are 1,800 men of working age. Well over half of these men are unable to report to work duty as a result of malnutrition and inadequate accommodations. The most frequently occurring diseases: 370 prisoners with dysentery, 102 with frostbite, 135 with festering wounds, 20 with conjunctivitis, 25 with lung infections, 63 with influenza, 30 with cystitis.

In certain cases, Jews with infectious diseases are selected and then, under the pretext of being transferred to a Jewish hospital or old people's home, are executed.

II.

K. employs a number of German Jews in his civil administration. They prove to be extremely hardworking and polite, and all speak excellent German.

There are repeated disputes between K. and the SS regarding the German Jews. The Security Police are in possession of the following confidential information:

> After K.'s first visit to the ghetto, the Jewish Elder Dr. Frank is said to have had the impression that K. would like to see the German Jews dealt with somewhat less severely than the Russian Jews, with whom they can in no way be compared.

> Dr. Frank is reported to have regular access to the general commissioner in order to file complaints. Proof: an oral complaint by K. about an old Nazi Party comrade who threatened to give a member of the Jewish Council of Elders a

beating and, if need be, put a bullet in his ribcage; a written complaint about an SS-Hauptsturmführer who beat a Jew for being insufficiently productive.

The Jew who works as a hairdresser in the general commissioner's headquarters and who shaves K. every morning is reported to have said that all Jews working at the headquarters are under K.'s personal protection. According to him, every Jew has the right to complain to K. about improper treatment.

The very fact that Jews are employed as hairdressers at the general commissioner's headquarters also arouses the displeasure of the SS. An SS-Hauptsturmführer reproaches K. for allowing his female employees to have their hair done by non-Aryans. K.: That's of no interest to me; I want my women and girls to look beautiful. The Hauptsturmführer points out that the hairdressers do not wear Jewish stars. K.: One can't expect that the German girls who come to have their hair done be forced to look continuously at Jewish stars.

"Stepchildren"

K., who continues to regard himself as a humanist, wants to revive the cultural life of the White Ruthenian people entrusted to him. Since the largest theater in Minsk has been destroyed during the fighting, he decides to establish a new municipal theater in another building. Plays are performed there for Germans as well as for the local population (with an emphasis on National Socialist or anti-Bolshevist and anti-Semitic dramas). Since there is no regular German theater company present in Minsk, K. is initially forced to rely on guest performances. In 1942, the municipal theater from Landsberg on the Warte performs in Minsk for three months. Productions include the well-known Gothic tragedy *Totila*.

> WERINGHARD:
> Und glüht und zuckt in dir nicht heischend alles,
> Mein blondes Schwesterlein im Arm zu halten?
>
> WERINGHARD:
> And doesn't everything inside you burn and ache
> To hold my blond young sister in your arms?

One day, K. notices a particularly attractive White Ruthenian physician. However, he is unable to obtain her name or workplace. After some consideration, he decides to convene a conference of White Ruthenian physicians in Minsk, and even to appear as a speaker himself. At the conference, K. is able to locate the woman again. He instructs his deputy to photograph her and to find out who she is. The next day, the physician is ordered to appear before Dr. Ermachenko, director of the local Self-Help Organization. Dr. Ermachenko informs the woman that General Commissioner K. has requested that she work as his housekeeper. The physician refuses. Dr. Ermachenko: We all have to make sacrifices for the White Ruthenian cause. The woman stands by her refusal. Dr. Ermachenko mentions the prospect of police intervention. The physician declares herself ready to accept the post.

K. would like to found a White Ruthenian Scholarly Society. However, since the idea finds little resonance among his superiors, he is forced to postpone his plans. K. himself is interested in the Schnurkeramiker (Indogermanic peoples ca. 5000–1800 B.C.), and he participates in the excavation of barrow sites around Minsk. German Jews support him in this as archaeologists.

> "We offer the White Ruthenians neither parliamentary antics
> nor democratic buffoonery. We offer them our own destiny:
> through labor, discipline, and morals we offer them progress
> and culture, soil and bread, the unfolding of the powers la-
> tent in them and the preservation of their kind."
>
> — Wilhelm K., "The White Ruthenians,"
> *Frankfurter Zeitung* (July 23, 1942)

Major Operation

At the beginning of March 1942, the SS organizes a major operation in the Russian ghetto in Minsk. The operation is officially
described as a resettlement. The Jewish Council of Elders in the
Russian ghetto is ordered to select 5,000 White Ruthenian and
Polish Jews for deportation. Each of the deportees is permitted to
take ten pounds of luggage.

K., who has been informed of the operation beforehand, does
not allow his German Jews to return to the ghetto after work,
keeping them the entire night at the general commissioner's headquarters. This arouses the suspicion of Jews in the Russian ghetto,
who begin to doubt the SS's account of the resettlement. At the appointed time the next morning, the assembly point is empty. As a
result, the SS calls in evacuation commandos, who drive the inhabitants of an arbitrarily chosen district of the Russian ghetto out of
their houses. A number of Jews attempt to avoid the transport.
They are either driven together by force or executed on the spot.
After the evacuation, the houses and streets are strewn with
corpses, which are later removed by inhabitants of the German-
Jewish ghetto. The evacuated Jews are loaded into freight cars at
the train station and transported to an execution site.

During the course of the operation, K. appears in the ghetto a
number of times in an aggravated state. Around 4:30 in the after-

noon, he returns with his personal aide-de-camp. A heated conflict develops between K. and several members of the Security Police. K. observes SS-Hauptsturmführer Stark beating Jews with a whip in order to drive them to the train station. He confronts the Hauptsturmführer, rebuking him in an extraordinarily sharp tone for his behavior. K.: "What! Aren't you ashamed as an SS leader to be standing around with a whip?" K. tries without success to remove the whip from Stark's possession. SS-Obersturmführer Burkhardt appears and attempts to intervene in the dispute. K. showers him with reproaches about events in the ghetto. All this occurs in plain view of the Jews and White Ruthenian policemen on the scene. In the course of the discussion, K. insults a number of SS officers, using expressions such as "swinishness" and "You'll be hearing from me about this later." Burkhardt regards the encounter as a "significant snub" for him in his capacity as an SS officer and an "Expert on the Jewish Question." Stark himself feels "roundly abused." After the dispute, K. remains in the ghetto for an extended period of time. According to "a not 100-percent authenticated report," K. is said to have passed out candy to Jewish children at this time.

SS-Hauptsturmführer Stark is so angered by the encounter that he immediately decides to get even with K. That same night, he enters the Sonderghetto without permission and executes K.'s three Jewish hairdressers. The next morning, K. notices their absence. He fears that the SS—despite their assurances—has included German Jews in the operation as well. He sends his District Administrator R. to Security Police headquarters. The police commander is unable to provide R. with any pertinent information. K. telephones the commander's superior, SS-Brigadeführer Zenner, and demands an explanation. Zenner, too, claims to know nothing about the matter. K. becomes increasingly agitated, screams into the telephone. Enraged, he announces that he holds the Security Service responsible for the disappearance of the three hairdressers. If they are not returned by evening, he will file charges

the evacuation of Jews from the German Reich had been strictly followed in every case, I have had each of the cases you complained about subjected to a thorough and *time-consuming* reexamination. As you can see from the enclosed compilation of the results of these examinations, the persons concerned are *without exception* Jews as defined by the law or Jews and Jewesses who, as the result of divorce and similar occurrences, are no longer connected to their German-blooded spouses and must therefore be considered Jews. I was not told how this list came into being. However, the only way I can explain its existence is that the information provided by evacuated Jews was believed blindly. One was thus more inclined to believe statements made by Jews than those made by German officials, officials who have subjected each individual case to the most exacting inspection according to the current detailed guidelines.

And this at a time when we have set about tackling the resolution of the Jewish Question in the German Reich and elsewhere. It is already known of many of the Jews included on the list that they have repeatedly sought to deny their affiliation to Judaism for every possible—and impossible—reason, just as it is in the nature of things in general that *Mischlinge ersten Grades* (half-Jews) are intent on denying their affiliation to Judaism on every occasion that arises.

I'm sure you will admit that in the third year of war there are more important military responsibilities for the Security Police and the Security Service than looking into the belly-aching of Jews, engaging in time-consuming investigations, and keeping so many of my men from other, much more important tasks. The only reason I have examined your list is to refute such attacks once and for all with documentary evidence. I regret that, six and a half years after the enactment of the Nuremberg Laws, I must still write such a justification.

Heil Hitler!

One Life

Despite this blow, K. refuses to give up. He discusses the case of Dr. Karl Loewenstein, a former lieutenant in the Royal Navy, with his old friend Reich's Minister Lammers. Lammers is sympathetic. He arranges that the case be presented personally to the Führer. Shortly thereafter, Reichsführer-SS Himmler orders that Loewenstein be released from the Minsk ghetto. At the beginning of May 1942, after several short delays, Loewenstein is placed on a passenger train traveling westward.

Final Solution

April 1942. On orders from the chief of the Security Police, SS-Obergruppenführer Heydrich, the following measures regarding the Jewish Question are implemented:

(1) The German Jews still alive in Minsk are no longer to be left to a "natural" death (freezing, starvation, disease, random shootings, and beatings), but are now to be included in the final solution to the Jewish Question.
(2) The deportation of Jews from Germany to Minsk, which was interrupted at the end of November 1941, is to be resumed.

The new transports of German Jews are no longer directed to the city of Minsk itself but rather to a former collective farm in the vicinity of the Trostenez estate, approximately fifteen kilometers southeast. Here, the deportees are killed immediately on arrival, initially with a bullet in the head, later in gas trucks. Between May and October 1942, no fewer than eighteen trains arrive from Theresienstadt, Vienna, Königsberg, and Cologne.

Adversary

The extensive organizational preparations required for these expanded measures against German Jews are entrusted to one of K.'s main adversaries, the current commander of the Security Police and the Security Service in White Ruthenia, SS-Obersturmbannführer Dr. Eduard Strauch.

Dr. Strauch (as evaluated by his superiors):

Common sense: existent

Stance toward the Nazi worldview: completely affirmative

Reactions: impulsive and explosive

Emotional life: not particularly well developed ("Strauch has great difficulty putting himself in the place of others.")

While Strauch is regarded as "courageous and extraordinarily cold-blooded," his superiors also note an imbalance in his character: "His personality is most strongly determined by an unwillingness to compromise, up to the point of rudeness, particularly in defending and enforcing ideological issues"—"a difficult personality with tendencies to dissatisfaction and carping."

As a strong supporter of the final solution to the Jewish Question, SS-Obersturmbannführer Strauch has difficulty getting along with K. Strauch expresses this politely to a civil servant visiting from Germany: K. does not possess the necessary *Ostfestigkeit* ("fortitude for the East").

Memorandum by Strauch (April 18, 1942): K. calls and relates the following: He has received a report several days ago that approximately fifteen Jewish men and women have been marched through the streets, covered with blood. In addition to this, the accompanying interpreter is said to have shot at the Jews in jail, thereby endangering the security officer working there at the time. K. demands an immediate investigation and punishment. He expects to be informed of the measures undertaken in the matter.

Strauch's response: I would like to request that you name those persons who have slanderously claimed that I allowed Jews or other people to be led through the streets covered with blood. The fact that we do not proceed gently should go without saying. No one—least of all the Reichsführer-SS or the Führer himself—would understand if I did not take the strictest measures to protect the lives of the men entrusted to me. In any case, the life of one of my own men is more important to me than that of a hundred Jews or partisans.

"Soft-Hearted"

At the end of May 1942, Albert Hoffmann, representative for Reichsleiter Martin Bormann, travels to Minsk as part of an official tour of the occupied Eastern territories. By the time he arrives in the city, Hoffmann is already quite skeptical. During the train ride, he has been informed of numerous irregularities there (excessive drinking, womanizing).

In Minsk, the Security Service informs Hoffmann about the following incidents involving General Commissioner K.:

(1) The White Ruthenian ballet (two-thirds White Ruthenians, one-third Jews or people related to Jews by marriage) has performed repeatedly before K. and his civil servants, at times even in K.'s own apartment. The girls have been regularly invited to dinner afterward. Once, they were even asked to take part in an evening get-together in their dance costumes, which they refused to do. Consequently, they were given nothing to eat.

(2) There have been significant drinking excesses, which are detrimental to the reputation of the German civil administration. For the most part, these excesses have taken place in House Potsdam, the living quarters of K.'s officials.

(3) K. made a gift of brassieres and panties to the ballet dancers, ostensibly because theirs were completely tattered. K. later reported with visible pleasure that he had been present at the fitting.

(4) During a walk through the ghetto, K. gave candy to Jewish children.

K. is questioned by Hoffmann about the accusations. He vehemently denies each one of them:

Regarding (1), K. insists that the White Ruthenian ballet has never danced in his apartment. Only once did they dance for the civil administration, and that was during the farewell party for SS-Obergruppenführer Erich von dem Bach. The girls did not meet with German personnel afterward but were simply served a meal in a side room. K. knows nothing about an invitation for the dancers to participate in an evening get-together in their dance costumes.

Regarding (2), K. has also heard about excessive drinking. He himself has not participated in a single instance of it. He also believes that womanizing is possible, although he knows nothing about the details. It is not his responsibility to stick his nose into private matters.

Regarding (3), K. explains: the Weizmann Trio was on tour in Minsk. During lunch, one lady in the trio—the daughter of a university professor—complained that she had been forced to dry herself with her own underwear. This had occasioned K. to have his district administrator give the lady a new set of underwear. Gifts to members of the ballet were out of the question.

Regarding (4), K. does admit to having given candy to several

Jewish children. This occurred in the following way. Once, the Security Service liquidated Jewish children in the Minsk ghetto in plain view of the White Ruthenian population. K. could not endorse this behavior. He had gone to the ghetto and requested that such measures be undertaken outside the city. On this occasion, he had been touched with human pity and given candy to several children who were crying the loudest. Three to five pieces.

Departure.   Hoffmann instructs K. that he must take forceful measures against excessive drinking and womanizing, but he needn't be more Catholic than the Pope.

In a Different Tone

Approval.   In June 1942, the SS plans a new wave of operations against the remaining Jews in White Ruthenia. The commander of the Security Police and the Security Service in Riga takes the following position on the matter: the economic value of Jewish skilled laborers is outweighed by their danger as potential supporters of the partisans. Asked for his opinion on the matter, K. explicitly endorses the standpoint of the SS. He requests that his territorial commissioners consult with the Security Service and then reexamine, using the strictest criteria, their need for the Jewish skilled laborers currently employed, and sort out all Jews not absolutely necessary for the economy.

Altered Logic.   Once again, K. submits an urgent request to his superiors, asking that they halt any further transports of German Jews to Minsk. Contrary to his argument eight months earlier, he now justifies this request through the ostensibly inferior work capacities of German Jews. K.: "I would like to point out that while there is no current economic need to introduce more German Jews into White Ruthenia, there are serious political objections to increasing the number of Jews here. Only a tiny percentage of German Jews are skilled laborers. Furthermore, we know from experience that their work capacities are extremely limited."

Testimonial.   In the middle of July 1942, SS-Brigadeführer Zenner is relieved of duty as senior SS and police leader in White Ruthenia. His superiors are dissatisfied with his performance (SS-Obergruppenführer von dem Bach: "Zenner has led an idle life here"). He is replaced provisionally by Walter Schimana, Commander of the Police Regiment Center, and then by SS-Gruppenführer Curt von Gottberg. On Zenner's departure, K. writes him an official letter of praise: "If, during your term of duty here, tens of thousands of our Jewish enemies have been exterminated, then that is also to your credit. You have consistently supported my goal of removing the natural enemies of the White Ruthenian people—the Russians, the Poles, and the Jews."

Cooperation.   On July 31, 1942, two days after the end of a major operation against the two ghettos in Minsk, K. files a report with the Reich's Commissioner for the East Hinrich Lohse. In the report, he emphasizes the accomplishments of his comrade SS-Obersturmbannführer Dr. Eduard Strauch:

Re.: Partisan control and Jewish operations in the General Territory of White Ruthenia
    In all our clashes with partisans in White Ruthenia, we have found that the Jews—in the former Polish part as well as in the former Soviet part of the general territory— have been the principal supporters of the partisan movement, together with the Polish resistance movement in

the East and the Red Army in Moscow. Consequently, given the threat to the entire economy, we must regard the treatment of Jews in White Ruthenia as a primarily political matter, one that cannot be resolved by economic, but only political criteria. After detailed discussions with SS-Brigadeführer Zenner and the extremely capable Head of the Security Service, SS-Obersturmbannfuhrer Dr. Strauch, we have liquidated around 55,000 Jews in White Ruthenia over the past ten weeks. In the territory of Minsk Land, the Jews have been completely eradicated—without endangering our labor supply. In the predominantly Polish territory of Lida, 16,000 Jews have been liquidated, in Slonim, 8,000 Jews, etc. An incursion by the Wehrmacht's Rear Area Command, about which I have already reported, interrupted our preparations to liquidate Jews in the territory of Glubokoe. Without bothering to contact me, the Rear Area Command liquidated 10,000 Jews—Jews we had already planned to eradicate systematically. In the city of Minsk, around 10,000 Jews were liquidated on July 28 and 29, including 6,500 Russian Jews—predominantly women, children, and the elderly. The remainder of those liquidated were Jews unfit for work, primarily from Vienna, Brünn, Bremen, and Berlin, who had been sent to Minsk last November on the orders of the Führer.

The territory of Slutsk has also been relieved of several thousand Jews. The same is true of Novogrudok and Vileika. Radical measures have been planned for Baranovichi and Hanzevichi. In Baranovichi, there are still approximately ten thousand Jews living in the city alone. Nine thousand of them will be liquidated in the next month.

There are still 2,600 German Jews in the city of Minsk. In addition to this, there are a total of 6,000 Russian Jews and Jewesses here, who remained with their work units during the last Jewish operation. In the future as well, Minsk will continue to have the largest number of Jewish work units, since the concentration of the armaments industry and the responsibilities of the railway here make this necessary, at least for the time being. The Security Service and I have set the number of Jewish workers at a maximum of 800, if possible 500, in all the remaining territories. This means that after completion of the operations currently scheduled we will have 8,800 Jews in Minsk and approximately 7,000 Jews in the ten remaining territories (including the territory of Minsk Land, which is free of Jews). There is no longer any danger that the partisans can continue to rely on Jewish support in the future. The Security Service and I would of course prefer that the Jews in the General Territory of White Ruthenia be eliminated definitively, as soon as the Wehrmacht no longer has any economic use for them. For the time being, we will have to take into account the needs of the Wehrmacht, which continues to be the main employer of Jews here.

In addition to this unambiguous stance toward the Jews, the Security Service in White Ruthenia must also repeatedly assume the difficult task of delivering new transports of German Jews to their fate. This is unduly taxing on the men of the Security Service both in material and emotional terms, and it keeps them from their actual tasks in the territory of White Ruthenia.

I would therefore be thankful if the Reich's minister would ensure that further transports of Jews to Minsk be stopped, at least until the partisan threat has been definitively overcome. I need a 100-percent deployment of the Security Service against the partisans and against the Polish resistance movement, both of which require all the personnel of the somewhat limited Security Service units here.

After completion of the Jewish operation in Minsk, SS-Obersturmbannführer Dr. Strauch reported to me with justified indignation that we had just received a transport of a thousand Jews from Warsaw, without instructions from the Reichsführer-SS and without the knowledge of the general commissioner.

I am in complete agreement with the commander of the Security Service that in order to prevent further unrest in White Ruthenia we must liquidate every Jewish transport that has not been ordered or announced by our superiors.

K.

K. in Conversation

Forced Assent.   An evening get-together at the Einsatzstab Rosenberg at the end of 1942. In the course of the conversation, the Jewish Question arises. K. turns to an SS officer and asks him to contact Commander Strauch so that the Fifth Police District can finally be placed under observation.

The SS officer: We know that the machinations of the White Ruthenian police are quite impenetrable.

K.: On the contrary, they are quite transparent. But I don't mean the White Ruthenians, I mean the Germans.

The SS officer: In what way?

K.: My best piano tuner was shot for no apparent reason.

During the conversation, K. calls the German police officer who executed the Jewish piano tuner a "swine." The SS officer is unable to object to this formulation, as K. announces in front of the other guests that Commander Strauch himself was outraged by the incident.

Strauch, upon learning of the conversation: There cannot, of course, be any question of outrage on my part!

Generation Gap (October 1942).   During a discussion, K. comes to speak about the author Georg Schmückle from Stuttgart. He praises Schmückle's work, including his novella *The Red Mask*. A National Socialist of the younger generation points out that the novella glorifies the "finance Jew" Süss Oppenheimer from Württemburg. K.: You young Nazis still don't have the right perspective on these matters. You are always afraid that your souls are endangered as soon as Jews are mentioned. Even as a student before the Great War, I listened to Mendelssohn and Offenbach and did not as a result give up my *völkisch* ideas. I cannot understand why we must act as if Mendelssohn did not exist, or why we are no longer allowed to perform Jewish works such as Offenbach's *The Tales of Hoffmann*. I limit myself here to the Jews of the nineteenth century, who, following their liberation from the ghetto, experienced an enormous cultural upswing. It is indisputable that Jews are artistic. The grounds for this lies in the 6 percent of their blood that is Nordic, and perhaps in Western and Romance influences as well.

K. (continuing): While you young Nazis do have the correct position on biological issues, you are off the mark on intellectual matters. In any case, I do not believe that Jewish contributions to the history of music, such as those of Mendelssohn, can simply be omitted without creating a gap.

Security Measures

At the end of October 1942, K. issues a "Decree Concerning Reports to the Police and the Security Service" to the senior department heads of his civil administration: "Reports to the police regarding offenses committed by members of the German authorities or by the White Ruthenians and Jews working for us must be presented to me first for approval. I request that senior department heads ensure strict adherence to this order by issuing a circular letter to those offices under their authority."

SS-Obersturmbannführer Dr. Strauch regards this decree as a measure aimed explicitly against his men and himself. Strauch: K. is concerned not about members of the German civil administration or about White Ruthenians but only about his German Jews, whom he wants to protect from the operations of the Security Police.

"We will clear the way without pangs of conscience, and then... 'the waves come crashing down, there is peace in the world.'"*

Partisan resistance in White Ruthenia presents a difficult and increasingly threatening problem for the Germans. None of the means employed to combat it, regardless of how ruthless or brutal, have yielded positive results. Partisans seem to spring out of the ground like mushrooms.

Albert Hoffmann, representative for Reichsleiter Bormann, after his visit to Minsk in May 1942: There is even a Polish resistance movement in White Ruthenia. The Security Service had planned to exterminate Polish intellectuals. Unfortunately, the civil administration did not go along with the plan. Hopes that the partisans would freeze to death during the first winter proved illusory.

---

*From a report by SS-Standartenführer Dr. Hubert Achim-Pifrader, head of the Combat Staff of the Security Police and Security Service.

Progress Report

The first half of August was, with the exception of two transports of Jews, rather monotonous. On 8/15/1942, preparations began for a major operation against bandits and partisans in the White Ruthenian territory.

On 8/27/1942, the entire detachment was mobilized against a partisan camp supposedly located at a particular site in a swamp. The operation was unsuccessful. After wandering through the forest for an hour, we came upon a swamp that was impossible to traverse. After firing the grenade thrower randomly into the swamp for fifteen minutes, we withdrew. A day later, we engaged in a night operation, which was also unsuccessful because the partisans were so well hidden in the village we searched that we were unable to find them. The village teacher, who attempted to flee after being interrogated, was shot by Sturmführer Hampe.

—SS-Unterscharführer Arlt

Motto: "Difficulties only exist in order to be surmounted!" (SS-Standartenführer Dr. Pifrader). Inspired by an implacable will to make White Ruthenia bandit-free and to bring peace to the territory, the Security Police tackle their difficult tasks with unabated energy.

SS-Obergruppenführer Erich von dem Bach, Himmler's plenipotentiary for Bandit Control Operations: "Experience teaches us that mass executions and the torching of villages, without liquidating the entire population or evacuating it in an orderly fashion at the same time, have only detrimental consequences for us. The decision as to whether a village should be burned down and whether its inhabitants should be liquidated or evacuated is solely and exclusively the responsibility of Security Service commando leaders."

In the fall of 1942, Hinrich Lohse, Reich's commissioner for the East, notes that a significant number of officials in the German civil administration participate voluntarily in mass executions. In November 1942, he finds himself forced to issue an explicit decree on the matter: "Occasioned by an individual incident, I hereby forbid office holders in the Eastern Administration from active participation in executions of any kind. Executions, in particular the liquidation of Jews, are the responsibility of the Security Police and the Security Service."

Operation Nuremberg (Nov. 1942).   Combat Group Gottberg reports: Total casualties:

(a) Enemy losses: 789 bandits, 353 suspected bandits, 1,826 Jews, 7 gypsies.

(b) German losses: 2 killed, 10 wounded.

(Not included in these figures: bandits, Jews, etc. who were burned in houses and bunkers.)

Operation Hornung (Feb. 1943).   SS-Brigadeführer Curt von Gottberg reports on his "most difficult operation to date":

Enemy losses: 2,219 bandits, 7,378 suspected bandits, 65 prisoners, 3,300 executed Jews.

German losses: (German comrades) 2 dead, 12 wounded; (foreign comrades) 27 dead, 26 wounded.

Spoils: 221.8 tons of grain, 13.8 tons of linseed and hemp seed, 60 horses, 9,340 cattle, 785 pigs, 5,490 sheep, 2 tons of flax and hemp thread, 65 sleighs.

Change of Policy (May 1943).   Due to an increasing shortage of labor power, SS-Obersturmbannführer Strauch, Commander of the Security Police and Security Service in White Ruthenia, issues the following decree: "The torching of villages and individual houses must stop. If it has been clearly established that the inhabitants of a village have supplied the bandits with provisions or information, they are to be conscripted for work service. In cases where there are compelling reasons why captured persons cannot be turned over to work service without endangering an operation, those persons are to be liquidated. Their possessions are to be confiscated and turned over to the next chief of staff or area elder for distribution among the local inhabitants. When liquidations occur in public, the inhabitants of the area should be informed of the reasons for this and presented with available evidence."

Under Way with the Wehrmacht.   The effects of this decree are not evident to Propaganda Leader Lauch (Civil Administration Minsk). On orders of General Commissioner K., Lauch takes part in a major SS and police operation directed by SS-Brigadeführer Gottberg in the Borisov district. Lauch is assigned to the Combat Group of First Lieutenant Kluptsch (Wehrmacht). After discussing suggestions about the use of propaganda with him, Lauch is forced to return to Minsk because of motor damage to a propaganda truck. Four days later, he returns with a new truck, meeting the combat group in Novo Yanchino. Here he finds two barns containing the corpses of executed partisans and "suspected bandits." Although the barns had been set on fire, the corpses inside were not completely burned and were partially eaten by animals. Lauch registers his objections about this state of affairs with Kluptsch. He requests permission to bury the corpses before the civilian population returns. Two days later, permission is granted, but only after several villagers have returned to the site and seen the partially burnt corpses.

First Lieutenant Kluptsch suffers minor injuries from a land mine. First Lieutenant Klitzing assumes command of the combat group.

Initial Success.   The next day, Lauch is able to hold two propaganda meetings, which, in his opinion, are well received by the local population.

He is forced to acknowledge, however, that the Wehrmacht does not properly understand his work. Two days later, when First Lieutenant Klitzing learns that partisans have disguised themselves in civilian clothing and are active in the surrounding villages, he orders that the villages be burned down and the inhabitants executed.

Propaganda Leader Lauch: Episodes like this make a particularly crass impression. In addition, both the police and the Wehrmacht rummage around senselessly in the villagers' houses, throwing furnishings, seeds, and other things into the courtyards and out into the fields. Slaughtered chickens are strewn about the villages. This creates a spectacle of senseless devastation and makes the worst possible impression on the local population. We must take a strict stand against this senseless slaughter of animals!

Since Lauch sees no possibility of engaging in effective propaganda, he decides to return to Minsk. He submits a report on the matter to General Commissioner K.

At around the same time, K. receives a similar report from his District Commissioner Langer regarding the actions of the SS in the Borisov district. K. forwards both reports to Reich's Minister Rosenberg and requests that the matter be presented at the Führer's headquarters.

Further Complaints.   K. receives a report from the administrator of prisons in Minsk: the gold bridges, crowns, and fillings of recently incarcerated German and Russian Jews are broken off one to two hours before scheduled police executions. K. forwards this report to Reich's Commissioner Lohse and also complains about Operation Cottbus, in particular about the Dirlewanger regiment, which is made up almost exclusively of convicted criminals from Germany. K.: With 4,500 enemy killed, only 492 guns were seized—that is, only 10 percent of the dead were armed; among the 5,000 suspected bandits executed, there were numerous women and children.

Reich's Commissioner Lohse is indignant: "The fact that the Jews are liquidated requires no further explanation. However, the things described in General Commissioner K.'s report from June 1, 1943, are beyond belief. What is Katyn in comparison with them?"

End Phase

At the end of June 1943, Reichsführer-SS Himmler orders that all Jews still in ghettos in the occupied Eastern territories be transferred to concentration camps; he forbids the removal of Jews from concentration camps for labor duty of any kind after August 1, 1943. Three weeks later, the Führer orders the removal of the entire population from the "bandit-infested" territories in the northern Ukraine and Russia-Center.

On July 13, 1943, there is a meeting of the Reich's Ministry for the Occupied Eastern Territories on the issue "Labor requirements in the German Reich, with a special emphasis on relations in the occupied Eastern territories." Participants at the meeting include: Reich's Minister Rosenberg, General Commissioner Koch, District Leader Dr. Meyer, District Leader Sauckel, Undersecretary Backe, Undersecretary Körner, SS-Obergruppenführer Berger, and General Commissioner K.

The shortage of labor power in Germany is discussed in detail. With the introduction of German women into the labor market (1.3 million in 1943), the German workforce has been completely exhausted. In Western Europe as well, there is essentially no further workforce to draw on. For this reason, the introduction of people from the east is urgently necessary.

Regarding the Issue of Extracting Labor Power from White Ruthenia. After expressing his appreciation for the bandit-control measures undertaken by the SS, K. points out that most of White

Ruthenia remains under the control of the German military administration. In order to exploit the labor power in White Ruthenia, K. emphasizes that the entire territory absolutely must be turned over to his civil administration. K.: "Only if we evacuate the general territory and transport the population to Germany in family units will we be able to meet the required quota of laborers." But he is opposed to the separation of families, since this would cause significant unrest in the country. Furthermore, it is essential that the evacuation occur peacefully, that transports and all other measures be well prepared and that the people be treated properly.

Regarding the Jewish Question in White Ruthenia. K. reports that the problem is currently being addressed in detail. He concedes that there are still several thousand Jews working in a sled factory in Minsk. While he does approve of the proposed transfer of the Jewish workers, he demands their replacement by other workers in order to maintain factory production. In a conversation with SS-Obergruppenführer Berger, K. claims that the factory would have to be closed immediately if the Jews were removed. Berger is skeptical: "I suggested to K. that he present the matter to Reichsführer Himmler (via the senior SS and police leader) and perhaps have the factory turned into a concentration camp. This would mean that K. would lose control of it. But if, as he claims, the only issue here is the production of sleds, then this would be no great loss for him."

"Sentimental Humanitarianism"

On July 20, 1943, SS-Obersturmbannführer Dr. Strauch arrests the seventy "house Jews" still working for K. and executes them. On his return from Berlin that same morning, K. discovers their absence and requests by telephone that Strauch report to him immediately. Questioned by K., Strauch explains that he had strict orders for the operation. K. would like to see the orders. Strauch replies that he considers verbal orders sufficient.

K. (outwardly calm): This is a serious encroachment on my sovereign jurisdiction. I was responsible for the Jewish workers, and it is unacceptable that the Reichsführer-SS or SS-Obergruppenführer von dem Bach interfere in my general commissionership. In addition to this, I regard the measure as a personal chicanery directed against me. I cannot, of course, arm my own men in order to prevent arrests by the Security Service—I must yield to force here. At the same time, I want to make absolutely clear that in the future I will refuse all cooperation with the police—in particular with the Security Police. I will no longer allow members of the Security Police to enter my headquarters.

Strauch (offended but also conciliatory): It is incomprehensible to me that we Germans should be at odds over a few Jews. Again and again I have seen my men and myself accused of barbarism and sadism, when we are only doing our duty. Even the fact that Jews scheduled to be liquidated have had their gold fillings removed—by a dental specialist and in accordance with regulations—has become a subject of discussion.

K. (highly agitated): This kind of behavior is unworthy of the German people, unworthy of the Germany of Kant and Goethe! If Germany's reputation is undermined throughout the entire world, it will be your fault. Besides, it is true that your men are actually aroused by the executions.

Strauch (vehemently protesting): It is regrettable that my men and I, having performed this unpleasant work dutifully, should be dragged through the mud in this way.

Settling Accounts

At the end of July 1943, SS-Obersturmbannführer Dr. Strauch is transferred to Bandit-Control Operations as the general staff officer for SS-Obergruppenführer von dem Bach. Shortly after assuming his new post, Strauch files an unsolicited thirteen-page report regarding General Commissioner K. with his new superior. In the report, he complains about the following:

(1) K.'s misguided personnel policy. Strauch boils this policy down to a simple formula: Anyone who is capable and effective is removed from office, while blockheads and bootlickers are kept on.

(2) K.'s personal behavior. Strauch reports that although there is almost no irrefutable evidence on this point, it is quite certain that before his wife's arrival in Minsk (in Sept. 1942), K. did occasionally engage in sexual intercourse with his female employees. Following Frau K.'s arrival, however, accusations of this kind were no longer made.

(3) K.'s negative attitude toward the SS and the police. Strauch: It is extraordinarily difficult to obtain unambiguous evidence for this, because K. does not say what he thinks. Outwardly, he is friendly toward the SS and feigns great esteem for Reichsführer-SS Himmler. Examples of this deceit: (a) K. offered SS-Brigadeführer Zenner the familiar form of *du*, and even used this familiar form of address at highly official occasions. However, at the same time, K. filed oral and written reports with the Eastern Ministry behind Zenner's back, emphasizing his incompetence. (b) Following Operation Swamp Fever, SS-Obergruppenführer Jeckeln was convinced that White Ruthenia had for the most part been pacified. K. agreed with this and even wrote Jeckeln a letter of thanks. In intimate circles, however, he ridiculed the Obergruppenführer and claimed that he had filed false reports with the Reichsführer-SS. (c) Following the successful Operations Hornung, Fohn, Cottbus, and so on, K. sent a confidential circular letter to his district commissioners, in which he requested further details about the actual successes

of the police. In this circular letter, he clearly cast doubt on the official figures reported by the police, thereby essentially accusing the responsible police leaders of lying.

(4) K.'s views on the Jewish Question [comprises eight of the report's thirteen pages]. Strauch: Here too, K.'s ambivalence is evident in the vociferousness with which he emphasizes that the Jewish Question must be resolved quickly and radically in all his official speeches and writings. His actual views on the matter, however, are revealed in the letters, statements, and decrees cited below. When K. feels attacked, he immediately claims that he, too, is a great opponent of the Jews: "As a decorated member of the Nazi Party, I take it as a matter of course that Jews are regarded as political criminals. I would most prefer if we could send the entire Russian Jewry as quickly and quietly as possible to their well-deserved fate." Strauch's interpretation of this: In my opinion, K. uses those speeches and writings in which he takes a public stand on the Jewish Question as a means to provide cover for himself. In conversations with me, he has repeatedly emphasized that we could keep alive without any difficulties Jews evacuated from Germany, since they do not speak the language here and thus pose no threat in regard to the bandits. Not a single Jew working for K. has been arrested without K.'s filing a complaint. One can indeed speak here of a "slavishness to Jews."

"A completely impossible attitude." Selected examples:

K. learned that a German Jew had been beaten by a police officer. In the presence of this Jew, K. confronted the police officer and asked him in a raised voice whether he was in possession of an Iron Cross, as the Jew was. Fortunately, the police officer was able to answer this question in the affirmative.

During a major ghetto operation, informants learned that the German-Jewish ghetto police, which consisted primarily of veterans of the Great War, was prepared to engage in armed resistance. In order to spare loss of blood on the German side, the ghetto police was told that there was a fire in the city and was ordered to report for fire-fighting duty. The men were then loaded into trucks and liquidated. In some inexplicable way, K. learned of the matter. He objected vehemently that it was cruel to eradicate these former front-line soldiers. In addition to this, he criticized the methods employed in this case as outrageous.

A departmental head filed the following report on November 7, 1942: While making rounds through the general commissioner's headquarters, he encountered a Jew lounging around. When asked what he was doing, the Jew answered: "I'm waiting for the boss." When asked who the boss was, he replied: "Herr K."

A number of Jews and Jewesses were arrested in the general commissioner's headquarters because they were not wearing Jewish stars. During interrogations, it was discovered that one of K.'s advisers had issued them identification cards as "Non-Jewish White Ruthenians" merely on the basis of their assertions that they were only one-quarter Jewish. Although K. was informed of this, he lodged a personal protest about the arrests. The adviser who acted negligently in the matter was not punished.

A Jew working as an electrical technician in the general commissioner's headquarters was supposed to check the telephone lines and repair them. He installed a listening device so that he was able to monitor all conversations, including those in the general commissioner's headquarters. The information obtained from these telephone calls was then passed on to other Jews. Following the technician's arrest, K. protested personally, repeatedly doubting the state of affairs as described by the Security Police.

Both K. and his wife have given German Jews—in particular hairstylists and tailors—foodstuffs, fruits, and vegetables.

Strauch: On the basis of these experiences, I am convinced that K. is, at the bottom of his heart, opposed to our Jewish operations. If he does not admit this openly, it is only because he is afraid of the consequences. He would agree to operations against Russian Jews because his conscience is assuaged by the fact that he regards them primarily as supporters of the bandits. Under these circumstances, it is in my opinion intolerable that K. remain in office.

Undermined

In Berlin, reports and complaints accumulate—both from K. and about him. SS-Obergruppenführer Anton Berger, Himmler's representative in the Eastern Ministry, is outraged about "the incredible frivolousness" of K.'s reports. Particularly irritating is the accusation that Berger himself has profited personally from a cattle transport in White Ruthenia. At the end of August 1943, K.'s old friend, Nazi District Leader Dr. Meyer, is sent to Minsk to deliver K. a serious warning.

The situation in Minsk becomes increasingly difficult. Acts of open resistance—including bombings and assassination attempts within the city—are on the rise. On September 9, 1943, there is an attack on the dining hall at Security Police headquarters in Minsk. Two days later, a bomb explodes in a laboratory of the Waffen-SS. At this point in time, the two ghettos in Minsk are closed down, their remaining inhabitants executed or evacuated.

In spite of everything, K. remains optimistic and loyal to the

Führer. In the third week of September, General von Bogen of the Wehrmacht appears in K.'s headquarters on orders from General Field Marshal von Kluge and announces that the General Field Marshal plans to move his residence to Minsk. In passing, General von Bogen mentions that the Führer has given the General Field Marshal authority to issue directives for the entire territory of White Ruthenia. K. refuses to believe this. He writes to Reich's Commissioner Lohse, requesting official confirmation of the communication and objecting to the "listless attitude" of the Wehrmacht.

A day later, on the night of September 21, 1943, a bomb explodes in K.'s bedroom. The left half of his chest is torn open, his left arm ripped off. The injuries are fatal. K.'s pregnant wife, who is lying next to him, is not injured but later suffers a nervous breakdown. Their three young children, asleep in another room, are also uninjured in the explosion.

That same night, as a retaliatory measure, the SS rounds up and executes an unspecified number of White Ruthenians. A special commission headed by SS-Sturmbannführer Bohndorf, appointed immediately after the assassination, comes to the conclusion that the attack was carried out by partisans. The commission finds that Jelena Masanik, a housemaid of K.'s with ties to the partisans, placed a mine of English origins under K.'s bed. Both the mattress and K.'s body deflected the explosion, explaining the absence of injuries to Frau K.

Among the leading Nazis, opinions about K. are not particularly positive. Goebbels: Between us, there was nothing much laudable to say about K.'s life. Himmler is reported to have said that K.'s death was a blessing for Germany, since otherwise he would have had to put him in a concentration camp.

A week later, there is an official state funeral for K. in Berlin. Reich's Minister Rosenberg gives the funeral oration. K. is posthumously awarded the Knight's Cross for the Military Order of Merit (with Swords). SS-Brigadeführer Curt von Gottberg is appointed the new general commissioner of White Ruthenia.

A RARE SENSE OF JUSTICE

On November 7, 1941, Dr. Karl L. is asked to appear the next morning in the offices of the Gestapo at Burg Strasse No. 26–27. L. was not at home when the Gestapo officers stopped by his apartment in Berlin-Weissensee, and his absence was no coincidence. Earlier in the fall, he had been notified by the Jewish Community that the Gestapo had ordered him to vacate the apartment before September 30. L. was allotted a room with his brother and sister-in-law on Hohenstaufen Strasse. Through his connections at the Foreign Ministry and the cooperation of the local police department, however, he was then permitted to move into one of the side rooms of his offices on Kurfürstendamm.

The housemaid neglects to call L. and inform him of the Gestapo's visit. He first learns of it in the evening, when he comes by to check on the apartment. Although he's been given notice, L. has yet to vacate the rooms completely. As usual, he has paid his rent in advance and feels no obligation to move out before December 31. He is also uncertain about what to do with the furniture. While he's in the apartment, an air-raid siren goes off. He gathers some valuables: a bundle of securities, a violin, an oil painting. The housemaid dusts the painting and packs it. L. gives her some money before taking the articles to his office. At last, the housemaid thinks, L. is going to flee the country.

That is what the Gestapo officers think as well when they open the safe in L.'s office the next day and discover the securities and a large amount of cash. L., however, has not attempted to flee. At 8:15 in the morning he reports punctually to room 313 on Burg Strasse. Although his two children and his ex-wife have emigrated to England, although his two companies have been "Aryanized" and officially no longer belong to him, although he is required as a *Volljude* (full-blooded Jew) to use the name Israel and wear a Jewish star, L. has remained in Germany. He is, after all, German, and has lived his entire life in Germany.

He has German friends, as well. The Gestapo officer at Burg Strasse informs L. that it was one of these friends who arranged for his arrest: retired Major Leonhardt Schliessmann, director of the National Club 1919 and an SS-Oberführer. The friendship between Schliessmann and L. dates back to 1922, when L. first came to Berlin from Upper Silesia. In 1933, L. took over a men's clothing company which had run into financial difficulties. Over the course of time, it became clear that in order to survive, the company would have to advertise in the *Völkischer Beobachter*. L. had never had any fear of contact with such organizations. The representative at the *Völkischer Beobachter*, however, objected that L.'s company was Jewish and refused to accept the advertisements; afterward, he notified the Reichstreuhänder der Arbeit (Reich's Trustee for Labor), which summoned L. to appear before its board. Schliessmann agreed to accompany L. to this meeting. During the negotiations, it was decided that the retired General Bering, a longtime member of the Nazi Party and an acquaintance of L.'s, should exercise codetermination rights over stock in L.'s bank. Advertisements were subsequently accepted in the *Völkischer Beobachter*. On Schliessmann's suggestion, L. then allowed additional stock to be represented by Aryan friends: 8,000 reichsmarks by the former Imperial Aide-de-Camp Count Detlef von Moltke and 7,000 reichsmarks by Schliessmann himself. In 1938, General Bering resigned as a trustee due to illness. Count von Moltke and Corvette Captain Fritz Albrecht assumed control of his shares. That same year, L.—no longer the official director of the A. Busse & Co. Banking House—was summoned to appear before the Deutsche Arbeitsfront (German Labor Front) and ordered to transfer his remaining stock to an Aryan. L. pointed out that according to the law, a joint-stock company was considered to be non-Jewish when less than 25 percent of it was owned by Jews. The chief negotiator responded: We determine what the laws are. L. turned over 8,000 reichsmarks of stock to his secretary, Fräulein M. In mid-November of 1941, two weeks after the Gestapo officers appear in L.'s apartment in Berlin-Weissensee, Schliessmann calls a board meeting of the Busse Bank. He appears in the offices on Kurfürstendamm with a Herr Schmidt, who alludes to irregularities in the company and threatens to report these to the authorities. Count von Moltke, Corvette Captain Albrecht, and Fräulein M. sell their stock to him at well below market value. Schliessmann is appointed deputy director of the company.

Detained

At the Gestapo offices on Burg Strasse, L. is asked various questions: Why hasn't he cleared out his apartment? Why hasn't he moved into the room assigned to him? Where did he stay during the month of October? Could he possibly think they didn't know where he was? Is he a member of the Bekenntniskirche (Confessing Church)? Is he aware that this is a criminal offense? Why is the Bekenntniskirche opposed to the Führer? L. is arrested and taken to the basement of the Gestapo building. The duty officer tells L. he's going to teach him what work is. L. is given a broom and ordered to sweep out the basement. Later, he is transferred to Tegel Prison. Official notation in the registration book: "Enemy of the State, Jewish operation."

When they learn of L.'s arrest, Count von Moltke and Corvette Captain Albrecht rush to police headquarters. They intend to lodge a complaint. The police officer on duty makes clear to them what they can expect if they continue to intervene for L. The two come to the same conclusion: they must break off the relationship immediately regardless of the circumstances. When Max Schmidt offers to buy their stock ten days later, they are actually relieved.

For four days, L. remains in Tegel Prison. On November 12, he is picked up by two Gestapo officers, who drive him to his apartment in Berlin-Weissensee. Here he is forced to sign a register of his assets and then ordered to pack. He is allowed to bring the following items: a small suitcase, a pillow, a wool blanket. He is also permitted to wear two pairs of underwear and two coats. Afterward, the Gestapo officers take him to the police station on Goethe Strasse. In the evening, he is brought to the Levetzow Strasse Detention Center (the synagogue).

The detention center is overcrowded. L. is forced to spend two nights on a folding chair. Although rumors abound, the official destination of the transport remains unknown. Shortly before departure, a bailiff serves L. with a judicial order: since he is an enemy of the state, his assets are to be confiscated for the benefit of the German Reich. It is a number of weeks, however, before the police clear out his apartment in Weissensee. In the interim, the rooms are occupied by Gestapo officers who drink and celebrate. The officers try on various suits and coats. They tell the custodian: Herr L. has a beautiful wardrobe.

Departure. After two days, preparations are complete. The identity cards of the 1,030 Jews at Levetzow Strasse are stamped: "Evacuated from Berlin to Minsk on November 14, 1941." The deportees are placed in disguised police vans, driven to the train station, and loaded directly into fourth-class railway cars. L. is lucky: he is issued the transport number 170, which means that he is seated in the second car behind the locomotive. The train is not heated; only the first two cars absorb some warmth. The trip lasts four days. Except for a small loaf of bread, cut into slices and smeared with spread, the deportees are given nothing to eat. Within twenty-four hours, the bread, distributed in Berlin, is hard as stone. The train stops in Warsaw, but no rations are distributed. Due to the threat of typhus, they are not allowed to drink any water. The authorities have great respect for epidemics.

Arrival

On November 18, the train arrives in Minsk. Latvian auxiliary policemen meet the transport, driving the deportees out of the railway cars with whips and rifle butts. L., who assumes the task of unloading baggage, is spared most of the abuse. The deportees are then marched through the city to an outlying district that serves as a ghetto for the local Jewish population. The district, which consists of rows of small wooden houses, is dilapidated and impoverished. On their arrival, the Berliners learn that they are the fourth transport from Germany. Over the course of the previous ten days, trains have arrived from Hamburg, Düsseldorf, and Frankfurt am Main. In the coming days, transports from Bremen, Vienna, and Brünn will follow.

Minsk.   After several days of waiting, the Berliners are assigned to wooden houses. The SS announces that in order to make room for them, 25,000 Russian Jews have been executed. Space, nevertheless, is cramped. Six to ten people share a single room. There are no mattresses; initially they sleep on the floor. Nor is there electricity or running water. For the entire ghetto there is only one pump. Dusk falls at four in the afternoon. With no light, one simply goes to bed. Rations: 300 grams of "soup" (water with 5 grams of buckwheat along with an occasional rotten potato), 150 grams of "bread" (inedible, even the horses refuse to touch it). There is no fat or salt. The winter of 1941 is particularly harsh; temperatures of 40 degrees below zero are not uncommon. After only a few weeks, some 700 of a total 7,300 German Jews have died from debilitation and "camp disease" (diarrhea).

Ghetto Police.   Shortly after his arrival in Minsk, L., who has a rather military bearing, is asked by an SS officer if he served in the last war. L.: In the navy. He is subsequently commissioned by the SS to organize a Jewish camp guard. The unit L. assembles consists primarily of former German soldiers and officers. They practice and drill daily. Responsibilities of the Ghetto Police: sentry duty (including night patrol), assistance with transports (food, patients, corpses), the performance of any other orders issued by the SS. At night, there are raids on the ghetto by marauding German soldiers and by Latvian policemen. L. reports this to the responsible SS-Oberführer, who orders that such persons be arrested in the future. This proves extremely difficult, as the Ghetto Police are armed only with wooden truncheons.

Sonderghetto.   In their ghetto, the German Jews are completely isolated from the outside world. Any contact with the local population, including that of the Russian ghetto, is strictly forbidden and, as is the case with almost all offenses in Minsk, punishable by death. Relations between German Jews and local Jews are made even more difficult by the fact that the German Jews speak no Russian, and many of them speak little or no Yiddish. In addition to this, the German Jews have been assigned to the houses of recently murdered White Russian Jews and appear to enjoy certain privileges. Their district is officially called the Sonderghetto or special ghetto; while Russian, White Russian, and

Polish Jews are required to wear only a piece of yellow cloth on their chests, the German Jews must wear a yellow Jewish star with the word *Jude* written on it. The former watch mistrustfully as German Jews place barbed wire between the two ghettos, unaware that this has been ordered by the SS. In the beginning, many German Jews imagine that they will enjoy special protection or be granted preferential treatment. After only a short time, it is clear that this is an illusion—one, however, that is difficult to abandon.

Supplementary Rations.   There are two ways to supplement the starvation rations in the ghetto. The first is barter, which is strictly forbidden and punishable by death. Here, the German Jews are always at a disadvantage. Lacking personal or familial ties, they are dependent on the local population. They trade their remaining belongings—clothing, gold, jewelry—for a piece of lard, a few potatoes, or a loaf of bread. The only other way to supplement rations is work. The SS, the Wehrmacht, the Organisation Todt, the German Civil Administration, and private companies are all in need of laborers. Sometimes work crews receive additional, if substandard, food. Sometimes they don't. After twelve hours of heavy manual labor along with physical abuse and humiliation, they return to the ghetto without having eaten anything.

Decision.   In the winter of 1941, three Berlin Jews flee the Sonderghetto. As head of the Ghetto Police, L. must report this to SS-Oberführer Schmiedel. On the following day, Schmiedel demands as a retaliatory measure that the Jewish Elder Dr. Frank draw up a list of three hundred prisoners to be executed. Horrified, Dr. Frank takes no immediate action in the hope that the matter will be forgotten. The next day, Schmiedel again demands the names of three hundred prisoners. L. is assigned the difficult task of assembling the list. He tries to negotiate. After some discussion, Schmiedel announces that he will accept a list of one hundred prisoners. Stalling for time, L. comes up with the idea of offering prisoners already suffering from advanced tuberculosis, who in all likelihood will not survive the winter. He draws up a list of thirty inmates with TB. Schmiedel finally agrees to the suggestion. The thirty are executed on the spot. The three escapees, inadequately clothed and without money or knowledge of the language, have not gone far. The next day, they are led back to the ghetto and executed before its remaining inhabitants.

Mistaken Identity.   In December 1941, the Jewish Elder in the Sonderghetto receives a series of inquiries from the German Civil Administration in Minsk, requesting details about the former lives of ghetto inmates in Germany. L. is reported as the only recipient of a civilian decoration—in 1935 he rescued a woman from drowning. Several days later, L. is notified that General Commissioner Kube is in the ghetto and wishes to speak to him. When he reports to Kube, the latter appears to recognize him. Kube believes that they studied together in Berlin.* L., somewhat bewildered, says nothing. Kube claims, furthermore, that they are related to one another—Kube's brother-in-law is married to the daughter of Counselor Abraham L. from the city of Paderborn. L. (hesitating): I do believe that my father is related to the family. In any event, the two have much in common: born in the same year, both are Upper Silesians, the one by birth, the other by choice; both fought for the Germans against the Poles in Upper Silesia following the Great War; and both were forced to flee to Berlin in the 1920s as a result. Kube is enthused. He demands that L. give him a résumé of his life and promises to present his case personally to the Führer. In the résumé, L. describes himself

---

*Kube apparently confuses him with another Karl L. (born in 1891), who studied at the University of Berlin for a semester in 1912 and later received a doctorate in law at the University of Munich (1922). In 1933, this Karl L. emigrated to the United States. After the war, he becomes a well-known professor of political science at Amherst College.

as follows: a *Halbjude* (half-Jew) converted to Protestantism, a first lieutenant in the Royal Navy, a member of the Freikorps in Upper Silesia, and a doctor of economics.

A Beating.   As head of the Ghetto Police, L. feels himself responsible for the welfare of the entire camp. He intervenes constantly, advising, warning, admonishing, and supervising the affairs of the Sonderghetto. In the second week of January 1942, an SS man requests a labor crew. Although, strictly speaking, this matter is beyond his jurisdiction, L. objects, refusing to release the workers: one week earlier they worked for the SS man and—despite his promises—received nothing to eat. The SS man takes L. aside for a private tête-à-tête. The result: L.'s upper and lower jaw are shattered, all his teeth are knocked out, his right eye is damaged, a number of ribs are broken, fingers on both hands are crushed, and he is kicked so hard that he develops a hernia. While unconscious, L. is doused with water, beaten further, then left to spend the icy night in an unheated cellar. He suffers frostbite on his hands and feet, develops a serious case of pneumonia. L.'s will to live, however, remains unbroken. Despite inadequate medical care and without any medication, his condition slowly improves.

Rescued.   In mid-April 1942, General Commissioner Kube appears again in the ghetto and informs L. that—together with Reich's Minister Dr. Lammers—he has presented L.'s case personally to Hitler. The Führer has ordered Himmler to release L. from Minsk. In the coming days, Kube continues, L. is to return to Germany. Three weeks later, an SS officer brings L. to the railway station and places him on a passenger train traveling west. The train arrives in Vienna three days later. Shortly thereafter, L. is transported to Theresienstadt and placed in solitary confinement in the camp prison. Only two other Berlin Jews will survive the Minsk ghetto.

Theresienstadt

After the Munich Accord in March 1939, the small garrison town of Theresienstadt—located sixty kilometers north of Prague—becomes part of the Protectorate Bohemia and Moravia incorporated into the German Reich. Theresienstadt is first mentioned as a possible site for a Jewish concentration camp on October 10, 1941, during a discussion of solutions to the Jewish Question in the protectorate. The Deputy Reich's Protector, SS-Obergruppenführer Reinhardt Heydrich, addresses the issue of placing Czech Jews in a ghetto: "Only a somewhat remote location or a small village or town with as little industry as possible should be considered. The Jews could be provided with ample work opportunities in the camp (producing small articles by hand such as wooden shoes, wickerwork for the Wehrmacht in the north, and so on). A 'Jewish council of elders' would be responsible for collecting these items and would receive in return the least possible sustenance containing a calculated minimum of vitamins, etc. (under the supervision of the Security Police). One possible location in Bohemia would be the old Hussite castle Alt-Ratibor. But it would be best if the Central Office for Jewish Emigration were to take over Theresienstadt. After the evacuation of the Jews from this temporary concentration camp (during which their numbers would be drastically reduced) to the eastern territories, the entire area could be expanded into a model German settlement." At the end of November 1941, the first transport of Czech Jews arrives in Theresienstadt.

"To Keep Up Appearances."   Shortly thereafter, Theresienstadt is assigned an additional function: it is to serve as a model camp for elderly, distinguished German Jews. On January 20, 1942, one day after SS-Sturmbannführer Adolf Eichmann has inspected the grounds of the garrison town, the following statement is issued in Wannsee: "It is intended that Jews over 65 years of age not be evacuated but instead sent to a ghetto for the elderly—Theresienstadt is to serve this purpose. In addition to persons of this age—approximately 30 percent of the Jews remaining in Germany and the Ostmark as of October 31, 1941, are over 65—seriously disabled war veterans and Jews with war decorations (Iron Cross First Class) will also be admitted to this Jewish ghetto for the elderly. With this one move, we will be able do away with the numerous interventions that have been made on behalf of such Jews thus far." The first transports of elderly German Jews to Theresienstadt begin in June 1942.

The former director of the Palestine Office in Prague, Jakob Edelstein, is appointed by the SS as the first Jewish Elder of Theresienstadt. On December 4, 1941, he travels with his staff to the garrison town. In Theresienstadt, Edelstein follows a policy of survival through labor, attempting in this way to keep alive young people in particular. If this policy ultimately fails, it is because the SS is, from the beginning, more interested in a final solution to the Jewish Question than in the limited labor capacity of undernourished prisoners. Given the limited possibilities in the concentration camp for effective resistance, Edelstein proves to be a clever tactician. Steadfastly, he attempts to delay transports to the east and to buy time.

The head of the Czech gendarmes, who guard the camp under the supervision of the SS, tells Edelstein how good the Jews have it in Theresienstadt: You are protected here, you don't have to serve on the front. Edelstein: Captain, you are welcome to convert.

The first seven months, Theresienstadt remains a transit camp for Czech Jews. Daily life in the camp is marked by substandard food, severe regulations (the strict separation of men and women, the death penalty for escape attempts and illegal communication via mail), work crews, and, above all, transports. Trains with Jews from the protectorate arrive continually in the camp. Beginning in January 1942, transports also leave Theresienstadt for the east (Poland). The SS determines the number of persons, the age group, the land of origin, or the category of people to be selected or spared. It is the Jewish camp administration itself that must determine which prisoners are to be placed on a particular transport. Although inmates do not know the destination, they sense that transports are something to be avoided at all costs.

Normalization.   The SS attempts to introduce hierarchies into camp life, not only because this is consistent with its own mode of thought but also because it wants to foster dissension among the prisoners. Edelstein, a socialist and Zionist, rejects the suggestion that the Council of Elders be given a special kitchen and requests no private quarters for himself. The members of the Council of Elders live together in a few modest rooms. This changes, however, in March 1942, with the arrival of their families in Theresienstadt. That same month, the Jewish leadership begins to allocate supplemental rations to those performing heavy manual labor at the cost of nonlaborers. It is also at this time that the SS announces the official grounds for exemption from transports to the east: separation of family members, over 65 years of age, war decorations, war disability (at least 60 percent incapacitation), valid Aryan "mixed marriage," foreign citizenship (limited), medically attested incapacity to be transported. Further grounds (not officially recognized): connections, bribes.

Jewish Self-Administration.   A ponderous bureaucracy develops in the camp—one that is anything but independent. The highest authority, as always, is the SS. Due to the various privileges that some members of the Jewish Self-Administration enjoy—including exemption from transports to the east—the bureaucracy balloons.

Organizational chart of the self-administration (abridged excerpts):

(1) Directorate
(2) Labor Department
(3) Internal Administration
(4) Economic Division
(5) Technical Division
(6) Finance Division
(7) Health and Welfare
(8) Child Welfare
(9) Leisure Activities

Regarding (1): The Directorate consists of the Jewish Elder, two Deputies, and the Council of Elders (12 members). Directly subordinate to the Directorate are: (A) Central Registration, (B) Central Office, (C) Bank of the Self-Administration, (D) Security Forces.

Regarding (A): The Central Registration includes the following departments: Central Index, Family Index, Transport Registration, Statistics, External Registration, Identification Office, Research Services.

Regarding (B): Central Office: Chancery of the Central Office (Central Receipt Department, Reproductions, Central Statistical Archive, Complaint Department), Personnel Office, Transport Division, Tariff Division, Division of Special Tasks (Genealogical Research, Book Registration Group), etc.

Regarding (2): The Labor Department consists of: Directorate (Office of the Directorate, Organization, Planning, Statistics, Personnel Registration, Revision Department), Registration of Laborers, Employment of Men, Employment of Women, Employment of Youths, Labor Control (Workplace Control, Employment Control, Manufacturing Control, Appraisal of Special Compensation, Workplace Accident Department, Examination of Agreements),

Supervision of Workers (Registration Department, Procurement and Distribution Department [Food, Clothing and Equipment, Lodgings, Hygiene, Leisure Time, Welfare for Sick Workers], Office for Work Productivity [Productivity Department, Status Registration, Wage Calculation], Employment Department, etc.).

Special Case

In the camp prison, L. remains completely separated from the other inmates. He is not permitted to speak with anyone or to leave his cell at any time, even to stretch his legs. He is, however, given a special diet and receives a German newspaper every day—something which not even the Jewish Elder Edelstein is permitted. These privileges inevitably arouse the attention of other camp inmates. L.'s preferential treatment, his German heritage, his apparent connections in Berlin, and the mysterious circumstances surrounding his arrival—his being the only known case of a German Jew transported back from the east—give rise to countless rumors.

On September 9, 1942, L. is ordered to appear in the camp commandant's office. Here, the commandant, Dr. Siegfried Seidl, and several SS officers await him. A brief discussion ensues. L. is asked a number of questions and then sent back to his cell. A week later, the camp commandant sends for L. again and informs him that he is to assume the leadership of the Jewish Security Forces in the camp. Seidl orders L. to introduce himself to the Jewish Elder Edelstein as the new chief of the Ghetto Police. L.'s appointment attracts particular attention in the ghetto, because up to this point the Council of Elders has been permitted to select the heads of the various departments of the Self-Administration itself. Eight days after L. takes office, his hernia is repaired by the physician-inmate Dr. Springer. L. recuperates in the camp hospital until the middle of October. Dentures are also made for him at this time.

During L.'s four months of solitary confinement, much has changed in Theresienstadt. With the arrival of elderly Jews from Germany and Austria, the makeup of the camp is altered abruptly. German-speaking Jews now constitute the majority of inmates. The average age in the camp is over sixty-five.* Many of the elderly German Jews come from wealthy or upper middle-class backgrounds and have been swindled by the SS: they were persuaded to turn over everything they owned to the Reich's Association of Jews in Germany in order to be allowed to live in the "health resort" or "old people's home" Theresienstadt. Frail and unprepared, exhausted and ragged, they arrive in the camp and are deposited in overcrowded casemates and attics.

Theresienstadt in September 1942: 56,717 inmates (= 1.6 square meters of living space per inmate); 38,912 nonlaborers, 12,000 more women than men; 3,349 deaths (1,938 of these from enteritis); 38 transports with 18,467 prisoners arrive in Theresienstadt, and 8 transports with 13,004 prisoners are deported to death camps in the east (7 of these to Trostenez near Minsk).

In the fall of 1942, the SS introduces a special *Prominente* or VIP status for inmates with high civilian and military honors. There are *A-Prominente*, who are named by the Gestapo directly in Berlin, and *B-Prominente*, who are proposed by the Jewish Council of Elders and then approved by the camp commandant. The privileges enjoyed by the *Prominente* include better accommodations (they are permitted to share a room in the *Prominente*

*The average age of prisoners deported to Theresienstadt: initial transports of construction crews: 31; remaining transports of Czech Jews from the protectorate: 46; transports of German Jews from Berlin and Munich: 69; transports from Cologne: 70; transports from Vienna: 73.

Houses rather than sleep in barracks or lofts), exemption from labor duty, and protection from being deported to the east. Some *Prominente* also receive—as does the Jewish leadership—double food portions, more frequent packages, and more extensive correspondence privileges. The total number of *Prominente* remains extremely small. Over the next two and a half years, fewer than two hundred inmates (including family members) are awarded this privileged status. L. is named an *A-Prominente*.

Servant of the Ghetto

L. carries out his duties as head of the Ghetto Police with a thoroughness that surpasses all expectations. He sets about reorganizing the Jewish Security Forces in accordance with the Prussian model. His first undertaking is to merge all the various security organizations in the ghetto. As head of the Security Forces, L. is already in charge of the Ghetto Police, the Orientation Service* and the Criminal Watch. After a brief but heated battle with the director of Internal Administration, L. succeeds in having the Fire Department, the Air Defense, and the Building Administration placed under his authority. The Economic Inspection Authority, which L. himself establishes in order to oversee the various economic departments of the ghetto, is also incorporated into the Security Forces.

L.: I am the most influential man in the camp.

Official regulations: "As the law enforcement agency of the superior authorities [i.e., the SS] and the Council of Elders, the Security Forces are responsible for maintaining peace and order in

---

*The Orientation Service assists newly arrived inmates adjust to Theresienstadt. In particular, volunteers in the service help elderly inmates locate their living quarters as well as family and friends. The Orientation Service also organizes lecture series and other activities for inmates.

the ghetto and for protecting the life, health, and property of ghetto inhabitants."

From the beginning, L. is aware of the difficulties of his office, caught between the demands of the German authorities on the one hand, and the interests of his fellow inmates on the other. He says to himself: You must demonstrate to the SS your own unimpeachability. Only in this way can you serve the common good. The camp commandant must be convinced that everything you say is unconditionally true, that all your assertions are airtight.

L.'s Maxims

Motto: "Everything for the ghetto!"

Guiding principle: "What is essential is the deed. Intellect without will is worthless. Will without intellect is dangerous."

Fundamental principle: "We are not a police state but the police within a state. Our watchword is, 'We are friends to the ghetto inmates. We don't want to punish, we want to help.'"

Watchword: (1) courtesy, (2) courtesy, (3) courtesy to our comrades in destiny.

"I am loyal to those who are loyal to me—unconditionally and without qualification." From the beginning, L. attempts to train members of the Security Forces to be prepared for any situation at any time. L.: In case of an emergency, regardless of where it arises or what it looks like, the organization I command must be so intact and well coordinated that it functions like a clock, free from any impediments, following only my orders. For this, it is necessary that the troops believe that their commander is unwaveringly loyal to them and that he receive, in return, the troops' unwavering loyalty. If my men are convinced of this, then I can demand from them what I want.

A Reliable Organ of Public Safety and Order

On May 14, 1942, three days before L.'s arrival in Theresienstadt, the Ghetto Guard is dissolved and replaced by an Order Guard as punishment for the guard's participation in the illegal delivery of letters. The new Order Guard is to fulfill its duties unarmed (i.e., without wooden truncheons) and is granted only limited privileges. On taking office, L. first reviews security conditions in the camp. The existing Order Guard is, in his opinion, more or less a band of smugglers whose principle task consists in relieving incoming transports of food, cigarettes, and other valuables. L. dismisses those whom he considers the most grievous offenders and introduces strict discipline. Because the remaining members of the guard place a great value on their original name, L. brings the matter up with the camp commandant and is able to arrange that they may once again be called the Ghetto Guard.

Responsibilities.   As a police force organized on a military basis, the Ghetto Guard carries out the sentry duties within the framework of the Security Forces' general responsibilities (see above). These duties include guarding prohibited areas, barracks duty, guarding prisoners, assisting with transports, general sentry duty, and the locating and arresting of camp inmates.

Role Models.   Members of the Ghetto Guard are required to dress in a neat and orderly manner both on and off duty, to behave respectfully and politely toward other ghetto inmates, and to be exemplary in every respect.

Daily Schedule (Summer).   06:00 hours: reveille, airing the beds. 06:30–07:00 hours: gymnastics, exercises, jujitsu, shadow boxing. Until 08:30 hours: washing, dressing, cleaning the quarters. 08:30–09:30 hours: drill and instruction according to a prescribed routine. Following this, report and briefing, breakfast, and then the taking up of sentry posts. The watch returning from duty have the afternoon free, so long as no further orders have been issued. If during this free time unusual incidents occur (i.e., there is a fire or a crowd gathers, etc.), the off-duty men are to return immediately to their barracks in order to be deployed as reinforcements. At 21:00 hours, every member must be in his bed in the barracks. By 22:00 hours, there is to be complete silence. At 22:00 hours, the duty officer in the room unscrews the lightbulb.

Watch Duty. The ghetto is divided into four districts. In each district, a watch consisting of a *Zugführer* (platoon leader), an *Aufführender* (deputy platoon leader), and ten to fourteen men perform street, traffic, and security duty in twenty-four-hour shifts. During the day, patrols are carried out by a single guard; at night, guards patrol in pairs. Two hours of active duty (in cold, hot, or bad weather, duty is reduced to half an hour) are followed by two hours of on-call duty and then two hours of standby duty, during which guards may rest.

The duty officer is responsible for order and security in his district. He is to inspect the guard posts at least four to eight times each day and night. In his absence, the deputy duty officer assumes these responsibilities.

Guards posted in the streets are to report any unusual incidents immediately, and all other events when they return to the watch room. In exceptional cases (fire, the gathering of a crowd, unrest, or special orders from the higher authorities), the required reinforcements are to move out to the location concerned under the command of the duty officer, leaving at least two men posted on watch. When required, further reinforcements may be called in from off-duty guards. The duty officer is to enter all occurrences into the log. A copy of the log must be presented daily to headquarters, at 06:30 hours and at 22:00 hours. Exceptional occurrences are to be reported immediately.

The senior duty officer enters the results of his inspection into the daily log. In every watch locale, there is a schedule book with an inventory of the watch's current duties. This book is to be supplemented as needed and checked monthly by the chief of the Ghetto Guard. The commander of the arriving watch is to assume control of the equipment and obligations of the guard stations from his predecessor and to confirm this in the log.

Required Salute.   Whether on or off duty, all members of the Ghetto Guard are required to greet the following persons:

by removing their caps: all uniformed members of the German Reich, as well as the Czech gendarmes*

by saluting: the Jewish Elder and his deputies, members of the Council of Elders, the chief of the Security Forces, the chief of the Ghetto Guard, all superiors in the Ghetto Guard, all members of the Ghetto Guard, the division leaders of the Criminal Watch and the Economic Watch as well as their deputies, and all other members of the Security Forces

Ranks.   When L. assumes control of the Ghetto Guard, the following designations of rank are in use: Wachmann, Aufführender, Zugführer, Abteilungsleiter, Dienstführender.† After consulting with the camp commandant, L. replaces these with the following ranks: Ghetto-Wachmann, Oberwachmann, Gruppenführer, Obergruppenführer, Zugführer, Oberzugführer, Kompanieführer, Dienstführer.‡ Officials in Berlin, however, object to these designations, since the ranks Gruppenführer and Obergruppenführer are already used for SS generals. In May 1943, L. is forced to introduce the following designations of rank: Ghetto-Wachmann, Oberwachmann, Schwarmführer, Oberschwarmführer, Haupt-

---

*The SS requires that all ghetto inmates greet uniformed members of the German Reich and Czech gendarmes in this way.
†Watchman, Deputy Platoon Leader, Platoon Leader, Section Head, Duty Leader.
‡Ghetto Watchman, Senior Watchman, Section Leader, Senior Section Leader, Platoon Leader, Senior Platoon Leader, Company Leader, Duty Leader.

schwarmführer, Schwarmmeister, Oberschwarmmeister.* Since these new designations never gain any currency among members of the guard, they end up sticking to the original ones.

Uniform.   While on duty, members of the Ghetto Guard are out-fitted with a service cap, a service belt, a service number affixed to a yellow armband on the left sleeve,† a whistle, an electric flashlight (without batteries), and a wooden truncheon. In addition to this, L. introduces a cockade in the shape of a four-leaf clover engraved with the letters GG, which is worn on the front of the service cap.

Service Cap (Austrian Model)
There is a yellow band two centimeters wide around the rim of the cap. The Oberwachmann's cap has a four-centimeter-long, half-centimeter-wide yellow braid above the bill of the cap, running parallel to it. The Gruppenführer's cap has a four-centimeter-long, half-centimeter-wide yellow braid in the center, vertical to the cap brim. The Obergruppenführer's cap has, in addition to this braid, the trimming of the Oberwach-mann's cap beneath the braid. The Zugführer wears a cap with a four-centimeter-long and half-centimeter-wide braid run-ning from the top of the cap down the middle. The Oberzug-führer's braid is the same as the Zugführer's, but a full centimeter wide. The Kompanieführer's cap has two of these braids. The commander of the Ghetto Guard has two two-centimeter-wide yellow braids below the top of the brim run-ning along the entire cap.

---

*Ghetto Watchman, Senior Watchman, Pack Leader, Senior Pack Leader, Chief Pack Leader, Pack Master, Senior Pack Master.
†Because the yellow armband becomes dirty too quickly and the number cannot be read when the armband is folded, L. has it replaced with a numbered metal badge worn on the left breast.

Accommodations.   When L. assumes his post, the Ghetto Guard is housed in the stables of the Magdeburg Barracks. L. regards this as degrading and unhealthy. He files a complaint with the Self-Administration and is given the former Hotel Deutsches Haus. Together with his men, he converts the hotel into a barracks: the attic is built out, a kitchen installed, and a large sick bay is set up. L. has the three-level bunk beds, which have been assigned to the Ghetto Guard, rebuilt into folding couches. He also arranges that old blankets be made into heavy coats with hoods and into warmly lined overshoes with wooden soles for use during cold-weather duty. Sentry boxes are erected to protect guards from rain and snow.

Privileges

L. convinces the SS and the Jewish Council of Elders to grant members of the Security Forces the following privileges:

First: transport protection (all members of the Security Forces and their families—i.e., spouses, children, parents, in-laws, and partners—are exempted from deportations to the east).

Second: luggage protection (all members and their families are exempted from searches by the "Beruskys," the Aryan women commissioned by the SS to look for contraband in the prisoners' living quarters and personal belongings).

Third: manual labor rations (double portions).

As a result of these privileges, L. is deluged with applications. For every opening in the Security Forces, there are over twenty candidates. This allows L. to make a careful selection. He employs only the strictest criteria, testing intellectual and moral capacities as well as physical ones. An additional requirement is knowledge of both German and Czech: members of the Security Forces must be able to communicate with every inmate in his or her mother tongue. The majority of those whom L. accepts are reserve officers in the Czechoslovakian Army. Over time, the Security Forces expand to 420 members.

The privileges enjoyed by the Security Forces are not welcomed by everyone. L. is able to attain them only with great difficulty and must continue to defend them even after they have been granted. Only after members of the Council of Elders have accompanied L. to a shift of sentry duty do they agree that it should be treated as heavy manual labor deserving of special rations. Transport protection is itself a sensitive subject, as the SS determines the number of prisoners required for a particular transport and any prisoner who is exempted must be replaced by another. An objection to such measures: one is usually aware of whom one protects but not of whom one endangers. L. rejects this argument: "The members of the Security Forces serve the general interest. They cannot perform this service if they are threatened with deportation." Although transport protection has been officially granted to members of the Security Forces, L. must be continually on guard to ensure that none of his officers is deported. Shortly after assuming office, while he is still recovering from his hernia operation, he learns that sixteen of his security officers have been scheduled for the next transport. In spite of his painful sutures, he does not return to his hospital bed before all sixteen have been removed from the list. L.: "During my term of office, not one person objectively protected from transport was deported."

Clean Hands. With privileges come obligations. The camp commandant puts the following condition on the preferential treatment granted to the Security Forces: the slightest infraction, even if only by a single member, will result in the dissolution of the entire organization. L. therefore insists that not only his security officers but their family members as well should do absolutely nothing wrong. When the mother of a Ghetto Guardsman misappropriates rations while working as a food server and is subsequently convicted by the Jewish Ghetto Court, L. dismisses the son from the guard. He announces to the remaining members of the Security Forces that while he deeply regrets this measure, he holds it to be absolutely necessary for the integrity of the entire organization. L.: Transport protection is not a gift. Those who enjoy its benefits must be aware that their personal behavior has to be beyond reproach and that they must avoid anything that might offend other camp inmates. That a person might enrich himself or herself at the cost of other defenseless camp inmates is intolerable for any member of the Security Forces. Through the illegal actions of his family, the Ghetto Guardsman has compromised the entire Security Forces; and there is no place in the Security Forces for compromised persons.

As a result, the family of the Ghetto Guardsman loses its transport protection. By order of the SS, persons convicted of offenses by the Ghetto Court are placed, along with their entire families, on the next transport to the east.

A Fanatical Defender of Justice

After assuming office, L. is outraged to discover that theft is widespread in the camp. In principle, any and all objects of value are stolen. Given the systematic malnutrition of camp inmates, however, theft of food and foodstuffs are the most frequent and significant offenses. Many inmates designate this as "organizing" rather than stealing, and justify it with the argument that they are taking from the SS and not from the camp community. L. rejects this position: "Those goods that are stolen are no longer available for distribution to the camp as a whole, since we have a fixed number of people here and have to make due with only those provisions allotted to us for a set amount of time. Such offenses are, in other words, crimes against the community. Furthermore, people steal not only to feed their families but also in order to resell the food at exorbitant prices."

Feeding at the Trough.   What L. regards as particularly grievous is the theft of common property by inmates in official positions— i.e., by members of the Jewish Self-Administration. In the food production centers, where there are numerous possibilities for "organizing," L. discovers "massive administrative corruption." This he cannot tolerate: "We live in a time of crisis, in which the majority of the population is condemned to go hungry. It is simply not right that a relatively small group of people is able to lead a better life at the expense of weaker inmates through trade in scarce foodstuffs."

Sources of Corruption.   L. locates the epicenter of corruption in the Central Provisions Office, the point through which all food-stuffs enter the camp. The Central Provisions Office supplies food to its branch offices, the Provisions Offices in the barracks, which then distribute provisions to the kitchens, the bread de-pots, and the House Elders. L.: A den of corruption. The Central Provisions Office also supplies foodstuffs to the Central Work Office, which distributes additional food to working inmates on the basis of a special premium system. L.: Another den of corruption.

Further Dens of Corruption.
  The Kitchens. One of L.'s most loyal officers reports that when dumplings are produced in the main kitchens, the kitchen personnel regularly set aside entire sacks of flour for their own use, even though they have reported it to the Central Provisions Office as having been used.
  The Butchers. According to L.'s estimates, up to fifty kilograms of meat are stolen every day.

The Transportation Department. L.: The transportation department provides vast territory for thievery. Many a stick of margarine, many a bag of sugar has disappeared here.

The Post Office. L. determines that packages sent to Theresienstadt by family and friends containing food and other valuables often reach their recipients only after they have been thoroughly plundered.

The "Sluice." Crime begins at the camp gates. The first thing newly arrived prisoners must do is pass through the "sluice." Here, they are robbed first by the SS, then by the Czech gendarmes, and finally by their fellow inmates. In the sluice, newcomers are routinely separated from their luggage. Anything that is not quickly reclaimed is regarded as abandoned. L.: It is, of course, difficult for the Ghetto Guard to determine which property has actually been abandoned and which has been stolen. That is the beginning of corruption!

"My Battle Against Corruption"

L. decides to act without regard for the consequences. His main goal is to ensure a just distribution of food. Everyone should get his fair share. In particular, L. seeks to protect elderly inmates, who are weak and frail and cannot defend themselves.

Kitchen Warfare.   Initially, L. directs his attention to the kitchens. To his astonishment, he learns that kitchen personnel enjoy special privileges. Not only are they served a nutritious and appetizing meal, but each member receives—with official approval—seven dumplings, while the remaining camp inmates receive only one. L. is not able to abolish this measure, which is supposed to counteract theft in the kitchens, but he does manage to have the size of the normal dumpling increased substantially. However, he does not want to be misunderstood here: it is corruption he hates, not the corrupt.

L.: "I do not regard the cooks as my personal opponents. I simply want to do away with injustices that harm the general welfare."

Reform Measures.   L. orders that every kitchen display a blackboard that informs inmates about the food being served. He also orders that a "sample portion" be exhibited every day and that a scale be present in every kitchen. When L. learns that meat is served only as goulash and that many camp inmates receive only sauce and no meat, he intervenes again. He demands that meat portions, even if they are only forty grams a week, be served in measurable form, as meat loaf, meatballs, or in slices. Here too, he encounters resistance, and forces the reform through only with great difficulty. Since he is repeatedly confronted with the objection that "there's no other way to do it," he decides to set up a model kitchen, open to all inmates, in the quarters of the Ghetto Guard. L.: The food in my kitchen tastes better and the portions are larger because nothing is stolen here.

Raids.   Having heard reports about misappropriations of food during deliveries from the Central Provisions Office, L. deploys three hundred members of the Security Forces for an unannounced inspection. L.: "The results are shocking. In most cases, the amounts distributed do not correspond with that to which individual camp inmates are entitled." An investigation of the bakery reveals that 10,500 dumplings have been officially distributed. In reality, however, the bakery produced an additional 1,400 dumplings, which the cooks rather than the workers received. The director of the Provisions Office and the director of the Bakery cannot explain the whereabouts of another 1,700 dumplings. A raid on meat deliveries shortly thereafter yields similar results. L. repeats such measures on a regular basis.

Economic Inspection Authority.   To ensure that the economic affairs of the ghetto are carried out in a lawful and orderly manner,

L. establishes an Economic Inspection Authority. This organization is responsible for inspecting and investigating every economic department of the Self-Administration at all times.* L. chooses the members of the Economic Inspection Authority with great care. Each official is an expert in his field: food chemists, leading figures in industry, executive accountants, master butchers and bakers, wheat and grain wholesalers, millers, warehouse managers, clothing manufacturers, master shoemakers, tailors, architects, a physician, a veterinarian, food importers and exporters, head cooks. In addition to this, L. appoints elderly camp inmates—who are no longer subject to work duty—to oversee the distribution of meals to frail and sick inmates.

Jurisdiction.　L.: "The Economic Inspection Authority is authorized to inspect all divisions of the ghetto and to place them under its supervision. It is superior to all those departments and, at the same time, the highest independent examining organ of the camp directorate."

Due to the repeated conflicts between the Economic Inspection Authority and the individual production centers, many members of the authority are not particularly welcome in the various departments. The Economic Division of the Self-Administration would like to take over the authority or to set up its own examining organ. L. refuses to permit this.

Further Reform Measures.　To ensure that the proper amounts of sugar and milk are distributed to inmates, L. introduces standard measuring containers—at first empty tin cans, later wooden receptacles. After a protracted search, he is able to locate calibrated weights, which he distributes to the various branches of the Provisions Office.

---

*The Economic Inspection Authority is also charged with presenting suggestions for improvements and with investigating all cases where it is suspected that the economic interests of the camp have been compromised.

In the Service of the Common Good

L. puts his heart and soul into his work; in the exercise of his duties, he has hardly a free minute. Conferences, inspections, meetings, briefings, court cases—the tempo is breathtaking. L. is everywhere at once. He feels personally responsible for the security of the entire ghetto. Once, during a roll call of the Security Forces, he is even said to have proclaimed, "I protect the Jewish Elder Edelstein with my own body, and have no fear of Camp Commandant Dr. Seidl"—a remark that causes much consternation among his subordinates.

Shortcuts.   L. regards the painstaking bureaucratic methods of the Self-Administration with great dissatisfaction: "Instead of granting the petitioners' requests in a timely manner and supplying them with the requested objects—if these are available—an extensive apparatus examines each case at great length and, after protracted consideration, decides whether the person concerned actually requires the requested object." L. fights doggedly against this administrative machinery. The plight of those submitting requests to the Welfare Office is all too clear to him; he regards the numerous examinations as completely unnecessary. L. doesn't talk, he acts. Goods confiscated by the Security Forces in the course of duty are immediately distributed to needy persons or institutions: fresh oranges and lemons to the Children's Home, vegetable and animal fat to the Tuberculosis and Typhus Wards, perishable foods to the Youth Welfare Office.

Issues of Jurisdiction.   L. intervenes everywhere, without troubling himself too much about the jurisdictions of the various authorities. Because no one seems to take responsibility for order in the ghetto or to investigate complaints quickly and thoroughly, he feels continually obligated to take matters into his own hands. Sometimes he even acts preventatively. He considers it his duty to protect the ghetto from unpleasant consequences that might arise from ignorance, neglect, or indifference. Often he finds little understanding for his actions, particularly among members of the Self-Administration. L.: People erroneously see in me a man who places himself arbitrarily above all authority. However, my view is that with respect to the security, peace, order, and general welfare of the ghetto, there can and should be no jurisdictions. A police force that is not in a position to act immediately and effectively soon loses all its power. What one might acquiesce to under normal conditions can—in times of emergency or in moments of danger—become an obstacle and even, under certain circumstances, have tragic consequences. This cannot be allowed to happen. First the common good, then the chain of command!

Presented with the possibility of assuming a seat in the Council of Elders, L. flatly refuses. He must, he explains, protect his freedom of action; as head of the Security Forces, he must remain independent in all respects.

Alone and Forsaken

In spite of L.'s interventions for the ghetto community, opinions about him remain divided. The modest successes achieved in his battle against corruption and theft bring him enemies as well as friends. L. often feels misunderstood. When, for example, he assumes control of the ghetto prison from the Czech gendarmes, he is given permission to punish minor offenders with three-day jail terms in the name of the Security Forces. This makes him unpopular among many inmates. L.: It is frequently overlooked that conditions in the prison have improved significantly and that my punishments do not have to be reported to the camp commandant. L.'s privileged position with the SS—he has constant access to the commandant's office and files a daily report there—also raises suspicions. L. himself believes not only that he understands the psychology of the SS (in particular that of Dr. Seidl, who loves everything military) but also that he is able to exploit that psychology. Even the fact that L. has been able to negotiate some benefits for the camp with the SS is viewed with distrust by the Council of Elders as well as by many inmates.

After some initial difficulties, L. develops a working if distanced relationship with the Jewish Elder Jakob Edelstein. Edelstein regards the Security Forces with skepticism: "I do not love the police; I merely make use of their services." L., for his part, acknowledges Edelstein's courage and intelligence in dealing with the SS, even while criticizing the Jewish Elder's insufficient energy in battling corruption. This situation changes dramatically at the end of January 1943, with the arrival from Berlin of Dr. Paul Eppstein, the former director of the Reich's Association of Jews in Germany, and from Vienna of Dr. Benjamin Murmelstein, the deputy director of the Jewish Community there. The SS announces a new hierarchy of power: Eppstein is named Jewish Elder and Edelstein and Murmelstein his deputies. Ostensibly, this occurs because of the new demographics in the camp, but it is also has the—not undesired—consequence of creating new discord among inmates. L., who has no inclination to subordinate himself to the Council of Elders, can get along with neither Eppstein nor Murmelstein—which doesn't appear to bother the SS in the least. The new Jewish Elder Eppstein, for his part, shows little interest in a battle against corruption. At this point in time, L.'s relations with the deposed Edelstein worsen. L. becomes convinced that Edelstein has spread false rumors about him. He breaks off the relationship, stops greeting Edelstein in public, and even refuses to shake his hand. Only L.'s relationship with the Rabbi Dr. Leo Baeck remains close. L.: "I feel as if I am alone in my battle against corruption. Instead of supporting me, leading members of the camp are insulted when I confront offenders."

Child of Sorrow.   To his great regret, L. discovers that there is even corruption in his own ranks. Some security officers do not move energetically enough against theft and misappropriation. Others actually participate in it. L.'s relations with members of the Criminal Watch become particularly strained. When conditions in the ghetto do not improve, L. threatens to dismiss the entire watch if the trade in stolen foodstuffs is not stopped within four weeks.

Given the lack of support from ghetto officials, L. decides to address camp inmates directly (Feb. 1, 1943): "Everyone can see for himself that my only goal is to maintain order and security in the ghetto. I consider it my duty and my mission to guard over the goods supplied to us, in whatever form that might be, and to ensure that those goods are used appropriately for the intended purposes. Goods should neither spoil due to inattentiveness nor be allowed to fall into the wrong hands. Everyone should get his fair share. However, I cannot be everywhere. I need the cooperation of every one of you. Do not buy from dealers, for they are selling your goods. Maintain discipline. Come to me openly with your complaints. I will listen to everyone. No one who comes to me with a request will be treated as if he were a disturbance. I am here to help. Please assist me in my battle against corruption. The integrity of the ghetto is at stake."

Decisive Action

From the beginning, L. is critical of the Council of Elders' food-distribution policy, which in his opinion unfairly favors children and laborers at the expense of elderly inmates. L.: Many of our old people have died from malnourishment. He argues, without success, that a portion of the undeliverable packages arriving in Theresienstadt—all of which are currently distributed to the children—should be given to elderly camp inmates. L.: "The children have a special kitchen, and their parents, relatives, and friends look out for them as well, while there is no one to care for those elderly inmates who have no relatives in Theresienstadt." The Council of Elders promises to investigate the problem and to implement the necessary measures.

All this takes too long for L., and he regards the proposed measures as insufficient in any case. In May 1943, he decides to take matters into his own hands. L.'s plan: to request that once a week the heavy manual laborers make do with half a meal for the benefit of the elderly. He organizes a one-week test run with members of the Security Forces: a soup is made from the collected rations and then distributed to elderly inmates. It appears to be a success. Already on the first day, L. receives letters and poems of thanks. To his dismay, however, he also discovers that those among the elderly who are more active have been able to obtain several servings of soup, while others, who cannot push their way forward, have received nothing. To combat this problem, he decides to have numbered meal tickets distributed to the elderly.

Encouraged by the preliminary results, L. writes an open letter to the manual laborers: "Today, I turn to you with a request, and I would be extremely pleased if you could give me an affirmative answer. When I was present at an autopsy recently, I noted with dismay that the corpses of deceased elderly inmates were nothing more than skin and bones. You all know that it is only possible to provide special rations for heavy manual labor because food has been saved—i.e., taken—from the rations of other inmates. If three thousand people were to forgo their additional rations for heavy manual labor—half a lunch once a week—then three thousand other inmates might eat their fill on that day. Wouldn't that be wonderful? Wouldn't it testify to your nobility? Please remember that you have parents or have had parents, and that all of you will be old yourselves at some point in the future. How would you feel if you were discarded as old and useless, or if no one cared for you anymore? I am convinced that when you consider this, you will support me and help our elderly and frail inmates. I would be overjoyed if you would agree to forgo half a lunch for one day a week in shifts, that is, once on Sunday, once on Monday, once on Tuesday, etc., for the benefit of the elderly and the frail."

The next day, L. is summoned to a special session of the Council of Elders, where he is sharply reprimanded by the Jewish Elder Eppstein. Eppstein objects that the undertaking far exceeds L.'s authority as head of the Security Forces and that it threatens to undermine camp discipline. He reminds L. that the Council of Elders has already investigated the problem of caring for the elderly and decided to seek approval from the camp commandant for its proposed measures. L. is forbidden to take any further action regarding the elderly, although he is allowed to complete his trial run with the Security Forces. L. concedes, but his relations with the Council of Elders remain strained.

A Question of Method

I.

L.'s relationship with Dr. Erich Munk, director of Public Health and a member of the Jewish Council of Elders, is particularly difficult. Munk is, in principle, opposed to L.'s modus operandi. Dr. Munk at a meeting of the Council of Elders: "We have made a city out of the camp; L. is turning that city back into a camp." In December 1942, there is a serious confrontation between Munk and L. A hospital patient reports to L. about misappropriations in the Infectious Ward: food and foodstuffs brought to the ward by parents and relatives of patients have not been passed on to the intended persons. L. decides to put things in order. He smuggles a nurse, who is in reality an officer of the Criminal Police, into the ward. The "nurse" is able solve the case quickly. Following this success, L. decides to send other police officers into hospitals and sick bays. However, when Dr. Munk learns of this plan, he states that he is opposed to having outside persons placed in hospital wards for surveillance purposes. He says he cannot sanction the use of spies. Despite L.'s objections, Dr. Munk refuses to alter his position.

L. is furious and takes up the matter with the Jewish Elder. L.: "It is insulting for members of the Criminal Watch to have their work designated as spying. I would have thought that a member of the Council of Elders would place the highest value on improving unacceptable conditions, particularly in the infirmaries, sick bays, and infectious wards. I have the impression that Dr. Munk—who has never lifted a finger to bring order and integrity into a hospital—is opposed, out of pure obstinacy, to my efforts to clean things up. Does Dr. Munk, because he is not up to his responsibilities, hide behind an insulting exterior? He appears to be a man who takes everything personally, thus bringing a particular bitterness into even the most trivial matters. He seems insulted by the mere fact that someone has attempted to address those problems that have unfortunately developed in the health system. Were I the director of Public Health, my sense of honor would not permit me to remain inactive while physicians violated their professional code of honor. What kind of Public Health Department seeks to suppress the very forces that are attempting to serve the public good?"

After a difficult battle, L. is permitted to have members of the Criminal Watch stationed as nurses in hospitals and sick bays.

II.

In early May 1943, a suitcase with medications arrives in Theresienstadt on a transport from Oppeln. The suitcase is picked up by two officers of the Criminal Watch and turned over to L. Since a significant number of security officers are patients in the Ghetto

Guard sick bay at the time, L. orders that the suitcase be given to the Ghetto Guard physician. When Dr. Munk learns of this, he files a written complaint with the Jewish Elder:

"Re: Suitcase with medications from Ratibor. Misappropriation by the Security Forces.

"A suitcase with medications arrived in the ghetto on the most recent transport from Oppeln. The supervising physician, Dr. Reinisch, ordered that the suitcase be turned over to the pharmacy. The criminal officers involved received this order but directed the bag instead to House L313 (the Ghetto Guard quarters). We would like to take the liberty of pointing out this incident to the directorate. We also request that action be taken against the head of the Security Forces and that the directorate ensure that in the future medications be turned over to the Central Medications Storeroom and not to the Ghetto Guard. We regard this incident as a violation of duty on the part of the criminal officers involved and would like to see the matter investigated. I take this opportunity to point out to the directorate the curious way in which medications were distributed to the physician at the Ghetto Guard sick bay. We hope that the chief of the Ghetto Guard will be kind enough to explain where these medications came from."

The Jewish Elder Dr. Eppstein requests that L. file a report on the matter and return the suitcase. L.'s response (May 14, 1943): "First, I would like to point out for the record that the term 'misappropriation' is an egregious distortion. The only thing that is correct in the director of Public Health's letter is that a suitcase with medications arrived here from Ratibor on the last Oppeln transport. The claim that Dr. Reinisch ordered that the bag be turned over to the pharmacy is false. I have myself repeatedly experienced how Dr. Munk, like a bull in a china shop, presents assertions as true without ever taking the trouble to see if his information is correct. Since I have come to know Dr. Munk quite well, I refuse to enter into a polemic with him, as I have no intention of trying to educate this man. The medical case—it is, in fact, a rather small suitcase—was discovered as abandoned property at the train station and was subsequently turned over to me. Given the terrible state of health among members of the Ghetto Guard, I ordered that the bag be turned over on that same evening to the Ghetto Guard pharmacy rather than to the Lost Property Office. Since I have in the past frequently turned over medications found in the course of duty directly to various institutions of the Public Health Department, I find it curious that the director of Public Health would write a letter at all, since he must be aware that the medications in question were turned over to a physician whom he himself appointed to the Ghetto Guard sick bay. I will give the director of Public Health the benefit of the doubt and assume that he has no idea what the word 'misappropriation' means. In any case, it is an impertinence to employ such a term in communications between departments, even if one does not understand its meaning."

Dr. Reinisch, however, confirms in writing that he requested that the two police officers turn over the medical suitcase to the Central Medications Storeroom, which the officers agreed to do. The suitcase was marked explicitly by Dr. Reinisch with a red cross to indicate that it contained medications so there could be no mistake about its being abandoned property.

The Jewish directorate repudiates L.'s letter emphatically: in an objective dispute about the delivery of a suitcase, L.'s response is intolerable, particularly when communicating with a leading member of the Council of Elders. Even if the director of Public Health's inquiry as to the whereabouts of the medical suitcase led to a difference of opinion, L. should not have responded with insults.

L. finds this repudiation incomprehensible: "In heading his letter to the directorate with the words 'Misappropriation by the Security Forces,' Dr. Munk made absolutely clear his intention of ridiculing and insulting the Security Forces—i.e., that authority in the ghetto which is responsible for combating misappropriation. I regret that the directorate has chosen to reprimand the response and not the original provocation. If the director of Public Health takes the matter personally, then he cannot complain when his impertinence is replied to in kind." L., however, insists that he is not vindictive: if Dr. Munk is willing to take the first step, then he, L., is prepared to retract his letter of May 14 immediately.

Dr. Munk, however, is unwilling to do this. Instead, on May 25, 1943, he submits a detailed letter on the matter to the Jewish directorate (excerpts):

Re: the question of jurisdiction. "The Department of Public Health is responsible for the storage and administration of medications arriving in the ghetto. It is obligated to account for its actions both to the Jewish Council of Elders and to the SS commandant's office. In particular, medications arriving on transports are supposed to be recorded as such in the entry book of the Central Medications Storeroom. On the basis of Dr. Reinisch's report, I was compelled to acknowledge that a division of the Security Forces had failed to bring a suitcase with medications to the Central Medications Storeroom, as Dr. Reinisch had requested. I described this state of affairs—attempting to characterize an action rather than a person—as misappropriation."

Re: the term "misappropriation." "The position taken by the head of the Security Forces led me to investigate the term 'misappropriation' more closely. In Paragraph 181 of the Penal Code, I found the following definition under the heading, 'Misappropriation become a crime': 'Misappropriation is to be treated as a crime when a person—by virtue of his public office (either federal or communal)—withholds or appropriates goods entrusted to him which are valued at more than 500 crowns.' According to Paragraph 461 of the Penal Code, when the value of those objects does not exceed 500 crowns, the misappropriation is regarded merely as a misdemeanor. The act itself, however, is still considered misappropriation."

L. cannot endorse this position. His response (June 16, 1943): In the first place, the suitcase with medications arrived in the ghetto as abandoned property and thus should have been turned over the Lost Property Office, which I, as head of the Security Forces, administer. In the second place, misappropriation requires a selfish intent, which clearly is absent in this case. Misappropriation is the acquisition of another party's property for one's own use. Who received the goods? The ghetto!

Dr. Munk (June 18, 1943): "The claim that this is not misappropriation because the medications from the suitcase were used to treat patients in the Ghetto Guard sick bay and were not kept by the head of the Security Forces for his own personal use is simply not correct. It is no different than if, for example, the head of the Security Forces were to order that a sack of flour or bread which arrived on a transport be turned over to the Ghetto Guard kitchen rather than to the Central Provisions Office. In this case, too, there would no selfish intent, and yet it would still be misappropriation." Dr. Munk now demands a public apology from L.

L. sticks to his position (June 24, 1943): "I ordered that a suitcase with medications—which arrived here as abandoned property—be turned over to the Ghetto Guard sick bay, rather than to the Lost Property Office, so that the necessary medications could be sought out. After this, the remaining medications were turned over to the pharmacy. I can no longer say how many medications were removed from the bag at this point in time. It cannot have been many in any case. Not thinking primarily of the jurisdiction of individual authorities in the ghetto, I ordered—in view of the urgent needs of the sick members of the Ghetto Guard—that these medications, i.e., goods intended for the ghetto, be turned over to an institution of the ghetto. Where is the misappropriation? I did not even turn over medications to particular individuals but rather had the physician appointed by the Public Health Department do so." L. offers no apology.

This is too much for Dr. Munk. Since the Jewish directorate refuses to take any action in the matter, he reports to the Camp
Commandant SS-Hauptsturmführer Seidl and requests that he be
allowed to resign from his post as director of Public Health. Questioned as to the grounds for this request, Dr. Munk explains that
the immediate cause is the self-authorized action on the part of the
head of the Security Forces with respect to an incomplete delivery
of medications to the Central Medications Storeroom. Dr. Munk
presents the original correspondence. SS-Hauptsturmführer Seidl
determines that the matter is too petty to be grounds for a resignation and demands that the Jewish Elder settle the matter to the
satisfaction of both parties within twenty-four hours.

That same day, the following document is drawn up and
signed by all the parties involved:

(1) The Jewish directorate establishes that the delivery of a
suitcase with medications, found at the train station, to the
Ghetto Guard pharmacy rather than to the Lost Property
Office constitutes an abuse of office. The Security Forces are
hereby admonished for this.
(2) The director of Public Health recognizes this and affirms
that this was not—as he claimed in his correspondence—a
matter of misappropriation by the Security Forces.
(3) The head of the Security Forces declares that in his letter from May 14, 1943, he did not intend to insult the director of Public Health.
(4) It is agreed by all parties that the matter has now been
settled amicably.

Two and a half months later, L. realizes that Dr. Munk was in
fact correct. The suitcase with medications did not arrive in the
ghetto as abandoned property. When the two members of the
Criminal Watch picked up the suitcase, it was marked with a red
cross and bore the name of a physician. Neither of these designa-

tions was present when the suitcase was turned over to L. In addition to this, personal items—an English razor, two fountain pens, and a bottle of methanol—had been removed. While L. was initially convinced that the two detectives had simply made a mistake, he now thinks otherwise. In a letter he apologizes to Dr. Munk, deeply regrets that he did not believe him.

Before the Fall

Public Relations.   All in all, the Ghetto Guard remains L.'s pride and joy. L.: "I can proudly say that the Ghetto Guardsman is a helper and friend of the ghetto. Each member of the Guard seeks to do credit to the collective of which he is a part." However, because of the severity with which its members perform their duties, the Ghetto Guard is not particularly popular with many camp inmates. For this reason, L. continually seeks to improve the Guard's image. In March 1943, an operetta, *The Ghetto Girl,* is produced under his supervision. The piece, written by members of the Ghetto Guard and performed by their children, presents the work of the Security Forces in an extremely positive light. The production causes a minor uproar in the camp.

Pinnacle.   Several months after L. assumed his post as head of the Security Forces, new members of the Guard were sworn into office. The ceremony took place on January 1, 1943, followed by a celebratory parade. The entire Ghetto Guard marched in goose step through the camp, which also caused quite a stir.

Over the next five months, the number of security officers increases significantly. A new swearing-in ceremony is long overdue. In the middle of May 1943, on the first anniversary of his leadership of the Ghetto Guard, L. stages a second ceremony—one that far surpasses the first. The celebration takes place in the courtyard of the Dresden Barracks, and more than 5,000 people participate in the festivities. There is a marching band, which even plays the Jewish national anthem. Members of the Ghetto Guard appear for the first time in their new blue-gray uniforms, made from bedspreads, complete with jacket pockets on both sides. After the ceremony, the entire Guard marches spiritedly before L., the Council of Elders, and thousands of spectators. L.: "The general opinion is that this was the most beautiful thing ever seen in Theresienstadt."

In the evening, there is a gala performance in the Ghetto Guard quarters (excerpt):

Ledec Quartet: harp quintet, first movement (Beethoven)

Ghetto Guardsman H.: prologue

Frau N.: aria from *The Huguenots* (Meyerbeer)

Herr N.: "Parable of the Rings" from *Nathan the Wise* (Lessing)

F.-L.: *Air palestinienne* (Kirmann)

Dr. S.: humorous readings

Irma G.: Jewish folk songs

Anny F.: Slavic potpourri

The Brothers G.: harmonica duo

Otto B.: "Theresienstadt, the Most Beautiful City in the World"

The parade—which takes place a day after the Warsaw Ghetto Uprising is definitively crushed by the Germans—is not appreciated by everyone. The next morning, the SS, which was also present at the celebration, confiscates the Ghetto Guard's new uniforms.

Ouster

On June 3, 1943, SS-Hauptsturmführer Seidl is relieved of his duties as camp commandant. The new commandant, SS-Obersturmbannführer Anton Burger, is less favorably inclined toward the Ghetto Guard than his predecessor was. Shortly after assuming his post, Burger issues a series of decrees directed against the Security Forces. In June 1943, L. is forced to dismiss 150 members from the Guard—they are deported to Auschwitz three months later under the pretense that they are to establish the ghetto police force in a new camp. At the end of July 1943, the SS orders that L. dismiss all members of the Ghetto Guard under forty-five years of age. On August 16, the new camp commandant orders L. to his office and suspends him from his post as head of the Security Forces.

Intrigue. Ten days later, L. is arrested by members of the Security Forces and put on trial before the Jewish Ghetto Court. Neither L. nor his lawyers are informed of the charges, and the entire proceeding is closed to the public. L. is accused of abuse of office and misappropriation. Members of the Council of Elders and the Criminal Watch, as well as several kitchen workers, appear as hostile witnesses during the trial.

On September 1, 1943, L. is convicted of the following offenses:

Abuse of office (excerpts):
(2) the improper distribution of confiscated foods to unauthorized persons or institutions (a glass of pork fat and a glass of marmalade, the contents of two sacks found on the street, a second glass of pork fat, a sack filled with onions, garlic, etc.)
(3) the issuing of extra ration cards to his orderlies
(4) the unauthorized exchange of two privately owned suitcases for two suitcases confiscated by the Security Forces

Misappropriation of the following objects valued at more than 500 crowns: a men's pullover; a pair of women's socks and a women's umbrella; a box of soap, powder, and perfume; a beefsteak weighing approximately fifteen ounces.

L. is acquitted of the following charges:

Abuse of office: delivery of a suitcase with medications to the Ghetto Guard sick bay instead of the Central Medications Storeroom, receipt of increased rations.

Misappropriation: the illegal acquisition of sixty bars of soap issued to L. for distribution by the commandant's office; the illegal acquisition of an undetermined amount of foodstuffs confiscated by the Criminal Watch.

L. is sentenced to a five-month prison term and the loss of his post as head of the Security Forces. He is declared unfit to hold public office.

L. himself does not deny the facts of the charges brought against him. He admits having distributed food on his own authority but insists that all the items involved, which included perishable goods, were turned over to various welfare institutions of the Jewish Self-Administration—meat and pork fat to hospitals, fresh oranges and lemons to sick children. He also attempts to convince the court that he believed himself, as head of the Security Forces, to have been justified in acting in this manner. In addition to this, he regularly informed the Jewish Elder of his actions. The court confirms that L. never confiscated food for his own benefit but points out that such goods were supposed to be delivered to the Central Provisions Office, which would then distribute them to the authorized persons and institutions. The fact that L. did not do this, the court argues, was injurious to the public good and therefore constitutes abuse of office.

L. also does not contest the fact that his orderlies were issued extra rations though so-called leftover meal tickets. However, he points out that this occurred at a time when the policy regarding leftover food had yet to be formed and that as head of the Ghetto Guard kitchen he was entitled to distribute such tickets at his own discretion.

Regarding the two suitcases, he explains that his two privately owned suitcases were damaged in the line of duty and that he replaced them with two suitcases of inferior value which were confiscated by the Security Forces. As head of the Lost Property Office, he was entitled to do this.

Regarding the charges of misappropriation, L. offers the following explanations:

The sewing box. He explains that it was a used cigar box covered with paper. New, it would have been worth approximately 1.90 marks. He states that he showed the box to the Jewish Elder and his deputy when they were in his room and that neither of them objected to it.

The pullover, socks, and umbrella. L. ordered the Lost Property Office to issue the items to his seventy-year-old former mother-in-law, who had arrived in Theresienstadt at the end of July 1942. After her death several months later, he returned the items to the Lost Property Office.

The beefsteak. After a meat raid, L. wanted to do something to help the sixty-nine-year-old Chief Rabbi Dr. Leo Baeck, who was in poor health. He sent for Baeck and ordered that a fifteen-ounce steak be fried for him. The Jewish Elder Dr. Eppstein was present when L. called for Baeck. L. informed Eppstein about the matter and Eppstein did not object to it. Dr. Eppstein admits this but claims that he assumed Baeck would consume the steak in L.'s office rather than in his private quarters.

The powder, soap, and perfume. L. insists that he has never seen any of the items.

The court does not take these arguments into consideration. Immediately following the trial, L.'s lawyers submit petitions for annulment and appeal. They dispute the notion that L.'s responsibilities as police chief were ever determined or limited in any way, or that there were clear instructions, either written or oral, concerning the distribution of confiscated foods in Theresienstadt. They also point out that no intent to injure was established during the trial, and that such an intent is necessary in order to demonstrate abuse of office or misappropriation.

Appeal.   Two weeks later, after the former Jewish Elder Edelstein has been questioned a second time, the Court of Appeals of the Jewish Ghetto Court issues its judgment, which essentially confirms the judgment of the lower court. In addition to the original convictions, L. is now found guilty of two further charges: having ordered that a suitcase with medications be turned over to the Ghetto Guard rather than to the Central Medications Storeroom and having accepted improper amounts of dietetic food. Because of the negligible value of the misappropriated objects, L.'s prison term is reduced to three months.

L. is particularly outraged by the accusation that he accepted excessive rations. He points out that after his arrival in Theresienstadt the camp commandant ordered that he was to receive special portions, and that he himself was the only member of the Security Forces who did not take his meals in the Ghetto Guard kitchen, despite its superior food. The sole reason for this, he argues, was to avoid the impression that he received larger portions on the basis of his position. L. submits two pieces of evidence: (1) A letter he wrote in November 1942: "After the fact, I realized that I had received sixty grams of cream and one-half sausage that

I was not entitled to. Since I do not smear my own bread, I did not notice this. I would like to request that you subtract this amount from my next portions. Best wishes, L." (2) A sworn statement from the chief cook in the Ghetto Guard kitchen: "During his frequent inspections, the head of the Security Forces, Herr L., rejected servings larger than a teaspoon with the explanation that this amount was sufficient. In fact, L. rebuked those who attempted to offer him larger amounts."

L. plans to petition the Camp Commandant's office to revise the Ghetto Court's judgment. His lawyer, however, advises him against this after learning from the Jewish Elder Eppstein that the sentence has been approved beforehand by the camp commandant. According to Eppstein, Eichmann's adjutant, SS-Hauptsturmführer Möhs, also approved the judgment and informed superiors in Berlin about it.

L.'s prison term begins in early October 1943. In his cell, he busies himself primarily with preparations for a retrial. Even in prison, he continues to cause unrest in the camp. The prison guard, who until recently was his subordinate, gives L. permission to walk freely through the ghetto. In addition to this, L. uses his writing privileges to submit complaints and offer suggestions to the Jewish directorate. When the prison guard is suddenly transferred, L. files a written complaint with the chief of detectives. In the complaint, L. refers to his own innocence and describes his incarceration as a form of house arrest. He also objects to the fact that as a former officer, who knows how to maintain discipline, his own word is not sufficient; however, he has voluntarily subjected himself to prison rules because he knows that he still has a role to play in Theresienstadt. L. is transferred immediately to a locked cell, and his writing privileges are revoked. During a search of his papers, prison guards discover a draft of a letter to the camp commandant, in which L. offers suggestions for carrying out a census of inmates during role call and makes disparaging comments about the Jewish directorate. As a result, an additional thirty days are added to his sentence for endangering public safety and order.

In February 1944, L. is released from prison. In order to prove his innocence, he convenes a disciplinary court consisting of seven former senior military officers, who declare unanimously that L. did not violate the officer's code of honor and that his behavior was beyond reproach. At the same time, L. also summons a disciplinary court of former civilian judges. This court is unable to issue a verdict, because a number of its members are deported to Auschwitz before the court can reach a judgment. However, two of the judges—Higher Regional Court Judge Dr. Arthur Goldschmidt and Regional Court Judge Dr. Otto Stargardt—submit expert opinions in which both sharply criticize the judgments of the Ghetto Court, designating them as miscarriages of justice.

Liberation

Following his release from camp prison, L. lives reclusively, no longer seeking an official position in the Self-Administration. In poor health, he is supplied with food packages by Leo Baeck. In the spring of 1944, the SS begins its *Stadtverschönerung* or "city beautification" program—an enterprise that succeeds in deceiving delegates of the International Red Cross about the true conditions in Theresienstadt during their tour of the camp in June 1944. After the inspection, work begins on a propaganda film in the ghetto. By the middle of September, filming is completed. Two weeks later, the Jewish Elder Dr. Eppstein is arrested by the SS and executed the same day in the *Kleine Festung* (Small Fortress) near Theresienstadt. The former Jewish Elder Edelstein—already deported to Auschwitz in November 1943—has been murdered in the extermination camp three months earlier. Benjamin Murmelstein becomes the third Jewish Elder of Theresienstadt. On September 27, 1944, two days after Eppstein's execution, mass transports from Theresienstadt to Auschwitz begin. Over the next four weeks, 18,400 inmates are deported to the extermination camp in Poland. When mass executions by gas are discontinued in Auschwitz on November 2, 1944, almost the entire Self-Administration of Theresienstadt has been murdered. Miraculously, L. is spared from the deportations.

The fall transports bring a definitive end to the camp community. By December 1944, only 11,000 inmates remain in Theresienstadt, almost all of them over 65. Only smaller transports arrive in the ghetto now: in February 1945, Jews from racially mixed marriages, then Hungarian Jews, and in mid-April inmates from other concentration camps. The SS begins to collect and destroy documents and evidence in the camp. At the beginning of May 1945, Theresienstadt is placed under the protection of the Red Cross. A few days later, Soviet soldiers assume control of the ghetto and impose a strict quarantine due to a typhus epidemic. On June 5, 1945, L. is arrested by a Soviet soldier during a walk outside the camp. At first, he is unconcerned, believes that the mistake will be resolved quickly. Several days later, however, instead of being released, L. is transferred to Pancrace Prison in Prague.

In late June 1945, Czech authorities begin an investigation against L. on charges of collaboration. Both Robert Prochník, Murmelstein's former assistant, and Jiří Vogel, a member of the Jewish Council of Elders, are questioned about L. by the National Committee for Theresienstadt shortly after the liberation of the camp. Neither of them incriminates L. with his testimony. During the course of the Czech authorities' investigation, which proceeds slowly and haltingly, L. is accused by three former members of the Criminal Watch—who had already testified against him before the Jewish Ghetto Court—of having abused and threatened Jewish police officers in Theresienstadt. They claim that L. was responsible not only for the dissolution of the Ghetto Guard but also for the deportation of two members of the Criminal Watch to Auschwitz. Two other camp inmates describe L. as a "devoted servant" and "stooge" of the Germans. Over the next fifteen months, a number of former Theresienstadt inmates are interrogated. Their testimony exonerates L. for the most part: he is described as a typical Prussian officer, who exercised a rigid or excessively strict control over the Jewish Security Forces. At the same time, witnesses mention L.'s interventions for subordinates and his relentless battle against corruption. Leo Holzer, former chief of the Jewish Fire Department, describes L. as a strict superior but one guided solely by his sense of duty. In a letter from London, Rabbi Leo Baeck insists that while L. may have made mistakes as head of the Ghetto Police, his intentions were always honorable. Even one of L.'s main opponents, the third and final Jewish Elder Benjamin Murmelstein—himself arrested on charges of collaboration—casts doubts on the accusations against L. and points to his "indisputable services" to the camp.

During the investigation, L. remains in Pancrace Prison in Prague. His cellmates are Germans, for the most part SS officers. The food in prison is meager and poor, which is particularly hard on L. after the years of malnutrition in concentration camps. The inmates' hunger is so great that they consume even grass and eggshells. In prison, L. is informed neither of the charges against him nor of the results of the investigation—it is not until February 1946 that he is interrogated himself. In March of that year, the investigating officers conclude that, on the basis of existing testimony, L. cannot be held responsible for either the abuse or the deportation of camp inmates. Three months later, he is transferred to a prison in the town of Litoměřice, three kilometers north of Theresienstadt. In August 1946, he is admitted to the prison sick bay. On January 9, 1947, shortly after several former members of the Ghetto Guard have been interrogated by authorities and have described L. as a strict but just superior, he is suddenly released from prison.

Homeless

After his release, L. stays with friends in Prague for several months, trying to recover his health. During this time, he files a petition with the Czechoslovakian government for reparations for his nineteen-month imprisonment in Prague and Litoměřice, which is subsequently rejected. L. would like to emigrate to Australia, where his elder son lives. In order to do so, however, he must first travel to England to obtain papers and passage. In mid-March 1947, L. flies from Prague to Amsterdam. He closes his eyes as the plane passes over Germany. In Amsterdam, he visits his seventy-five-year-old sister—his only surviving sibling—before traveling to his younger son in Petersborough, England.

Getting to Australia proves difficult. Australian dockworkers refuse to unload Dutch ships, and English ships are not allowed to take foreign travelers. Only with great effort is L. able to reserve a berth on an Egyptian ship sailing from Marseilles. Almost a year later, in February 1948, he departs for Australia.

Melbourne.   L. finds work in a factory, the United Woolen Mills, which is run by a Jewish philanthropist. After the many years of hunger and misery, he finds the immense island impressive. Excerpt from a letter (1948): There is truly a surfeit of everything here. Bones with plenty of meat on them, fat, lard, margarine. One scarcely notices that there was ever a war.

At seven in the morning, L. is in the spinning mill. Because his coworkers are Czechs, Hungarians, Slovaks, Poles, and Germans, L. is forced to speak German in the factory. He spends his free time with other "Theresienstadters," whom he meets in Melbourne. He swims in the ocean, goes to the movies. On the screen, he sees for the first time a completely demolished Germany, something which arouses mixed emotions in him. After the film *A Foreign Affair*: "I had not imagined that the damage was so great. Despite my terrible anger at the Germans, I was nevertheless shocked." After the film *Berlin Express*: "I did not expect such destruction—but even so, it was unfortunately not enough."

In spite of this, L. continues to entertain the thought of traveling to Germany in order to deal with his restitution claims—or perhaps even to live there. His job at the spinning mill is strenuous, and he is getting older. In September 1950, L. reserves a place on a steamer to Germany, but then decides not to go. He is uncertain. Because his last residence was in the current East Sector of Berlin, he fears that he won't receive a pension in the West Sector. However, his various petitions for reimbursement prove difficult to manage from Australia. Problems have already arisen with his first damage claims. After a number of months, L. receives permission to emigrate to West Berlin. He remains uncertain. Then his situation in Australia changes drastically. In April 1952, he is dismissed from his job at the spinning mill. His application for an office job at the Melbourne railway is rejected because he's sixty-five. The West German government promises him a small pension. A friend advises him to emigrate to England. L.: "No, I'm still German. I don't want to become a British citizen. I'll just have to bite into the sour apple and attempt to make it on 170 marks a month until my restitution claims have been settled."

Homecoming

At the end of July 1952, L. takes a steamer from Melbourne to Rotterdam. He arrives in Berlin on September 19. For several weeks, he lives with an old friend before renting a room in an apartment in Berlin-Wilmersdorf. He is initially awarded a pension of 165 marks a month. The rent for his room is 47 marks, not including gas and electricity. In addition to this, there are medical costs (physicians, medications) as well as lawyer's fees for his reimbursement trials. L. begins a protracted battle to right the wrongs that have been done to him.

Compensation

L.'s hopes for prompt compensation prove to be illusory. During his first months in Berlin, he is forced to live on money borrowed from friends, because even his basic pension as a "politically-racially persecuted person" has yet to be approved. He requests that his claims be processed in a timely manner. The *Entschädigungsamt* (Compensation Office)* in Berlin informs him: It is not possible for us to process your compensation claims—which were first filed in January 1952—at this time. It would be an indefensible injustice to those persons who filed their claims at an earlier point in time and who also have financial difficulties, if we did not process claims in the order in which we received them. L.: I would like to point out that I originally filed my claims on November 19, 1951. In fact, I filed a claim with the Central Office for Assets Administration in Bad Nenndorf already in 1947, before the issue of compensation or reimbursement had been dealt with officially. The Compensation Office in Berlin, however, maintains that it first received L.'s claims in January 1952. L. will simply have to wait.

Categories of compensation:

PrV: politically-racially persecuted person

B: damages to body and physical health

C: damages to freedom

D: damages to assets

E: damages to professional and economic advancement

F: damages for wearing the Jewish Star

---

*Two separate authorities in the Federal Republic of Germany process reimbursement claims made by victims of Nazi persecution: the *Entschädigungsamt* (Compensation Office), which is responsible for damages to the victim's person, and the *Wiedergutmachungsamt* (Restitution Office), which is responsible for damages to the victim's property and assets.

Category B [Damages to body and physical health]. L.'s B-pension is processed relatively quickly. On July 6, 1953, a number of the physical injuries listed in L.'s petition are recognized by the Regional Court in Berlin to be the result of Nazi persecution. The court, however, refuses to recognize that injuries to L.'s heart and eyes have been caused by persecution. L. finds this ruling incomprehensible: "My eyes and heart were in perfect order before my imprisonment. The damages I have are the direct result of the abuse I suffered in Minsk." He files an appeal the next day. The officials at the Compensation Office, however, are unyielding. In August 1953, L. submits a medical report from a surgeon, confirming that his heart problems are the direct result of a serious injury to the thorax. The Compensation Office informs L. that the original decision can be altered only by the Regional Court, following a hearing on the matter. L. petitions the Regional Court in Berlin which rejects his appeal as unfounded.

In June 1954, L. requests that the Compensation Office approve a medical examination of his stomach. At the beginning of August, the request is rejected. One week later, L. files a written complaint: "In registering damages to my health, I reported only those injuries sustained as a direct result of serious mistreatment. I would have felt like a hypochondriac to have included the fact that my stomach no longer functions properly, or that my respiratory system has never been the same since the severe bronchitis and pneumonia I experienced as a result of my being left outside in an open basement, soaking wet, in the terrible Russian winter of 1941–42." L. submits a medical report from an internist, Dr. Felix M. Excerpt from the report: "L. weighs approximately 130 pounds; not only have we been unable to increase this, but L. has actually lost weight recently. All subjective complaints and objective changes can be traced back to the effects of an extended imprisonment in a concentration camp." The Compensation Office refuses to alter its position.

L., however, does not give up. In early January 1955, he submits the following medical reports. (1) A report from Dr. H., a former Theresienstadt inmate and physician, who testifies that between 1943 and 1945 he treated L. for numerous illnesses and various complications. (2) A medical report from an ophthalmologist, Professor V., who confirms that L.'s eye problems are the result not of old age but of trauma. (3) A report from the director of the City Hospital in Berlin-Steglitz, Professor R., who concludes in his detailed evaluation that L.'s serious health problems are in all probability the result of the grave injuries he suffered during his imprisonment between 1941 and 1947.

Later the same month, L. writes again to the Compensation Office: With reference to the medical reports submitted by Professor R. and Professor V. to the Regional Court in Berlin, I would like to request that my medical injuries be recognized as the result of political persecution. I have no interest in a retrial. My heart causes me problems. Even with medication, I cannot sleep. I am plagued by headaches. I have no interest in a larger pension or in financial compensation. My sole desire is that the health problems listed above be recognized as the result of political persecution; that I receive medical treatment for them; and, above all, that I finally have peace and quiet. Is that such an unjust request?

In February 1955, L.'s heart problems, intestinal problems, and respiratory problems are officially recognized as having been caused by Nazi persecution. Only in December 1957, one month after L. has had an eye operation and submitted two additional medical reports from physician-inmates in Theresienstadt, are L.'s eye injuries recognized as the result of persecution.

Category C [Damages to freedom].   L. files for imprisonment damages for a total of 1,856 days—from his arrest by the Gestapo in November 1941 to his release from the Czech prison in Litoměřice in January 1947. The Compensation Office, however, recognizes only 1,276 days of imprisonment. From the decision (Feb. 13, 1953): "The further claims for monetary damages resulting from the imprisonment from May 9, 1945, to January 9, 1947, cannot be awarded, because the concentration camp Theresienstadt was ~~liberated~~ occupied by Soviet troops on May 8, 1945. According to Paragraph 1 of the Berlin Indemnification Law, damages cannot extend beyond May 8, 1945."

Category D [Damages to assets].   Even before returning to Berlin, L. had received the following communication from tax officials in Berlin-Weissensee: "A detailed search of existing income tax records yielded no positive results. The records concerned were presumably destroyed during the war." As a result, L. is dependent on eyewitnesses. He collects sworn affidavits from friends and acquaintances, which testify both to his affluence before the war (chauffeur, servants, trips abroad) and to his character in times of need (in particular, his interventions for inmates in Theresienstadt). However, because the majority of L.'s claims regarding his assets are also covered by the Restitution Office, he ends up withdrawing them from the Compensation Office. In January 1955, the Compensation Office awards L. financial damages for the Jewish Assets Tax he was forced to pay in 1939; and in December 1959, L. is compensated for his travel costs from Australia to Germany in 1952. L.'s petition for his emigration costs from Theresienstadt to Australia via England and for a "passport tribute" he was forced to pay to the Gestapo in 1939 so that his ex-wife could travel to England are both rejected as unfounded.

Category E [Damages to professional and economic advancement].   L. demonstrates convincingly that his annual income sank drastically after 1936. On November 19, 1957, he is awarded compensation in the form of a monthly pension.

Restitution (Material)

Between 1952 and 1960, L. files more than twenty reimbursement claims with the Restitution Office in Berlin. Items claimed include: stocks, securities, household articles, promissory notes, real estate, cash, paintings, and a musical instrument. Over the course of years, the Restitution Division of the Regional Court in Berlin rejects most of L.'s claims as either unfounded or nonreimbursable.

L.'s chief object of interest is the A. Busse & Co. Stock Corporation, of which he was sole owner and director. During the Weimar Republic, the corporation was an investment house. Following the Nazis' seizure of power in 1933, the company was forced, as a result of the political and economic circumstances, to cease its banking activities and reduce its operating capital significantly. By the time racial laws were introduced in Germany in 1935, the corporation claimed only two major assets, both of which had been acquired during the 1930s: two apartment buildings in Berlin-Borsigwalde and the HBG—Gentlemen's Clothing Company.

Apartment Buildings.   L.'s first restitution claim is a petition for the return of the two apartment buildings in Berlin-Borsigwalde from their current owner, Frau Frieda B. At the beginning of 1942, shortly after Max Schmidt took over the Busse Stock Corporation from L.'s trustees—Count von Moltke, Corvette Captain Albrecht, and Fräulein M.—Schmidt sold the buildings to Frau B. for 30,000 reichsmarks. At the restitution trial, Frau B. claims that the houses were purchased legally from an Aryan. However, L. has evidence that Frau B. did not buy the houses in good faith, that she knew they were actually owned by a Jew. The witness named by L. is not interrogated by the court. Frau B.'s lawyer argues that his client is in possession of an identification card from the organization Victims of Fascism, that she is officially recognized by that organization as a victim, and that it would be a particular hard-ship for Frau B.—who was sentenced to a ten-year prison term during the Hitler era for actively supporting Jews and served one and a half years of that sentence—to be forced to return the houses. The court rejects L.'s petition on the grounds that he was no longer the majority owner of the Busse Stock Corporation when the houses were sold.

HBG—Gentlemen's Clothing Company.   L. encounters similar difficulties with his petitions for damages regarding the Gentle-men's Clothing Company (HBG or Herrenbekleidungsgesellschaft). In May 1942, Max Schmidt sold the HBG to three businessmen. Shortly thereafter, Werner Henning was appointed director of the company. Over the next two years, there were several increases of operating capital, including one in 1944 involving Schmidt. In February 1945, Henning fled to Hamburg. An employee of the company illegally assumed control of the HBG and then sold it to a third party after the war. At the end of 1945, the employee was forced to pay Henning over 60,000 reichsmarks as compen-sation; in 1949, Henning was awarded a further 16,500 deutsche marks. During L.'s restitution trial, Henning's lawyers argue that their client purchased the HBG from an Aryan corporation. The court agrees with this position. L.'s petitions for reimbursement are consistently rejected: in a partial decision by the Restitution Court (Jan. 27, 1956); in a decision by the Third Court of Ap-peals (Mar. 2, 1958); and in a decision by the Highest Restitution Court (Dec. 13, 1962). On February 10, 1966—one and a half years after the defendant Henning's death—the Restitution Court again rejects L.'s reimbursement petition in a final decision.

Busse & Co.   In 1947, shortly after his release from prison in Litoměřice, L. contacted the district attorney's office in Berlin and requested that criminal charges be brought against Max Schmidt for blackmailing his trustees into selling the Busse Bank. The district attorney, however, concluded from his investigation that Schmidt did not exercise direct pressure on the trustees and thus did not acquire the Busse stock illegally. After his return to Berlin in 1952, L. establishes the following: that Count von Moltke died in 1944, that Major Schliessmann was picked up by the Russians in 1945 and has not been seen since, and that Corvette Captain Albrecht and Fräulein M. are penniless. Albrecht certifies in a sworn affidavit to the Restitution Court (1953) that both he and Moltke sold their stock only because of threats from Schmidt. Fräulein M.—interrogated by the Gestapo directly after L.'s arrest and threatened with internment in a concentration camp because of her illegal relationship with him—asserts that she agreed to sell her stock only after a mutual friend, who had known Schmidt from earlier business dealings and had characterized him as ruthless, advised her to do so. Schmidt denies making threats of any kind. Employees at Schmidt's company, now located in Ansbach, Bavaria, submit a written affidavit testifying that Major Schliessmann was not a fanatic Nazi and that they, the employees, knew of cases in which he actually used his influence to assist racially persecuted persons and foreign workers, even removing them from concentration camps and bringing them to Schmidt's company. They claim that Schliessmann became an SS officer only because he was required, as president of the National Club 1919, to assume a representative position in the Nazi Party.* Because Schmidt answers correspondence from L.'s lawyers and from the Restitution Court only when threatened with legal action, the Busse Bank case is drawn out over years. In 1956, the Restitution Court rejects L.'s petition for reimbursement. The

---

*These statements are contradicted by Schliessmann's SS file, which documents how he sought for years, in vain, to be promoted to the rank of SS-Brigadeführer, even leaving the Protestant Church in 1944 and reporting to Himmler that he was now *gottgläubig*. Excerpt from Schliessmann's SS file: "Schliessmann has consistently maintained close ties to SS comrades and has always sought to serve the SS. At the outbreak of the war, he repeatedly informed the Gestapo about persons hostile to the state."

court's justification: "A corporation which is designated in the sales contract as Aryan and which has an Aryan director and Aryan stockholders cannot be regarded as persecuted at the time of sale, even if the stock was originally given to Aryan persons by a racially persecuted owner who had, by and large, transferred the stock to them legally." L. immediately submits an appeal: in the first place, Count von Moltke and Corvette Captain Albrecht were only trustees, they never actually had the stock in their possession and therefore were not entitled to sell it; in the second place, L. never voluntarily sold stock to Aryans, but rather was forced to do so by the Reich's Trustee for Labor and the German Labor Front. In January 1960, L.'s appeal is rejected by the Restitution Court. At the end of 1960, the court also rejects another petition in the same matter, which L. filed against the German Reich for forcing him to transfer his stock to trustees. The court's justification: "At issue is a simple case of extortion, typical of those carried out by Nazi officials, one which does not, however, provide any legal basis for reimbursement or damage claims."

Restitution (Ideal)

In 1957, a document from L.'s past resurfaces—a certificate issued by the Berlin Police Department on July 8, 1936, confirming that L. saved a woman from drowning the previous year. Immediately after the rescue, L. was nominated for a life-saving medal. However, shortly before the medal was to be awarded, a high-ranking police officer visited L. on behalf of the police chief in order to suggest that L., as a non-Aryan, might voluntarily decline the award. L. was in no way prepared to do this; rather, he insisted on the medal, to which, according to regulations, he was entitled. After a long discussion, L. was able to convince the police officer—who was not a Nazi—of the correctness of his position. The police chief, however, did not dare make the nomination official. Instead of the medal, L. received a written certificate.

After a number of inquiries, L. establishes that while life-saving medals have been reintroduced in West Berlin as of May 28, 1953, they are not being awarded retroactively. An acquaintance of L.'s discusses the matter with Berlin's minister for internal affairs. The problem: the city's lawyers are unaware of any legal options that might permit the belated conferral of a medal. L. is advised to seek support from a public figure, preferably one living abroad. This person might then endorse his petition in a letter to the federal president of Germany.

L. writes to his friend Dr. H. G. Adler, who has recently published a detailed study of Theresienstadt and who, as a result, has become acquainted with the current president, Theodor Heuss. L. even encloses a sample letter for Adler: "Since, in addition to material restitution, there is also such a thing as ideal restitution, I take this opportunity to ask whether you, Herr President, might belatedly confer a life-saving medal on Herr L." In spite of L.'s repeated inquiries, Adler—who doesn't regard the matter as very promising—postpones writing the letter.

In 1961, L. is forced to accept that his life-saving medal will not be awarded retroactively. Particularly irritating is the fact that at precisely this time a certain Herr Katz—currently a successful junk dealer in southern Germany and formerly an inmate and provisions director in Theresienstadt—is awarded the Order of Merit of the Federal Republic of Germany for his interventions on behalf of fellow camp inmates. L.: I never met a provisions director whose actions weren't detrimental to his comrades. What a horrendous battle I had to fight against the Central Provisions Office simply in order to force them to use calibrated weights. I would have understood if I had been given such an award as compensation.

Working Through the Past

L. continues to intervene on behalf of his fellow Theresienstadt inmates. When he is not occupied with his own reimbursement trials, he assists friends and acquaintances—free of charge—in filing their compensation claims, since many of them live abroad and have difficulties dealing with the local authorities. L.: One can't just sit back and do nothing.

In addition to this, L. continues to work on a manuscript about his imprisonment in Minsk, Theresienstadt, Prague, and Litoměřice. Already during the war, he began to put his experiences in writing. As a result of his numerous trials and disputes, he was compelled to reflect at length about events in the camps, making considerable efforts to explain and even justify his actions. While waiting to sail from England to Australia, he begins to organize these memoirs into a manuscript. In the following years, the report expands, eventually encompassing more than three hundred pages. L. finds the process of writing therapeutic. The more he writes, the freer he feels. The hatred he felt for Germany and the German people begins to dissipate.

The past, however, cannot be mastered so easily. There are other former concentration camp inmates, who, spurred on by their own experiences, also write about life in the ghetto. The first comprehensive book on Theresienstadt is published in 1953. Its author, a Czech Jew named Zdenek Lederer, presents L.'s role in the camp in a less than flattering light, even suggesting illegitimate privileges and abuses of power on L.'s part. The accusations cut deep. L. considers taking Lederer to court in order to force a retraction. Two years later, Adler publishes his detailed study of Theresienstadt. While Adler's judgment of other leading figures in the camp is severe and, for the most part, negative, he evaluates L.'s role as head of the Security Forces positively: "L. was able to accomplish many things for the camp in his dealings with the SS. As far as his subordinates were concerned, he did what was in his power. His orders were short, decisive, and martial. He did not shy away from attacking abuses unequivocally, in particular theft and corruption. In so doing, he unfortunately proceeded undiplomatically and became embroiled in an ever-widening battle against almost every department [of the Jewish Self-Administration], so that he ended up making more enemies than was necessary. Had he been no less energetic in his engagement but more conciliatory and careful in form, he could have achieved many beneficial things for the camp—more gradually perhaps, but for that all the more lasting. Thus, he was, in the best sense of the term, a knight in shining armor, without, at the same time, being able to avoid those errors which arose from his lack of insight and inadequate knowledge of human nature." Adler's judgment, however, is by no means the last word in the debate over L.'s role in Theresienstadt. In a critical review of Adler's book, the former head of the camp library in Theresienstadt points to the peculiar fact that L. was convicted of crimes by the Ghetto Court but was not subsequently deported to Auschwitz, as was standard procedure at the time. After Adler translates the review from Czech into German, L. composes an angry rebuttal.

L. himself writes bluntly about corruption in Theresienstadt and about his ruthless battle against it. In his manuscript, he makes grave accusations against the Jewish Self-Administration, in particular against the three Jewish Elders of Theresienstadt. Publishing the report proves to be extremely difficult. Even though L. is prepared to contribute a limited sum of money himself, a number of publishers reject the manuscript.

An evaluation of the manuscript by an editor (written at the request of the Christian-Jewish Society in Berlin): "The reader has the feeling that he is witness here to a self-justification—one that is essentially not intended for his ears if he was not in Theresienstadt himself. If the reader were an inmate in that camp, it would seem safe to assume that he does not necessarily want to be reminded of that time. The goals of the Christian-Jewish Society are not treated in this work, nor was this, in my opinion, the intention of the author. Were we to present this book to younger readers, it would give them a false impression of what happened, since most of the problems dealt with here appear to have been caused by the inmates' own comrades in destiny. When L. writes, for example, that 'Murmelstein is responsible for the death of thousands of people,' young readers will deduce from this that the Jews actually exterminated themselves. Because the manuscript is written exclusively from the perspective of a single individual, it cannot, in my opinion, be reworked into a novel—which might allow for greater mutual understanding. On the other hand, it is not objective enough for a scholarly report."

An evaluation of the manuscript by a staff member of the Yad Vashem Archives in Israel: "Dear L., I have read your letter and the enclosed documents with great care and interest. I was pleased to find, in a letter from Dr. Adler, an evaluation of your manuscript which is similar to my own ('a personal report of extraordinary documentary significance'). That is what counts when evaluating a manuscript before it is published in book form. But—and I want to emphasize this—even Dr. Adler has reservations about whether everything here can be published ('one shouldn't make accusations in public that one can't prove'). My objections go somewhat beyond this, as I fear that your memoirs, even in cases where you are absolutely correct, could very well provoke a negative reaction. Such a dark portrait of those Jews who held leading positions in Theresienstadt would necessarily have such an effect. For a book is read not only by our friends but also by our enemies, who seek in such books—particularly in those written by Jews—material to use against us. They take great pains to find such material. You know this yourself from experience."

In 1956, L.'s chapter on Minsk is published in a slightly revised form in *Aus Politik und Zeitgeschichte,* the supplement of the weekly newspaper *Das Parlament.* In October 1957, the first of

L.'s twelve Theresienstadt chapters—significantly abridged but nevertheless containing serious accusations—appears in *Die Mahnung,* a publication of the Association of People Persecuted by the Nazi Regime. L.'s brief chapter on his incarceration in Czech prisons after the war is never published.

Light and Shadows

In October 1957, Grete Salus, a former Theresienstadt inmate, publishes a personal memoir in *Aus Politik und Zeitgeschichte.* Her report includes an extended discussion of living conditions in the ghetto. Excerpt: "In Theresienstadt as well, there was a bitter struggle, carried out under suffocating conditions, against sickness, hunger, vermin, and deportation. Everyone fought for themselves, for their families and their close friends—there was no energy for anything more than that. The elderly inmates needed to be fed quite differently than they were, but we also had thousands of children in the camp who had to be saved at any price. This was only possible by providing them with a better diet than that of the adult inmates. The cloth was simply not big enough for the entire table. Some part of it always remained bare. We tried many alternatives, we calculated and experimented. There simply wasn't enough to go around. We had to maintain the ghetto on our own. There was hard, unpleasant work that had to be done, such as cleaning out the sewers, loading the various foodstuffs, transporting corpses and sick people, and everything else that is necessary in such a community. The people who performed these tasks were given more to eat—they had to be rewarded in some way. Over time, a bonus system developed for various kinds of labor to ensure that it was done properly. There were also numerous patients with lung disease. In order to keep them alive—they were mostly children and adolescents—we had to provide them with better food. Where could this food come from given our limited provisions? Some group had to be disadvantaged. And since, initially, there were almost more elderly inmates than younger ones, it was the elderly who had to bear this burden."

In a letter to an acquaintance in Israel, L. comments on the article, objecting to the fact that the author never mentions corruption in Theresienstadt. The letter is forwarded to Salus, who writes to L. in the middle of November 1957: Dear Herr L.! Forgive me for responding to your letter to Frau Dr. Kör. I admit that I take the Jews' side. How could I do otherwise? I myself do not believe that it would be appropriate for us to write exhaustively about corruption in the ghetto administration. After all, the Germans are the perpetrators here, not the Jews. By providing precise information about what occurred, we cannot, unfortunately, make anything good again—on the contrary, we can do considerable damage. And this, I imagine, would suit many of the guilty parties—to blame the Jews for the death of so many people. Black is not always black. Life has taught me that this color has many shades. I am certain, however, that you will not agree with this statement. I myself am firmly convinced that our imprisonment in Theresienstadt as a community of families necessarily promoted corruption. In any event, the elderly inmates could not have been saved by a piece of bread. They starved to death primarily because their bodies could not digest the kind of food they were given. They needed fat and protein in a more concentrated form. In normal life, corruption is abhorrent to me, and I would fight against it with every means possible. However, the life that human beings were forced to live in the camp certainly cannot be measured by the same standards. Jews are just as good and as bad as other people. Why should we, the survivors, bear witness against those who are no longer alive—to the satisfaction in this case of a considerable number of Germans? I myself cry out bitterly about the fact that this community, rooted in scarcity and need, was ever brought into existence. But I can't bear to go into the details. Is the rest of the world so infallible? Don't crimes against humanity occur continually? Should we spread the so-called truth about Theresienstadt to such a world? Where is the pure and incorruptible judge? As I suggested in my article, we must place a seal on this and sink it in the deepest mine of oblivion. It cannot be very uplifting for our children to have to read about this in the future. Above all, I can see no pedagogical value in it, either for our Jewish youth or for the Germans. I am a teacher and live here with Jewish children. I can well imagine what a shock this would be for them. I hope that you can understand what I mean. Your Grete Salus.

L.'s response (Nov. 29, 1957): My dear Frau Salus! I was greatly impressed by your article. It is very well written and very interesting. I am certain that it will have enlightening effects in Germany. However, I cannot agree with the thoughts expressed in your letter. The entire world knows that there was corruption in every jail, in every concentration camp, in every form of incarceration during the war. It is also well known that the SS only selected, and only retained, those inmates they could rely on. If corruption arose in concentration camps, the blame lies primarily with the SS, who appointed these miserable creatures in the first place. I am certain you have read in the newspaper that there have been, and will continue to be, trials in Germany against former kapos. Last year, before visiting America, I made a tour of Israel, and I must tell you that I was enormously impressed with what has been accomplished there. For this reason, I cannot imagine that they, too, will not understand when the truth is told. I simply have too high an opinion of the Jewish people to believe that they won't. No, Frau Salus, where there is light, there are also shadows. And the light has a much more powerful effect, when, rather than hiding the shadows, one shows them as well. If you study the statistics, you will see that the mortality rate in Theresienstadt began to rise in July 1942, which is when corruption began to increase. It then declined sharply in October 1942,

right hand, has overexerted his left hand, which itself was injured as a result of Nazi persecution. Taking this into consideration, the court now proposes a settlement that would allow the orthopedic injuries to L.'s left hand to be included in his federal treatment plan. On February 11, 1971, the Compensation Office decides to accept this settlement and to recognize that the injuries to L.'s left hand were caused by persecution.

"That the just may also receive justice..."

In February 1960, following the Restitution Court's final rejection of L.'s claims regarding the Busse Bank, L.'s lawyer files an immediate appeal. At the end of that year, the Third Court of Appeals reverses the lower court's decision, ordering that the case be sent back to the Regional Court for review. Over the next three years, there is no progress on the case. In an effort to speed up matters, L. writes to the head of the Restitution Court (Oct. 2, 1963): Dear Herr Director! I would be grateful if the hearings regarding my case could be continued. I am seventy-six years old and have already had my first stroke, albeit a minor one. I would like to be able to enjoy the money due to me before I become senile. Respectfully yours, L.

First Success.   In January 1965, the Restitution Court rules that in the case of the Busse Bank, the defendant Max Schmidt must pay L. damages in the amount of 24,500 reichsmarks (= 2,450 deutsche marks). The court rejects L.'s claims for further damages. Lawyers for both parties file immediate appeals.

Two years later, on January 23, 1967, the Third Civil Court of the Court of Appeals in Berlin rules that L. is entitled to damages for the disenfranchisement of Busse Bank stock with a nominal value of 33,000 reichsmarks. The Court of Appeals orders that the case be sent back to the Regional Court for a ruling on the real amount of damages, as well as for a ruling regarding the loss of further Busse Bank stock with a nominal value of 5,000 reichsmarks.

At roughly the same time, the Third Civil Court of the Court of Appeals in Berlin rules in the case of the HBG—Gentlemen's Clothing Company that L. is entitled to a share of the company amounting to 14,000 reichsmarks (1,400 deutsche marks)—this after L.'s claims in the matter have been consistently rejected by the courts for more than fifteen years. The executor of the estate for the deceased defendant, Werner Henning, informs the court on February 14, 1968, that if this settlement is approved, the bankrupt Henning estate does not have the assets to pay its share of the damages (1,250 deutsche marks).

At the end of October 1968, the court decides that is necessary to obtain an expert opinion on the following questions regarding the HBG—Gentlemen's Clothing Company: (1) How much was L.'s interest in the HBG worth at the time of his deportation? (2) How much is this interest worth at the present time? (3) How much would this interest have been worth if the business had continued to operate up to the present time, if it had not been sold by Schmidt and if it had been run in the same fashion as it was before L.'s deportation?

Due to a number of unfavorable coincidences, it takes the court almost four years to find an expert who is able to produce such a report. A year later, in August 1973, the report is submitted. Conclusions: (1) The value of L.'s interest in the HBG—Gentlemen's Clothing Company at the time of his deportation: 15,000 reichsmarks; (2) the value of this interest at the present time: 32,000 deutsche marks; (3) the value represented by this interest if the company had continued to be operated in the same fashion up to the present time: 40,000 deutsche marks.

At the beginning of 1974, L. is still waiting for a ruling. On January 28, he writes to the head of the Regional Court: Dear Herr Director! I would be greatly appreciative if you could schedule a court date for me in the near future. I am eighty-six years old. How much longer must I wait? For this reason, I have decided to accept the expert opinion.

In July 1974, L. declares that, given his advanced age and the extended length of the two trials, he is willing to accept damages in the amount of 20,000 deutsche marks in the case of the HBG—Gentlemen's Clothing Company and damages in the amount of 30,000 deutsche marks in the case of the Busse Bank.

Max Schmidt offers L. 3,000 deutsche marks "in order to be rid of the matter, which is burdensome for me as well." L. refuses the offer. The Henning estate informs the court that, after payment for the services of the deceased executor of the estate to the executor's heirs, assets in the bankrupt Henning estate currently amount to 529.59 deutsche marks.

On August 9, 1975, L. dies while taking a cure in Bad Neuenahr-Ahrweiler.

Two years elapse before the Regional Court in Berlin is able to locate L.'s heirs in Australia in order to ask them whether they wish to pursue the two unsettled cases. L.'s younger son, Horst L., responds on August 28, 1977: My deceased father pursued these legal actions for years in order to receive the justice due him; I will continue to pursue them.

Shortly thereafter, Max Schmidt dies, deeply in debt.

On December 11, 1979, the Regional Court in Berlin writes to L.'s heirs: "Both reimbursement claims are in themselves justified. However, they are not enforceable because the businessman Max Schmidt died with a debt of DM 1.5 million. If you do not expressly file within three months for the continuation of the two trials, which have now become pointless, the court will assume that you have withdrawn your claims in both cases."

Since the court does not receive a response within the three-month deadline, it proceeds under the assumption that the petitions have been withdrawn. The two cases are considered settled.

Precautionary Measures

The sixty-seven-year-old widow Klara D. lives in the town of Bayerisch Gmain near Bad Reichenhall. After the death of her husband in 1924, she leads a reclusive life, rarely leaving her home. On December 9, 1938, one month after the Reichskristallnacht, unknown perpetrators pin a note to her front door reading: "All Jews get out now!" D., who has taken the anti-Jewish measures very much to heart and lived in fear that someone might do her harm at some point, takes an overdose of Veronal. In the early morning of December 10, the housemaid finds her lying unconscious in bed. For three days, D. wrestles with death. During this time, the housemaid notifies a number of physicians in Reichenhall, all of whom refuse treatment, referring her to the Jewish physician Dr. O., who finally takes on the case. D. dies on December 13, 1938.

In the monthly bulletin of the Reichenhall Police Station, it is reported that D. took a fatal overdose on December 13, 1938. Whether the date was recorded incorrectly here in order to avoid embarrassing respectable citizens or in order to ignore the last sufferings of an old woman or simply in order to prevent additional paperwork, remains unclear. The report closes with the following words: "The town of Bayerisch Gmain is now *judenfrei.*"

Structural Transformation
of the Public Sphere

At the end of August 1942, the retired transport worker Wilhelm H. writes the following inscription on the interior wall of the public toilets at Mariannenplatz in Berlin: "Hitler, you mass murderer, you must be murdered, then the war will be over." Duly reported to the authorities by other visitors of the toilets, the inscription is immediately removed. Twice over the next eight weeks, the seventy-three-year-old pensioner writes the same demand at the same location, as the printer Max R. is able to determine during repeated visits to the facilities. When, at around 5:00 P.M. on October 28, 1942, H. appears again in the public toilets and begins to write on the wall with blue crayon, R. is there to observe him. In order to catch H. red-handed, R. does not intervene at first. When H. has finished writing the words "mass murderer," R. makes a citizen's arrest.

In Custody

At the local police station, H. denies having written anything on the bathroom walls. As no writing implement can be found on his person, he is released on his own recognizance. Two weeks later, on November 13, 1942, the police arrest H. in his apartment and bring him to headquarters for questioning. This time, H. admits to having written the inscription. When asked why he did this, he explains that he receives two monthly pensions totaling 78.80 reichsmarks and must pay 34.05 reichsmarks a month rent.

Five days later, H. is transferred to preliminary detention at Plötzensee Prison in Berlin. The senior district attorney: "Even if the seventy-three-year-old accused does not otherwise appear to have ever engaged in harmful political activities, the suspicion that a crime has been committed here according to Paragraphs 80ff. of the Penal Code [conspiracy to commit high treason] cannot be dismissed." He turns the case over to the *Volksgerichtshof*, or People's Court.

Investigation

Curriculum Vitae.   Wilhelm H., born on 1/13/1869 in Klein-Rietz, currently resides at Berlin SO 36, Pückler Strasse No. 44, married, Protestant, without previous convictions. After attending elementary school, H. worked as a farm laborer until the age of twenty. From 1889 to 1892, he performed his military service as a soldier in the Thirty-fifth Infantry Regiment in Brandenburg on the Havel. Following this, he moved to Berlin, where he worked as a transport laborer for various companies. After thirty-five years, disabled.

Financial Situation.   H.'s apartment on Pückler Strasse consists of a room, a kitchen, and a hallway. Monthly rent: 34.05 reichsmarks. H.'s disability pension amounts to 57.30 reichsmarks a month. His wife receives a pension of 21.50 reichsmarks. H. has no additional income, as he is disabled. His wife earns four to five reichsmarks a week as a cleaning woman. During the winter, the couple regularly receives fifteen to eighteen reichsmarks from the Winter Relief Work. They do not receive financial support from other sources, for example from their children. They have never had lodgers. Despite their limited income, Frau H. does contribute to charities. The couple is not in debt.

State of Health.   During questioning, H. claims to suffer from spells of dizziness. He says his nerves aren't so good anymore.

Political Views.   H.'s neighbors confirm that he leads a reclusive life. No one can recall hearing him make politically disparaging remarks. He is not known to have read a particular newspaper or to have flown a flag on special occasions. H. reports himself that he was never politically active or the member of a trade union. Before the Nazi assumption of power, he voted for the Social Democratic Party.

Interrogation

On January 16, 1943, H. is brought before the investigating magistrate. The magistrate questions him about his motives. Was he dissatisfied with the political, social, or economic conditions in Nazi Germany? H. responds that the cost of living, especially during the war, has become too expensive. He used to be able to buy more with his pension.

H. is asked to explain how he came to commit the crime. He responds that during walks he frequently engaged in conversations with people he didn't really know, as one is wont to do when strolling through public places or sitting on park benches. Often they talked about the political and economic situation, and these people spoke unfavorably about conditions in the Reich. In the course of the conversations, it was said that the Führer was to blame for the current war, for the resulting sacrifices, and for the present restrictions on the standard of living. H. agreed with this position. Consequently, he resolved to bring about a quick end to the war, but did not feel capable of doing so himself. For this reason, he decided to call on other people to act and at the same time to inform them as to why this was necessary. From the summer until the end of October, he then wrote secretly in blue crayon on the interior wall of the men's public toilets at Mariannenplatz: "Hitler, you mass murderer, you must be murdered, then the war will be over."

Question: Does H. admit that through his actions he stirred up the populace, agitated against the government, and called for acts of violence against the Führer? H. contests this. He only thought that things would be different if the Führer wasn't there anymore.

People's Justice

On January 22, 1943, a Herr Wagner (director of the Central Department for the Supervision of Justice at the Staff Office for the Nazi District Leader of Berlin) telephones the People's Court. He informs the district attorney on the case that, given the gravity of H.'s assault on the Führer, the Nazi district leader of Berlin (Dr. Josef Goebbels) would like to see H., despite his advanced age, executed for the crime. The district attorney promises to discuss the matter with the senior Reich's attorney and to keep Herr Wagner abreast of developments. At a brief meeting between the district attorney and the senior Reich's attorney, it is decided that H. should be prosecuted and given a death sentence as quickly as possible. Informed that the Nazi district leader of Berlin is interested in the case, Senior Administrator T. at the People's Court promises to schedule a court date in the first half of March. T. would like to inform Dr. Goebbels of the date himself.

Indicted

Three days later, on January 25, 1943, the Reich's attorney's office submits its indictment. H. is accused of the following crimes:

(1) Calling for the Führer to be killed (Paragraph 5 of the Decree for the Protection of People and State)
(2) The high treasonous act of attempting to alter the constitution of the German Reich through violence, whereby the crime was aimed at influencing the masses by means of the written word (Paragraphs 80ff. Section 2, Paragraph 83 Section 2 of the Penal Code)
(3) Aiding and abetting the enemy during a war against the Reich and harming the military powers of the Reich (Paragraph 91b of the Penal Code)

Examined

As the end of January 1943, the senior Reich's attorney at the People's Court requests a medical evaluation of H.'s mental competence. Was H. capable of recognizing that his inscriptions, directed at random unknown persons, called for the murder of the Führer?

The resident physician at Plötzensee Prison (Feb. 23, 1943): "I have examined the pensioner Wilhelm H. on numerous occasions. He is a seventy-four-year-old man with a chronic ailment in his left hip, advanced arteriosclerosis, and high blood pressure. Psychologically, he appears to be in fairly satisfactory condition; I was unable to find any serious deficiencies of intellect or memory. However, we do need to take into account his egocentric attitude, which is characteristic and normal in elderly people, as well as his inability to adapt to new situations. Given these circumstances, I think that H.

does meet the prerequisites for Paragraph 51 Section 2 of the Penal Code (diminished accountability). Paragraph 51 Section 1 of the Penal Code (legal incompetence) does not apply here."

In the Name of the German People (Top Secret!)

On March 8, 1943, H. is tried before the First Court of the People's Court. The proceedings last an hour. H. is convicted of the charges and sentenced to death.

From the decision: The wording of the inscription—"Hitler, you mass murderer, you must be murdered, then the war will be over"—is clear. There is nothing about the sentence or its meaning to quibble over. Given H.'s selection of a public location, the inscription must be regarded as a call on the populace to kill the Führer of the German Reich. Nor can there be any doubt as to the seriousness of H.'s intentions here. Through his call to murder, H. sought to bring an end to the war, and this goal remained unaltered, as his repeated writing of the inscription demonstrates beyond any doubt.

Since H. wrote his demand quite legibly in crayon on the wall, it could be read by all German comrades visiting the toilets, and this in a neighborhood made up primarily of manual laborers. In addition, the designation of the Führer as a mass murderer and the claim that the war would be over if the Führer were dead both created the appearance of oppositional movements in the Reich and stirred up visitors of the public toilets against the Führer and his Nazi regime, inciting them to acts of violence. In selecting public toilets for this purpose, H. consciously sought to influence the masses through propaganda, because, as he admits, he believed that in this way his inflammatory slogans would be read by many German comrades.

In the fourth year of the war, at a time when the German people are engaged in the most profound struggle for their freedom, H. has placed himself on the side of the enemy. If, as H. desired, the Führer had actually been killed, the German Reich would have been robbed of its supreme leader and an indescribable disaster might have arisen for Germany. And all of this because H. desired greater buying power for his pension and because he himself wanted to lead an "adequate and contented" life. H.'s old Marxist views—evident in his past votes for the Social Democratic Party—resurfaced at the moment when he believed National Socialism didn't offer him enough for his personal needs. He has placed the life of the Führer and the fate of the entire German people at risk in a reckless and wanton manner, and all this merely for his own personal well-being. In so doing, H. has expelled himself from the community of German people, who share a common destiny, and thus has passed sentence on himself. He deserves to die. Given the necessity of protecting the Führer, the people, and the Reich, H.'s personal circumstances— such as the fact that he has no previous convictions and that both the medical expert and the court believe it possible that his mental capacities are diminished—cannot be taken into consideration as mitigating factors. The People's Court has thus sentenced H. to death, a punishment which, given the heinousness of the crime, also takes into account popular German sentiment.

Due Process

In prison, H. is quiet and unassuming, and has little contact with other prisoners. The division warden reports: The prisoner Wilhelm H. has conducted himself well in this institution, and his work has been satisfactory. He appears to feel remorse for his crime.

On April 1, 1943, the district attorney at the People's Court informs the Reich's Ministry of Justice that he has received no statements supporting a pardon for H. In addition to this, he has been informed by the director of the Central Department for the

Supervision of Justice at the Staff Office for the Nazi District Leader of Berlin that Dr. Goebbels himself regards the death sentence and the execution thereof to be imperative.

Position taken by the cognizant official at the Reich's Ministry of Justice (Apr. 13, 1943): "There is nothing to object to in the judgment, either in factual or legal terms. The condemned man has confessed and has been convicted of the crimes he is accused of in a convincing manner. The crimes themselves are extraordinarily serious. In the fourth year of the war, the condemned man has—for purely selfish reasons—removed himself from the German front, placed himself on the side of the enemy, and called for the worst thing that could happen to Germans at the moment. The persistence of his criminal intent is evident in his repeated inscriptions calling for the murder of the Führer. The interests of state resolutely demand the elimination of this vermin. I therefore recommend *execution*."

One week later, the Reich's minister of justice decides not to exercise his right to grant a reprieve, but rather to let justice run its course.

On May 2, 1943, H.'s court-appointed attorney, Dr. Gerhardt R., submits a final plea for mercy: Until his criminal act (i.e., until the age of 73), H. lived an orderly life and grew old without dishonor. He has never belonged to a labor union and has lived in the same building for forty-two years as a transport worker. He enjoys a good reputation and is held in esteem by the other people in the building and, in particular, by his family members, including his three sons-in-law.

Silence

At approximately 7:00 P.M. on May 10, 1943, H. is led with his hands tied behind his back to the execution site at Plötzensee

Prison. According to the protocol, he is calm and composed, allowing himself to be placed on the guillotine without resistance. From the official presentation of the prisoner to the announcement that the sentence has been carried out, the execution lasts sixteen seconds. H.'s corpse is released to the Anatomical-Biological Institute at the University of Berlin for educational and research purposes, with instructions to observe absolute secrecy.

Preliminary draft of a press release: "The pensioner Wilhelm H. from Berlin, who was sentenced to death by the People's Court, was executed on———, because he repeatedly wrote the inscription(s) ~~'Hitler, you mass murderer, you must be murdered, then war will be over'~~ in a public toilet in the southeast of Berlin from the late summer to October 1942."

On instructions from the Reich's minister of justice, officials refrain from issuing a press release or any other announcement concerning the execution.

THE INABILITY TO DIGEST

On June 25, 1941, three days after the beginning of the German offensive against the Soviet Union, SS-Gruppenführer Erich B. bids farewell to his family and heads eastward in his automobile. For the occasion, his wife has prepared a little celebration on their estate in Breslau-Burgweide. The children, dressed in their Sunday best, form an honor guard with the conscripted servant girl. Eberhard, the youngest, presents his father with a bouquet of roses; Little Heini says, "Come back soon!"; Ines stands before him, tears in her eyes. In the stifling summer heat, B. sets off for Warsaw. That evening, "deep in the land of the Polack," he recalls the endearing faces of his children. He writes in his war diary: "How much more splendid their childhood is in our wonderful, well-kept home than mine was! To ensure that this generation has it better than we did—that is what we are fighting for." The next day, he reports as senior SS and police leader for Russia-Center to his new superior, General von Schenckendorff, the rear-area commander of the Army Group Center. B.'s assignment: the pacification of eastern peoples behind the front.

Go-Getter

Militarist.   In 1914, at the age of fifteen, B. is a volunteer in the Royal Prussian Army. At the age of eighteen, he is a lieutenant with the Iron Cross First and Second Class.

Pauper.   B.'s father, an impoverished aristocrat, was a traveling salesman for an insurance company. The military offers B. the possibility of social advancement. After the Great War, B. is a member of the Freikorps in Upper Silesia and an active officer in the German Army until 1924. During the 1920s, he runs a taxi-cab business in Berlin with three motorized carriages, before purchasing a small farm in Dühringshof with his wife's dowry. National Socialism provides him with a second opportunity for advancement. In January 1930, B. becomes a member of the Nazi Party, in February 1931, a member of the SS.

"A One-Hundred-Percenter."   Weltanschauung: very good National Socialist. Personal characteristics: loyal and honest, strongly impulsive, in many cases unrestrained. Himmler is said to have called B. "the best stallion in his stable."

Warhorse.   B. despises the bootlickers surrounding the Führer and the Reichsführer-SS. Better a lone wolf than a court jester.

Master Race.   Physicians reproach B. that his entire family suffers from overeating. B.'s diary entry from October 19, 1937: "Obesity and gluttony lead to mental lethargy and foul moods, which, in turn, give rise to the inferiority complexes I suffer from."

Posterity.   Fate can strike most cruelly at one's own children. B. worries about the passive nature of his elder daughter. In the next generation, he can detect no drive for social advancement. Does this imply a return to the social status of his parents? Is it the result of a congenitally weak will or their mother's pampering?

Power Struggle (1935).   As head of the Gestapo in Königsberg, B. becomes entangled in a running battle with Erich Koch, the Nazi district leader and president of East Prussia. B. complains to his superiors about corruption and "separatist strivings in the province here." Mutual accusations follow. The Führer takes Koch's side in the dispute. B. is transferred to Breslau.

Rehabilitated.   B. dedicates himself to his work with renewed devotion, eventually reaping praise and recognition from Himmler. In June 1938, he is promoted to senior SS and police leader for the Southeast (East Upper Silesia). Already in 1939, the SS plans the evacuation of Jews from the Altreich, as well as from Danzig, Posen, East Upper Silesia, and South Eastern Prussia. In September 1940, B. complains that he has still not been able to get rid of the Jews in East Upper Silesia.

Combat

July 1941.   From Warsaw, B. moves eastward behind the advancing German front, to Bialystok, Grodno, Baranovichi. In White Russia, he begins a bitter struggle against "partisans" and "plunderers."

Heroic Deeds.   The SS Cavalry Brigade under B.'s command is charged with searching, pacifying, and securing the Pripet Marshes. In the middle of August, the Second SS Cavalry Regiment (Mounted Division) files a report on their operations from July 27 to August 11, 1941:

Battle impressions: none

Pacification: Jewish plunderers were executed. Only a few craftsmen employed in the repair workshops of the Wehrmacht were spared.

Driving women and children into the marshes did not produce the intended results, as the marshes were not deep enough for them to sink into. In most cases, there was solid ground (probably sand) at a depth of only one meter, so that submersion was not possible.

It was also striking that the local population was, on the whole, well disposed toward the Jewish sector of the population. However, they did assist energetically in rounding up the Jews. Local law enforcement, comprised in part of Polish policemen and former Polish soldiers, made a good impression. They provided active support and participated in the battle against plunderers.

The total number of plunderers, etc., executed by the Mounted Division: 6,526.

To sum up, the campaign can be designated as a success.

B.'s entry in his war diary (Aug. 3, 1941): In the past days, the men in the Cavalry Brigade have fought like heroes.

During the Same Week.   Since the First Company is fired on as it withdraws from Jazyl, B. orders that the entire male population of the town be executed.

Kulturvolk.   On August 15, 1941, Reichsführer-SS Himmler visits Minsk, and witnesses an execution of Jews. B. expresses concerns to Himmler about the coarsening effect of such mass executions. The Reichsführer commissions SS-Obergruppenführer Arthur Nebe to look into more "humane" forms of liquidation. After a failed attempt with dynamite at a White Russian insane asylum, gassing methods are investigated.

Rest and Recuperation.   Following Himmler's visit, B. is back on his estate in Breslau-Burgweide for two days. "The children's happy play touched my heart. Forgotten, for several hours, the difficult work in Russia."

Back in Minsk.   B. reports on August 20, 1941: "The following localities have been razed to the ground: Turov, Zapesochye, Dworzec, Pohost, Sleptsy, Ozerany, Siemuradze, and Choczen." Four days later, B. organizes his first Ukrainian police battalion composed of voluntary defectors. The battalion later takes over time-consuming mass executions for the German police.

An Injustice.   Although partisan combat requires of both officers and troops significantly stronger nerves than regular combat does, the Wehrmacht is much more liberal in awarding military decorations for regular combat.

The Loving Father.   After the German civil administration assumes control of the western part of White Russia at the beginning of September 1941, B. moves eastward with his staff to the city of Mogilev. He establishes his quarters in a former children's home. His living room and bedroom are huge halls with a view of the garden and the city.

Exemplary.   B. is not one to sit around in his office pushing paper. He prides himself on having actively participated in every campaign of his SS and police units.

Evening Hours.   The SS men sit around the campfire and sing military songs. A radio truck from the Deutschlandsender's propaganda company records the festivities. B. hopes that Mommy and the children don't miss the broadcast, so that they can hear Daddy's voice again.

Military Training.   B. at a course on partisan combat in Russia-Center: "Where there are partisans, there are Jews, and where there are Jews, there are partisans."

The Spirit Is Willing

In spite of his successes, B. feels listless and sluggish, something he initially attributes to his new surroundings. Excerpt from his war diary (Sept. 29, 1941): The long eastern nights are stifling. They may also give rise to that certain melancholy found in the hundred million masses of dull Slavs. I feel it in my own body.

Sonderaktion.   On October 2 and 3, 1941, 2,270 Jewish men, women, and children—a third of the remaining Jews in Mogilev—are executed on B.'s orders.

Bellyache.   Two days later, B.'s vague discomfort assumes a more concrete form. After a glass of wine, he feels a stabbing pain in his abdomen. At first he thinks it is only a harmless kidney-stone attack. The next day, however, the pain is so intense that he's forced to take a narcotic. He remains in bed the entire day. A week later, he's still suffering.

Back to Work.   After ten days, B. is finally free of pain. Since the Wehrmacht has been lax in preventing the return of the local population and thereby provided indirect support for the partisans, B. decides to establish a civilian detention camp in Mogilev. On October 19, 1941, a further 3,720 Jewish men, women, and children are executed in the city. Less than 1,000 Jews—skilled laborers and their families—remain alive.

Civilized.   During the third week of October 1941, the Reichsführer-SS pays a visit to Mogilev. In the midst of the destruction, B. wants to make an impression on Himmler. At dinner on the first evening: white tablecloths and flowers, clean orderlies and waitresses, musical entertainment by a Russian pianist and a balalaika player. B.: "We Germans cannot abandon our cultural interests here, if we want to avoid sinking to the level of this eastern race." On the second day, a visit to Field Marshal von Bock: Words of praise from the field marshal about B.'s work. B. still awaits the bar to his Iron Cross First Class.

On the Battlefield.   Ten days later, the pain has returned. In the midst of mop-up operations, B. is crippled.

Promoted.   Telegraph from the Reichsführer-SS (Nov. 3, 1941): "My dear B.! The Führer has named you SS-Obergruppenführer and General of the Police effective 11/9/1941. My heartfelt congratulations. In friendship, HH." Because of a kidney-stone attack, B. is forced to postpone the promotion celebration.

Revived.   Due to continuing abdominal pains, B. flies to Breslau on November 13, 1941, where he is examined by an internist at the university hospital. Afterward, he spends a few days at the Police Convalescent Home in Berlin-Wannsee. He drinks several bottles of French red wine with the home's director and SS comrades. In the morning, a steam bath; in the evening, an opera (*Siegfried*). B.: "A spiritual bath. The music gives me the purest life." Following this, a day in Breslau-Burgweide with the children. Hide-and-seek in the garden.

Iron Will.   Back in Russia, the weather is cold, not very pleasant for B.'s weakened abdomen. In spite of this, he carries on. His friend SS-Gruppenführer Hildebrandt congratulates him on his promotion, asks about his illness. B.: "I'm healthy enough. In any case, I won't think of slacking off until we reach the Ural Mountains."

Decorated.   On December 5, 1941, the still ailing B. is awarded the bar to the Iron Cross First Class.

Optimist.   During a visit, Colonel von Bismarck, recipient of the Knight's Cross, informs B. that the commander in chief of the Army Group Center, Field Marshal von Bock, suffers from a stomach disorder and is, as a result, a pessimist. B., on the contrary, is an optimist. When asked about the grounds for this, he answers: "Adolf Hitler."

Reenergized.   B.'s dejection is dispelled. He has new battle assignments! Telegraph from Reichsführer Himmler: "You are to be supplied with new forces at once: the Second Police Battalion from Kauen, a police battalion from Tilsit, and a police battalion from Minsk. In addition to this, one Latvian and two Lithuanian police divisions, comprising a total of 1,000 men. As for your kidney infection, my most heartfelt wishes for a quick recovery. As soon as the situation allows, you must take a convalescent leave." B. telegraphs back: "The Reichsführer's statement regarding the promised medical leave is incomprehensible to me, as I was already supposed to go in October but have repeatedly refused to take leave during movement at the front. Am indignant that my leave would even be considered before the definitive stabilization of the front."

Christmas.   There's a Christmas tree in the living room and an Advent wreath in the bedroom. B., however, is not at all in the mood for Christmas: "One has no time for such celebrations or even for one's own personal well-being when one has stood in the service of his people for decades." On the first day of Christmas, B. is together with his men. The men drink liqueur. B. drinks tea, eats a cheese bread, and promptly has a kidney-stone attack. The next two days and nights, he has severe cramps.

New Year's.   At the beginning of January, B. notices extensive intestinal bleeding. Two weeks later, Himmler calls from the Führer's headquarters, asks about the troops and B.'s health. B. is touched. For the troops, he requests another shipment of field ovens. As for his own health, he has no time to be sick while as the troops are fighting.

Starvation Diet.   The pain doesn't go away. To lessen the continuous bleeding, B. stops eating altogether. He drinks only coffee.

Slacker.   As a result of his blood loss, B. feels constantly exhausted. In order to avoid anemia, the physicians recommend surgery. At the end of January 1942, B. requests that the Reichsführer-SS grant him a four-week leave at a military hospital. B. would like to be treated in the area so that he can continue to oversee operations. Himmler, however, insists that the surgery be performed at the SS Military Hospital Unter den Eichen in Berlin-Lichterfelde.

Course of Treatment

In February 1942, B. undergoes a serious hemorrhoid operation. In the course of postoperative treatment, the physician notices that B. has become accustomed to excessive doses of morphine. Informed of this, the Reich's Physician-SS, Professor Dr. Grawitz, files a report to Himmler. Himmler orders his adjutant, SS-Obergruppenführer Karl Wolff—an old friend of B.'s—to visit the patient in the hospital. In Berlin, Wolff finds B. for the first time in their friendship in a completely unsoldierly, almost tearful condition. B. begs Wolff to defend him against the intrigues of his physicians and to explain his condition to Himmler. In a long conversation, Wolff makes clear to B. the urgency and significance of this crisis in his life, emphasizing that the outcome will determine whether or not B. is released again for active duty on the front. Before departing, Wolff appeals to B.'s sense of honor. B. promises to overcome his addiction as quickly as possible and get back to being his old self.

Three days after Wolff's visit, B. writes a letter to Himmler (Mar. 4, 1942): "Dear Reichsführer! I have asked my wife to deliver this letter to you. First, I would like to thank you most humbly for all your concern, particularly for the friendly birthday wishes conveyed to me by Count H. I believe I am now over the main hurdle. It was all so much more painful than I had thought it would be, as I had not taken any time until then to care for myself. But when Wolffie came here and, in particular, when you phoned from the Führer's headquarters, I knew that I was being looked after with touching care. You mustn't worry overly about me, for through your training we have all become such that we are unable—even when we are ill—to forget our duty to our men. Day and night I think only of the decisive moments which lie before us, and which we will master. To my great pleasure, the army group sent me a bouquet of flowers. I hope very much that in four weeks I am completely fit for active duty. Once again, I thank you for your care and concern. I remain your loyal and grateful B."

On the same day, Dr. Grawitz also writes to Himmler, who received an alarming report from SS-Obergruppenführer Wolff a few days earlier. Grawitz writes:

"After the immediate postoperative effects subsided and the healing process began, we encountered in the past eight days some difficulty in restoring normal intestinal activity. The reason for this is that after the operation the patient's intestines were sedated with opium for several days, as is routine with such procedures. [. . .]

"(The delayed recovery and the relatively long-lasting soreness are unfortunately typical with hemorrhoid operations, as the mucous membrane of the anus cannot be immobilized completely but rather remains in motion through the continuous activity of the sphincter muscle.)

"At the same time, the patient's difficult general condition and, in particular, his nervous state of exhaustion were apparent on his arrival for treatment from the eastern territories.

"Since the psychological treatment of the patient is not easy—he suffers in particular from mental images related to executions of Jews that he himself directed, as well as other difficult experiences in the East!—I have assumed personal supervision of the treatment to a great extent and have sought repeatedly to support on a daily basis the recovery of his spiritual equilibrium as well as the personal well-being of his wife, whom I have permitted at her own request to care for her husband during his stay in the hospital. I was forced to take this unusual step, which raises unavoidable if thoroughly surmountable difficulties, since the spiritual care of the patient, as described above, constitutes a significant factor in his overall recovery.

"I have waited so long to file this interim report, Reichsführer, because I did not want to alarm you unnecessarily about these problems, problems which after all are not life threatening and about which I wanted to form my own opinion first.

"The difficulties described above were related primarily to the patient's medical treatment and to his environment, and I was convinced on the basis of medical examinations and the overall situation that we would be able to overcome them in a short period of time. The fact that the patient is today objectively healthy and subjectively lively confirms my prognosis. I sincerely regret, Reichsführer, that, as a result of the aftereffects of the narcotics, SS-Obergruppenführer Wolff obtained a completely distorted view of the matter during his visit here on Saturday and that, as the result of this, you received the inaccurate impression that we were providing SS-Obergruppenführer B. with insufficient and incorrect care. Let me assure you once again that from the very first day of treatment I was well aware of the magnitude of my responsibility to you, Reichsführer, particularly with regard to this SS officer. I hope that in the foreseeable future B.'s recovery will confirm for you the correctness of my statements here.

"In regard to my prognosis for further recovery, I add the following: I hope that in two to three weeks B. will have completely recovered physically and be ready to take a climatic convalescent cure for several weeks without any special medical treatment."

Five days later, B.'s appetite has increased, and his local discomforts have lessened. Professor Umber, the director of the West End Clinic in Berlin-Steglitz, is brought into the case and attempts to raise the patient's self-confidence and self-esteem. He provides B. with vigorous encouragement, appeals to his will to recover.

Dr. Grawitz's interim report to Himmler (Mar. 9, 1942): "I am somewhat concerned at the moment with the patient's emotional state. Fear of his hemorrhoidal condition had already caused B. to starve himself qualitatively and quantitatively for months during his tour of duty in the East. B.'s delayed and somewhat difficult recovery has been the result of the severe physical, nervous, and mental state of exhaustion in which he was admitted to the hospital. Now that he has begun to improve physically, he torments himself with certain feelings of inferiority ('an exaggerated sensitivity to pain, loss of control, a lack of concentration') and with concerns about being completely ready to serve you, Reichsführer, in the near future. I have repeatedly assured Herr B., most recently this morning, that he will certainly regain his old vigor and productivity after several weeks of thorough climatic convalescence. I am completely convinced of this myself, although I also foresee that he will continue to be plagued by frequent symptoms of depression for quite some time to come."

In the third week of March, B. is released from the hospital. From his estate in Breslau-Burgweide, he writes a letter of protest to Himmler (Mar. 31, 1942): "Reichsführer! After being permitted to leave my sickbed for increasing stretches of time each day,

I had myself released from the SS military hospital. Because my experiences during the first half of my hospital stay caused the first emotional shock of my life, something I confess openly to you, Reichsführer, I wanted to leave the hospital atmosphere as quickly as possible. The minor follow-up treatment with olive oil that Professor Umber has ordered and the attempts to walk again, the massages, and the training of the completely flabby muscles can be done just as well at home. In the coming days, I will begin my convalescent cure in Karlsbad since the physicians still consider hiking in the mountains to be too strenuous. I would like to request, my Reichsführer, that you excuse me for the time being from reporting in detail about my illness, since I am slowly becoming your old B. again and would like to expunge from my memory all that I have gone through. However, I do want to defend myself with all my might against one particular interpretation, an interpretation which, for certain reasons, confuses cause and effect. It is not true that I entered the hospital as a completely exhausted and worn-out man. As your old fighter, whose energies return daily, I must defend myself—despite the continued innuendos made at my sickbed—against such a distortion of the facts. I do not believe, my Reichsführer, that during your visit to the military hospital shortly before my operation you had the impression that I was a mentally or physically broken man. I agreed to the operation only because the physicians predicted a complete recovery within four weeks and because I wanted to be 100 percent healthy for the major battles in the coming spring. Until fourteen days before my operation, I was in daily contact with Mogilev through radio and courier. Even on my sickbed, I was notified personally of each military operation, before the troops moved out, in order to discuss the deployment. In my hospital room, I received the nurses who had been mobilized from Berlin to Mogilev and Bobruisk. Procurements, supplies, trucks, etc., I kept all the reins in my hands. That doesn't look like a collapse, does it? Only when the cramps set in and, from the paralyzed intestines, the poisoning of the body and then the soul began, could one speak of a collapse. And here it was less the incredible physical pain that led to the breakdown than my conviction of a false diagnosis by the physicians and the threat of a shameful 'straw death' at a time when every soldier has the right to a decent death in battle. So I thank you, Reichsführer, for your intervention following Wolff's visit. For I no longer had the strength to defend myself. At once, the internist SS-Sturmbannführer Dr. Liebau was consulted, something that had not been possible earlier. I also owe much to SS-Hauptsturmführer Dege and Professor Umber for the fact that my lower tract has slowly begun to resume its functions. The experts may know their domain of expertise very well, but they refuse to see anything that doesn't fit into their preconceived notions. Such anomalies are simply attributed to mental complexes.

"I will prove to you this year, Reichsführer, that your old warhorses don't knuckle under, even in the face of such trials and tribulations. In loyal gratitude, Heil Hitler! Your B."

Restored

Back from his convalescent cure in Karlbad, B. writes in his diary (end of April 1942): There is an enormous vacuum in my memory. But that doesn't matter, for a book of war memoirs is after all not a history book of my past illnesses. Around March 1, I went through a serious crisis as a result of incorrect treatment by the attending physicians. It was a matter of life and death, as intestinal cramps set in. Mommy nursed me back to health at considerable self-sacrifice. What I've learned from the illness in terms of spirit and character is this: Everyone must die! It is so easy to say this when one is young and healthy. When, however, one is touched by death during a prolonged condition of suffering, then even the most courageous soldier stands in utter disbelief before this inexorable fact. In this case, the religious person has a much easier time than someone who is *gottgläubig* and has to rely on his own reason. The final gate through which we all must pass remains terrifying and incomprehensible, despite the fact that life continues in our own children. "You unknown God." There is pain that is so incomprehensibly horrible that it weakens not only the body but the soul as well. It all seems so meaningless when one considers that often good people die an excruciating death, and the worst people die an easy one.

What B. finds most troubling: the thought that even children and innocent animals sometimes suffer an agonizing death.

Question: Has the illness strengthened him spiritually, or has it made him weaker? Only the battlefield can provide an answer.

Back in Mogilev, B radiates composure and energy. He feels healthy, is full of confidence, and is profoundly happy about all the work he has. B.: I sleep like an innocent child, fly with the carefreeness of an eighteen-year-old lieutenant, and feel myself superior to everyone and everything. The long illness, during which death was continually present at my bedside, seems to have served its purpose. I am more balanced spiritually. Perhaps this fortunate condition also means that I am prepared for death, in order to accept my God-given fate. True happiness does not comes from outside; it rests in our own hearts.

Ready for Combat.   As B. flies by smoldering villages, his desire for action burns in every fingertip.

Return

B. is forced to crack down sharply, as there have been serious drinking excesses during his absence. On his first evening in Mogilev, he is with his officers until four in the morning, developing plans for future campaigns. B.: We are here to fight, not to lead a comfortable existence.

Back to Business.　During the first three months following B.'s return, 81,000 partisans are put out of action.

Tactics.　B.: If the moment of surprise is lost—for example, through the chance appearance of civilian inhabitants—then the location should be given up immediately, if the bothersome witnesses cannot be disposed of silently.

Old Ailment.　At the end of August 1942, B. is bedridden for two days with abdominal pains. In September, he takes a two-week convalescent cure in Karlsbad with his wife.

Selfless Dedication.　Back in Russia-Center, B. radios Himmler: "With the next supply convoy, 10,000 pairs of children's socks and 2,000 gloves are being sent from Mogilev to the Reichsführer-SS as Christmas gifts for SS children, to be distributed at the discretion of the Reichsführer-SS."

Ambitions

On August 18, 1942, the Führer declares Himmler to be responsible for all partisan operations located outside the operational areas and rear areas of the Wehrmacht. Two weeks later, B. suggests to the Reichsführer-SS that he himself assume overall control of the entire battle against the partisans. Himmler agrees, appointing B. plenipotentiary of the Reichsführer-SS for bandit control on October 23, 1942 (with retention of his post as senior SS and police leader for Russia-Center). B. establishes a command central that directs the overall planning of operations to which all

SS and police units and their attached formations are subordinate. B.: A terrible responsibility to the German people.

As plenipotentiary for bandit control, B. plans the following operations against partisans and "suspected bandits": Operations Munich, Albert II, Franz, Water Nymph, Föhn, Wet Triangle, Daredevil I, Daredevil II, Maybug, Seydlitz, Nuremberg, Hamburg, etc.

Given Germany's increasingly difficult war situation, B. is ordered to combine antipartisan operations with the conscription of foreign laborers for work service in Germany. At the end of February 1943, he issues new combat guidelines:

"The total destruction of the bandits remains the supreme law of bandit control. This is, however, not identical with the destruction of all human life in the bandit territories. Only the bandits themselves and their accomplices should be put to death. Elderly people, women, and children not directly involved should be spared, even in the immediate vicinity of the combat zones. Men who are not directly involved with the bandits should be registered and requisitioned for work service. Combat group commanders are responsible for deciding whether captured bandits should also be registered and requisitioned for work service. Reprisals against relatives of bandits are permitted following an examination of the justification and necessity of such measures. In each individual case, the names, reasons, and evidence should be recorded. The destruction of the bandits must be coordinated with the extensive registration and requisition of humans, animals, and grain. Every potential laborer must be registered and turned over to work service. Even former bandits can work in Germany, thereby allowing German laborers to be used on the front.

"White Ruthenia is the source of food for an entire army. This source must never be allowed to dry up. It is precisely in the bandit territories that we must be successful in registering and requisitioning goods and laborers, for such success means, at the same time, the removal of the bandits' lebensraum. Every ton of grain, every cow, every horse is more valuable than a dead bandit. Insufficient provisions for our troops at the front requires that we support them through extensive transports from the German Reich, and this worsens the food situation of our families at home. The totality of the war requires not only soldierly deployment in battle but also the sensible registration and requisition of all assets that can contribute either as labor power or as economic goods to our ultimate victory."

Further Responsibilities (End of June 1943).   Following a briefing by Himmler on the growing partisan threat, the Führer declares "bandit control" to be the exclusive responsibility of the Reichsführer-SS. B. is appointed head of Bandit Control Units.

Pressure to Succeed.   Himmler's control of all antipartisan operations leads to increased rivalry between the SS and the Wehrmacht. B. and his men feel compelled to prove themselves worthy of this enormous responsibility. In the Bandit Control Units, shooting prizes for individual achievements are introduced. B.'s chief of staff, SS-Brigadeführer Herff, notes as the result of this competition a tendency to deal even more ruthlessly with partisans and "suspected bandits." In the middle of July 1943, he complains about this in a personal letter: "There are certain things that I am simply not *prepared* to do or even to consider in any shape or form. One of them is altering official reports. In my opinion, the reports sent from here to the Reichsführer have been doctored! Yesterday, a Nazi Party leader and general commissioner published reports, without meaning to or knowing that he had (they were intended for the Führer), which indicated that on 6,000 dead 'partisans' only about 480 firearms were found. In short, *everyone is executed* in order to increase the enemy dead and, in doing so, to increase one's own 'heroic deeds.' There must be dead bodies, regardless of where they come from. Otherwise the respective combat leader is not a leader or a soldier. That he will not be decorated if he doesn't do this goes without saying. Yesterday I immediately raised this question regarding the issue of '6,000 / 480' (see above). The answer? 'You don't seem to realize that the bandits destroy their own weapons in order to escape death and to wash themselves of guilt.' How easy it must be to defeat these bandits, when they destroy their own weapons!"

Three days later, there is a brief meeting between Herff and his commanding officer. Herff declares that he's had enough. B.: Consider your decision carefully. You could damage your reputation here, but you could also gain great honor.

B.'s diary entry (July 28, 1943): My chief of staff is to be relieved of duty, since he's not up to his responsibilities.

Relapse

To B.'s dismay, the German Siegfried, in spite of all his ruthlessness, appears to be no match for the subhuman Asian. In January 1944, as the Red Army advances westward, B. is removed from antipartisan combat and transferred to the front in Kovel. During the fighting there, B.—who was already slightly ill in the fall—develops sharp abdominal pains. After two months, he can bear the cramps no longer. He files a report with the Reichsführer-SS.

Himmler's response (Mar. 12, 1944): "My dear B.! I have heartfelt sympathy for your dreadful and difficult situation and can only express my admiration, as a soldier and as a man, that you have stood so tall and fought so valiantly with your combat group despite such serious health problems. I request that you leave for Karlsbad without reporting to me, have yourself examined there, and then take the time to have a sufficiently long cure. You have six to eight weeks for this. Following the cure, you must be obedient and take several weeks of convalescence and vacation at home. After the aforementioned six to eight weeks, I am certain you will be completely recovered."

In Karlsbad, B. is examined by the internist Dr. Rupert. On March 22, 1944, Dr. Rupert files a report with Dr. Grawitz, who forwards it to Himmler:

B. arrived at the Höhen Villa on Saturday evening, and I was able to pay him a visit on Sunday morning. From our lengthy conversation, I learned from B. that his primary complaints are caused by an irregularity of bowel movements in the form of constipation and by a weakness of the anal sphincter muscle. My examination of B.'s internal organs following our conversation was negative. The rectal examination indicated that the mucous membrane of the anus was extremely sensitive to even the gentlest palpation. *The sphincter, however, continues to function well and the previous hemorrhoid operation was quite successful. What Herr B. lacks, rather, is the concentration for the innervation of his sphincter.* Given Herr B.'s nervous psychological disposition, I attribute this incapacity to the fact that during combat hygienic measures such as cleansing baths and the like are lacking and that through this the complaints described above have worsened. Under normal conditions, however, when all such hygienic measures can be met, I am convinced that we can achieve a most far-reaching recovery and that Herr B. will be free of complaints in this respect. The prognosis for this case is thus favorable and I hope that through purely conservative measures such as baths, the regulation of bowel movements, the appropriate diet, etc., we can attain a complete recovery. I would like to refrain from drastic measures such as the massage of the anus and will thus carry out an electrical treatment of B.'s sphincter muscle that causes no sensations or feelings of pain.

Herr B. has already begun with these measures and is very satisfied with the accommodations as well as the treatment here. I hope that the complaints described above—taking into account the patient's nervous and labile constitution—will greatly improve and that Herr B. will be able to take part in brief and also very intensive military deployments. However, given these circumstances, I would advise against longer deployments, even if they are less intensive, since they often entail a lack of hygiene that can lead to a worsening of this kind of illness.

Impatient.   One month later, B. reports to the Reichsführer-SS that he is feeling better and would like to return to the front. Himmler, however, insists that B. remain in Karlsbad: "I am pleased that your health has improved. I merely expect from you that you will not terrorize the physicians, but will instead allow yourself time to recover. There is no sense in breaking off a cure fourteen days too early. Here I must appeal vigorously to your knowledge and to your sense of obedience. I expect you to report to me on May 15, no sooner."

Temporary "Retirement"

Disappointments.   In May 1944, Himmler informs B., who is recovered and resting at his estate in Breslau-Burgweide, that he will not receive the Knight's Cross for his deployment in Kovel. At the beginning of July 1944, B. is awarded the Bandit Control Badge but, in accordance with the strict regulations, merely in bronze, since he was able to participate in only twenty-eight days of combat. Consolation from Himmler: Be proud of the badge in spite of this. What matters is your own sense of having fulfilled your duty, and that is something you truly deserve.

Truest of the True (July 20, 1944). B.'s heart is heavy. "How can such an attempt on the Führer's life be possible?"

Call to Action. An emergency telephone call from East Prussia on August 2, 1944. B. is to report immediately. "Huge mess in the Government General."

Intensive Deployments

B. is entrusted with suppressing the Warsaw Uprising. As commanding general, all units in the city—Wehrmacht, SS, police, and civil administration—are subordinate to him. Himmler promises B. the Knight's Cross if he retakes Warsaw.

B.'s diary entry (Aug. 7, 1944): "Rows of burning houses and mountains of corpses." B. expects a major offensive at any time from the Red Army, which, however, proves content to remain on the other side of the Weichsel River and wait out the battle between the Germans and the Polish Home Army (AK).

On August 23, 1944, B. bleeds again, for the first time since his operation.

Bloody Hand-to-Hand Combat. With heavy casualties among the civilian population, the Germans are gradually able to retake the city.

Feverish Heart. At the beginning of October 1944, the Polish Home Army capitulates. B.: "This day will go down in history. I am so proud for my sons. I am negotiating on my own authority with the Poles—in other words, big-time politics." As promised, B. is awarded the Knight's Cross.

Supreme Honor. One week later, B. is received by the Führer at his headquarters. Hitler thanks B. for Warsaw and for earlier deployments, and confers on him special powers in Budapest.

Operation Panzerfaust.   After international protests about the deportation of Hungarian Jews to Auschwitz, Admiral Horthy, the imperial administrator of Hungary, attempts to negotiate a peace agreement with the Soviet Union. With the Red Army one hundred fifty kilometers from Budapest, Gestapo officers kidnap Admiral Horthy's son. B., who is still suffering from intestinal disorders, orders that the palace be stormed. Horthy capitulates. A day later, B. writes in his diary (Oct. 17, 1944): "My assignment is completed. Once again, diplomats and politicians have the reins in their hands. There will be plenty of people who claim the success for themselves. It is enough for me to know that through my toughness, intransigence, and political shrewdness, I have prevented a catastrophe for the German military forces. Self-promotion would be unworthy of me. One day world history will bring to light the true facts."

While B. once again travels to Karlsbad for a convalescent cure for his ailing abdomen, the leader of the fascist Arrow-Cross Party, Ferenc Szálasi, is named Hungary's head of state. A week later, 50,000 Hungarian Jews are ordered to be deported to Germany for work service, as Auschwitz is scheduled to be closed in the near future. In November 1944, death marches to Germany begin.

Recovered.   Ten days after B.'s arrival in Karlsbad, the internist Dr. Rupert files a report with Dr. Grawitz (Nov. 1, 1944): "B.'s state of health continues to improve, which is evident in particular in his increased interest in the course of the war. Herr B. is also very lively and active and in the best of moods, so that in all probability I will not be able to keep him here much longer. His thoughts are already at the front, an indication of general recovery. Objectively, his abdominal complaints have improved, and it appears that the galvanization and faradization of the sphincter were quite successful. The anus muscle is very strong and the cotton-wool bandage has not been soiled, which means that Herr B. can be deployed for intensive military operations of short duration in the near future."

Until the Bitter End

In the middle of November 1944, B.'s convalescent leave in Karlsbad is abruptly interrupted. Himmler assigns B., as commanding general of the Fourteenth SS-Corps, to rebuild the collapsed front in Alsace-Lorraine. At the end of January 1945, B. is relieved of this assignment and sent to Pomerania as commander of the Tenth SS-Corps. In May, he is captured by American forces.

Tactical Silence

In August 1945, B. is turned over to the American Counter Intelligence Corps; at the beginning of October, he is transferred to the military prison in Nuremberg. B. proves to be a willing interlocutor. During repeated interrogations, he provides detailed reports about the course of the war but is at the same time extremely careful not to incriminate himself. As a senior SS officer, B. voluntarily assumes a general responsibility for the war but denies any direct participation in war crimes. He claims that he always protected the Jews, that he was himself related to Jews by marriage (two of his sisters had Jewish husbands). He reports, for example, that he left open an escape route for the Jews by preventing his police units from occupying the Pripet Marshes, and that he informed local rabbis of this and advised them to flee there with their congregations. He also claims that he sabotaged plans to build a gas chamber in one of his buildings in Russia-Center. At the same time, B. has no qualms about speaking openly of his Nazi comrades and their actions or about testifying against them in court. Between 1945 and 1949, he appears as a witness at more than twenty trials: at the main war crimes trial in Nuremberg, at the Wilhelmstraße trial, at the Ohlendorf trial, at the Rasse- und Sieldungshaupamt trial, at the trial against the South-West generals, as well as before the Dutch Legal Commission, the Czech Military Court, and the Denazification Chamber in Prague.

Advantage of this strategy: the Allies treat B. merely as a witness. No charges are ever brought against him.*

Disadvantage: B. is regarded as a traitor by the comrades he incriminates. In the courtroom at Nuremberg, Göring calls him a "*Schweinehund.*"

Reparation: B. provides Göring with a poison ampoule, so that the field marshal can take his destiny into his own hands.

Denazification

At the end of January 1949, B. is released from military prison and transferred to the Detention and Labor Camp in Nuremberg-Langwasser. Shortly thereafter, investigations begin for a denazification trial against him. At the end of March, he is transferred to the detention camp in Eichstätt. B. continues to assert his innocence. He claims that his responsibilities in Russia-Center were purely military, that as head of Bandit Control Units he had no authority to issue orders, merely inspectoral powers. B.: "I spent the entire year of 1943 trying to eradicate the partisan plague in honorable combat."

---

*Walter H. Rapp, chief of the Evidence Division at the International Military Tribunal in Nuremberg, writes in a report in October 1946: "As for himself, he [B.] feels a great guilt and he only hopes that he could pay with his life for what he considers his past errors—but at the same time he says, 'as long as you [Mr. Rapp] are here I don't think that I will be tried because I seem to be more valuable as a witness than as a defendant.'"

Illness-Profit.   In August 1949, B. composes a seven-page single-spaced report entitled "My Resistance Against the Excesses of the Nazi Weltanschauung and Against Its Orders," which he submits to the Denazification Court in Nuremberg. In the report, B. offers a detailed description of thirty-two cases of his resistance, including point number 13: "A nervous breakdown from January to June 1942 due to the insane policies in the East. As a protest, I reported sick and was transferred to the SS-Military Hospital in Berlin-Lichterfelde."

At the end of 1949, the camp director in Eichstätt files a complaint with the Bavarian State Ministry for Special Assignments about the repeated and often extended leaves of absence from the camp granted to B. The Denazification Court in Nuremberg sharply repudiates any implication of preferential treatment on its part. On March 21, 1950, the Bavarian State Ministry orders that B. be tried before the Denazification Court in Munich as a major case, but concludes at the same time that there is no danger of B. attempting to suppress evidence or flee the country. Two months later, the ministry orders that he be released from the work camp.

In November 1950, B. is indicted. Particularly incriminating evidence includes: (1) the letter from Dr. Grawitz to Himmler on March 4, 1942, in which the Reich's Physician-SS reports that B. suffers from mental images related to executions of Jews that he himself directed; (2) a sworn affidavit from a lieutenant general in the Ordnungspolizei, in which he asserts: "The war against the partisans had the sole purpose of eradicating the Slavic and Jewish population."

Two weeks later, B. submits a detailed response to the indictment.

Regarding the Grawitz report: B. claims that he was in a life-threatening situation at the time, as Dr. Grawitz, "the inspirator of the euthanasia program," wanted to have him declared mentally ill. In addition to this, he attempted to get Himmler as well as his superiors in the Wehrmacht to put a stop to the executions. "Only when General von Scheckendorf informed me that his talks with Quartermaster-General Wagner had failed did I break down in screaming fits that lasted for days. Even now I am not ashamed of this breakdown, for unfortunately I am not as cold-blooded as those people who still today deny everything that the entire front spoke about with utter indignation in 1941."

Regarding the lieutenant general's affidavit: "As far as partisan control is concerned, I remain full of pride and gratitude to God for all the measures I took and the orders I gave. In the same situation today, I would act now exactly as I acted then. At a time when the world was a madhouse—as it is again today—I held aloft the banner of humanity. In doing so, I saved the lives of hundreds of thousands of people on both sides, and it is not my fault if ultimately the bloodlust on both sides prevented my efforts from being 100 percent successful." B. also points out that the Western powers have adopted in their Korean campaign the very service regulations for partisan combat that he himself developed in Russia.

At the end of March 1951, the Denazification Court in Munich classifies B. as a major offender. The court rejects as implausible his claims that he intervened for more humane methods of combat, and it regards his refusal to execute civilian prisoners in Warsaw as a tactical maneuver in the face of Germany's catastrophic war situation. The court sentences B. to ten years in a labor camp, including in the sentence two years for the time he has already served. B.'s assets are confiscated for use as reparations; his legal claims to a pension of any kind are revoked.

After this judgment, B.'s lawyer immediately files an appeal. Before the Court of Appeals in Munich, B. claims that he was forced against his will to assume a leading position in antipartisan operations; already in 1943, as head of Bandit Control Units, he saved the lives of 250,000 Jews and 100,000 Poles for purely humanitarian reasons.* The Appeals Court, in turn, cites a report from February 1943 about Operation Nuremberg—in which SS-Brigadeführer Gottberg announces that 3,508 partisans, 8,230 suspects, and 3,300 Jews were executed—at a point in time when B. had long been Himmler's plenipotentiary for Bandit Control. In a report to Himmler about Operation Cottbus, B. also informed the Reichsführer-SS that the local civilian population had provided voluntary, even fanatic, support for the partisans, requiring in response the "elimination of all humane considerations" on the part of the Germans. On December 23, 1951, the court rejects B.'s appeal with the stipulation that five years of custody in military prisons and detention camps count toward the original ten-year sentence. B. never serves the remaining five years of the sentence. After the trial, he refuses to report to the work camp. "Then let them come and get me; I wouldn't think of turning myself in." No one comes.

1954.   The district attorney's office in Nuremberg abandons its preliminary investigations of B. as an accomplice to murder. "The accused continues to be a suspect in the extermination of large portions of the population in the East. However, our investigations have failed as yet to provide sufficient evidence to warrant filing charges against him." The Regional Court in Nuremberg-Fürth removes B. from the threat of criminal persecution.

---

*Rapp, now legal adviser for the United Nations Korea Reconstruction Agency in New York, writes to the Denazification Court in Munich and puts in, as former chief of the entire Evidence Division at Nuremberg, a good word for B.: "Personally, I would like to add that Herr B. was, in my opinion, one of the most cooperative and honest witness-prisoners that I encountered during my entire work in Nuremberg, which involved thousands of people."

A Matter of Faith

B., in search of a secure ethical foundation and the reinstatement of his officer's pension, converts to Protestantism. In 1955, the Bishop of the Evangelical-Lutheran Church in Bavaria writes on his behalf to Undersecretary Dr. Meinzolt in Munich: "B. is a man of character, who is seriously attempting to learn from his past mistakes and to abide by the laws of our democratic nation. Up to now, he has strictly refused to associate with groups that continue to endorse the ideas of National Socialism." The pension is not reinstated. B. converts to Catholicism. Two years later, in November 1957, a new plea for clemency on B.'s behalf—this time with the support of the Catholic Church—is submitted. The Bavarian State Ministry of Justice grants B. a "clemency pension," revocable at any time, for his service as lieutenant during the First World War.

Tried and True

In December 1958, B. is arrested on charges of having ordered two SS men under his command to execute the SS-Oberabschnittführer in Königsberg, Anton von Hoberg und Buchwald, during the Röhm Putsch in 1934. In the belief that the two men, Karl Deinhard and Paul Zummach, are dead, B. has consistently denied the accusation for years. In prison, he is unexpectedly confronted with one of the two men, his former chauffeur Zummach. B. admits to having ordered the execution.

Two years later, the trial begins in Nuremberg. B. on the first day of the proceedings: "I was an absolute Hitler man until the end, and I still am today. I remain true to him, if no longer to National Socialism."

After the witness Zummach is found hung in his cell, B. retracts his confession. "You will never learn the entire truth." In

February 1961, the court finds B. guilty of manslaughter and sentences him to four years and six months in prison.

Memory Gaps

In 1957, B. appears as a witness in the trial against his former rival SS-Obergruppenführer von Woyrsch for acts of violence by the SS against Nazi storm troopers during the Röhm Putsch. Three years later, the district attorney's office in Nuremberg determines that B.'s sworn testimony at the trial—that he himself had refused, as head of the Gestapo in Königsberg, to permit violence against storm troopers during the Röhm Putsch—was false. The district attorney initiates investigations against B. for perjury. Confronted with indisputable evidence, B. claims that as senior SS and police leader in Russia-Center he suffered a mental breakdown in January 1942 and underwent psychiatric treatment in an SS military hospital as a result of this. Since that time, he has no longer been able to rely 100 percent on his memory. If he did, in fact, make the false statements he is accused of, he can only explain this as a consequence of his breakdown.

On August 18, 1960, B. is examined by a court-appointed physician. He reacts mistrustfully to the doctor: "Himmler also tried to get at me in this perfidious way." During the examination, B. scorns the Reichsführer-SS, claiming to have had a great hatred for him: "Himmler was jealous of me because I was in Hitler's good graces, and he tried at every possible turn to get even with me or to make a fool of me."

Excerpt from the physician's report: Aside from flat feet, nothing pathological. Medical history: B. reports that as a child he had measles and scarlet fever; in 1915, a war injury to his left shoulder; in 1918, a poison-gas attack without permanent injury; between 1923 and 1945, he claims to have had five hemorrhoid operations.

Results of the examination: B. is still mentally alert and aware of the present, calls his life "not unhappy," and remains a completely unbroken man. He shows no symptoms of dementia. On the contrary, in the course of our discussion he proved very adaptable and nimble. Question: "The war, however, could not have been won?" Answer: "No one could have foreseen that, and we had to fight." Objection: "But even a victory, as the SS imagined it, would not have been a victory." Answer: "That is Spengler's doctrine. I respect it and can understand it, but even if it is true, we had to fight. That wasn't wrong." This kind of statement indicates a fully capable and active mind. It seems, therefore, reasonable to assume that a physically ill and anemic person might have suffered from a depressive phase at the time, a phase that did perhaps have some temporary clinical significance. However, following a reactive phase of this kind, nothing remains. And that is precisely what I have been able to find, nothing. In any case, the patient demonstrated a brilliant memory for both the past and the present.

Three months later, the court is able to locate three of the physicians who treated B. at the time and to question them about the case. The physicians report that B. was a very difficult patient, that he was admitted to the military hospital in a state of significant emotional unrest, and that after the operation he was even given to maniacal behavior. At the time, B. was extremely sensitive to noise and pain, and it was necessary to seal off the hallway where his room was located. Dr. D.: "Out of fear of pain, B. invented for himself a peculiar, completely roughage-free diet and bathed the entire day. There is no doubt that at the time I found his behavior psychologically outlandish." None of the physicians, however, can recall anything about a nervous breakdown or psychiatric treatment.

The court rejects B.'s explanation. In the middle of November 1961, he is convicted of perjury and sentenced to an additional six months imprisonment.

Undigested

In 1958, B. appears as a witness in the Einsatzkommando trial in Ulm, conducted against ten former German police officers for the execution of Jews and Communists near the German-Lithuanian border. In the course of the proceedings, the court determines that several police units under B.'s command participated in the executions. As a result, the district attorney's office in Nuremburg resumes its investigations of B. for war crimes in Russia-Center. Investigators, however, continue to have difficulty obtaining concrete evidence. Witnesses refuse to provide clear information about B.'s cooperation as senior SS and police leader in Russia-Center with local Einsatzgruppen and their Einsatzkommandos; and they become silent as soon as they are questioned about the chain of command.

1959.   In response to newspaper reports about criminal investigations against B., the following unsolicited letters are sent to the district attorney's office in Nuremburg (excerpts):

Reinhold G.: All male inhabitants were executed on the spot, regardless of whether they had anything to do with the partisans. These atrocities interfered with the recruitment campaigns of other German authorities. The one authority had orders to recruit people for labor in Germany, the other had orders to eradicate them. When questioned about this absurdity, Herr B. offered the following explanation: I alone am responsible for what occurs in my territory. Russians and Jews are not humans but subhumans who have to be eliminated. If you don't have the nerves to watch the executions, then you should have yourself transferred back to Germany.

Dr. Otto W.: We were forced into leather club chairs and given red wine. From 10:00 P.M. to 2:00 A.M., B. spoke without interruption, mostly of his personal experiences. We hardly got in a word during these four hours. B. held a monologue as if in a manic state, so that I began to wonder if he was on morphine. He reported mostly about his own "heroic deeds" and those of other SS leaders. One number in particular etched itself in my memory, when he said: "On my orders, 380,000 Jews have been executed." I left at 2:00 in the morning.

Harald K.: Incidentally, it was also the case that when Herr B. appeared, everyone shook with fear. In his sleeping quarters, B. had six or seven loaded revolvers lying on a night table. At the slightest sound, he simply shot at the windowpanes. We all said that he suffered from a persecution complex. In his quarters, he had the entire works of Heinrich Heine. On his bathroom table, he always had an immense number of perfumes and floral waters.

A Special Commission Erich B., composed of five police officers, is assigned to the case by the Bavarian State Police. The commission seeks to determine B.'s responsibility as senior SS and police leader in Russia-Center for the actions of the police units under his command.

Excerpt from a report by the Special Commission Erich B. (Nov. 2, 1959): The current interrogations of staff officers have provided no evidence for concrete charges against B., as the staff members were—as expected—not only extremely reserved in their statements but also claimed that they were unable to remember even the most basic information. We strongly suspect that influential staff officers met long ago to prepare for the expected interrogations.

Over the next three years, more than three-hundred police officers who were active in Russia-Center between May 1941 and December 1942 are interrogated by the special commission. In spite of all the difficulties, investigators are able to gather evidence against B. in three mass executions:

Bialystok (July 1941). Fifteen witnesses confirm B.'s presence at the execution site; several recall a motivational speech that B. gave to police officers, in which he justified the executions, designating them as "necessary."

Mogilev (Oct. 19, 1941). A Ukrainian unit under B.'s command participated in a mass execution of Jewish women and children.

Bobruisk (summer of 1942). B. is reported to have been present at an execution of Jews and/or to have ordered the execution.

In August 1962, B. is convicted by the Regional Court in Nuremberg in an unrelated case for the murder of five Communists in 1933. The court sentences him to three consecutive life terms in prison. Nine months later, when the judgment becomes final, B. begins his jail term in Munich. Shortly thereafter, the criminal investigation against him for the execution of Jews in Russia is abandoned. The district attorney in Nuremberg explains (June 10, 1963): "In light of the murder convictions, it appears justified and expedient to abandon provisionally the current case against B. pursuant to Paragraph 154, Section 1, of the Penal Procedure Code,* especially since a conviction of the accused in this case would in all probability only be as an accessory to murder." The case is turned over to the district attorney's office in Mannheim, which is responsible for the codefendant Hans Giese, an intimate friend of B.'s and his special adviser for foreign units and for the Jewish Question in Russia-Center.

---

* "The district attorney can refrain from prosecuting a crime (1) if the sentence that can result from the prosecution of that crime is of no significant consequence in comparison to a sentence that has already been imposed or could be imposed on the accused for another crime, or (2) if, in addition to this, a sentence for this crime is not likely to be imposed within an appropriate period of time, and if an actual or expected sentence imposed on the accused for another crime appears to be sufficient both for the punishment of the accused and the defense of the legal system."

For six years, the district attorney's office in Mannheim investigates Giese. At the end of July 1969, the senior district attorney in Mannheim reports: "Our failure to obtain unambiguous evidence for the probable course of events is due primarily to the fact that Giese has suffered for quite some time from pronounced mental and perceptual disturbances as a result of premature sclerotic breakdown, and thus he can no longer be interrogated." The district attorney's office in Mannheim abandons its criminal investigations.

Despite numerous reports about incriminating evidence against B. from other district attorney's offices as well as from the Central Office of State Judicial Administration for the Investigation of Nazi Crimes in Ludwigsburg, the district attorney's office in Nuremberg refuses to resume its criminal investigations of him. In the middle of February 1972, B. is released from prison. He dies three weeks later in a Munich hospital.

AN AUTHORITARIAN
PERSONALITY

In December 1942, R. is transferred to the extermination camp
Treblinka. R. is a calf-sized dog, with black and white spots. In
Treblinka, R. joins up with SS-Oberscharführer Kurt Franz. He
recognizes the Oberscharführer as his master. R. regularly accompanies Franz on his rounds through the upper and lower camps.
During these rounds, it sometimes happens that Franz sics R. on
Jewish prisoners with the words, "Human, get the dog!" R., however, also goes after prisoners without orders, when Franz merely
yells at them. He always attacks the object of Franz's wrath. Because R. is the size of a calf and his shoulder height roughly that
of an average human's lower abdomen, he frequently bites prisoners in the buttocks and sometimes in the genitals as well. R. is
often able to knock weaker prisoners to the ground and tear them
limb from limb.

At the end of November 1943, the extermination camp is
closed down. R. is brought to Ostrow to Dr. S., superintendent of
the local military hospital. After some time, R. enters into a new
master-dog relationship with the physician. Now R. is lazy and
good-natured. He normally lies under or next to the desk in his

new master's study. In the military hospital, R. is called "the big calf." He never harms anyone.*

Attempt at an Explanation

In 1965, the Regional Court in Düsseldorf takes up the matter of R.'s behavior in Treblinka. How can one explain the fact that in the camp R. was a rapacious beast and then afterward a gentle, lazy creature? Witnesses offer credible testimony that even in Treblinka, when SS-Oberscharführer Franz was not present, R. was a completely different animal: one could pet him and even tease him. In regard to R.'s biting: witnesses confirm that Franz did carry out general obedience training with R. However, no one is aware of any special exercises aimed at encouraging R. to attack buttocks or genitals. Dr. S. reports that he often brought R. with him when he examined row after row of naked soldiers in Ostrow to see if they were fit for duty on the front. There, according to Dr. S., R. never exhibited an inclination to bite any of them.

At the end of January 1965, the court calls as an expert witness the director of the Max Planck Institute for Behavioral Research in Seewiesen / Upper Bavaria, the internationally famous Professor Konrad Lorenz—a former member of the Nazi Party, who after 1945 has himself found new masters. On February 4, 1965, Professor Lorenz appears before the court and offers the following testimony. The story, as a whole, is credible. A dog is the reflection of his master's subconscious. Under an aggressive master, a dog may bite a human and then exhibit nothing of this character trait when the master himself changes. It is a recognized fact of behavioral psychology that one and the same dog can be

---

*In 1944, R. is evacuated to Schleswig-Holstein. Two years after the war, he is put to sleep because of old-age infirmities.

well-behaved and harmless at one moment, dangerous and vicious at another. The latter is the case when the dog is sicced on a person by his master. Sometimes, it is sufficient that the master merely shout at a person for the dog to go after him. A short time later, the same dog can play harmlessly with children without there being any cause for concern. He can also exhibit the same behavior toward adults to whom his master speaks in a gentle tone—he is friendly to these people as well. He adapts himself entirely to the moods and whims of his master. From the photos presented to him by the court, he, Professor Lorenz, can see that R. was not a pure-bred Saint Bernard but rather a mongrel, and mixed breeds are particularly sensitive animals. Once such a dog has reached six or seven years of age, he can adjust to a new master only with great difficulty; exceptions, however, are possible. When he enters into a new master-dog relationship, his character might change completely. Therefore, the fact that R. exhibited no inclination to bite under his new master, Dr. S., is not particularly unusual. This phenomenon has been confirmed through experiments.

Summing up, Professor Lorenz explains that R.'s biting behavior might have developed without any training expressly for that purpose. When a dog bonds with its master, he knows intuitively what his master's intentions are.

The Regional Court in Düsseldorf accepts this explanation, and holds SS-Oberscharführer Franz responsible for R.'s attacks, even when these occurred without explicit orders. In 1973, Konrad Lorenz is awarded the Nobel Prize for his research on animal and human behavior.

A New Beginning

In April 1939, three weeks after the Munich Accord has divided the remaining territory of Czechoslovakia into a Protectorate Bohemia and Moravia, incorporated into the German Reich and a Slovakian state "under German protection," Dr. Ivan E. recognizes the new situation. The White Russian nationalist, exiled in Prague, seizes the initiative and addresses a letter to Hitler, in which he outlines the plight of his nation and offers his services for a bilateral cooperation with Germany. He calls himself Johann, professes to be a Germanophile: his wife is a Bessarabian German woman; only under German leadership can his country be free. Over the next two years, Dr. E. is in Berlin on numerous occasions in order to promote German–White Russian cooperation. As the Wehrmacht advances toward Moscow in the late summer of 1941, Dr. E., who has developed close ties to the Eastern Ministry, is assigned a responsible position in the civil administration of occupied "White Ruthenia." In the middle of September, he closes his "not absolutely impeccable" medical practice in Prague and drives to Minsk in a privately owned automobile.

Self-Help

Dr. E. is assigned the establishment of a White Ruthenian Self-Help Organization (WSO), which is attached to the public health and Volkspflege division of the general commissioner's office in Minsk. As director of the WSO, Dr. E. is responsible for the following activities:

The collection of "voluntary donations" (money, foodstuffs, valuables) from the local population. A quarter of the collected items remains in the locality, a quarter in the district, the rest is transported to Minsk. Here, the donations are brought to a storeroom and then redistributed under Dr. E.'s supervision.

Mediation between the White Ruthenian and the German peoples. On the one hand, Dr. E. is supposed to convince White Ruthenians that the German occupation is a liberation and that the possibility exists of receiving assistance from the German authorities. On the other hand, he is responsible for introducing those Germans residing in White Ruthenia to the local inhabitants' inferior culture.

Advising General Commissioner Kube on cultural and political issues. Dr. E. is included in discussions about the not yet reopened school system in White Ruthenia.

The establishment of a White Ruthenian Self-Protection Organization. Dr. E. is appointed supreme commander of the local guard. The former Czarist officer, who fought with Generals Denniken and Wrangel against the Bolsheviks, holds training courses for officers.

Trials and Tribulations

The country is poor and ravaged by the war. The local population's initial encounters with the new occupying forces inspire little trust. Dr. E., who has lived abroad for more than twenty years, is received with skepticism and reservation by his compatriots. Exiled politicians in Berlin accuse him of slavishly towing the German line. Partisans consider him a traitor, threaten him and his coworkers with death.

The SS regards Dr. E. mistrustfully as well. While Reichsführer Himmler does support the establishment of a White Ruthenian territory in order to fragment the greater Russian Empire, he has not yet decided whether the preservation of the White Ruthenian people should be supported or promoted at all. The Security Police in Minsk fear that Dr. E. could, through the WSO, become a popular White Ruthenian leader and thereby pose a threat. SS-Brigadeführer Curt von Gottberg complains in Berlin: This gentleman from Czechoslovakia has spread completely erroneous notions about the White Ruthenian people and White Ruthenian independence. Up to now, the WSO has only done harm and driven the population crazy. In addition to this, the Self-Protection Guard—clothed, armed, and trained by the Germans—defects in entire squadrons to the partisans.

Dr. E. enjoys active support only from the German civil administration. A coworker at the general commissioner's office in Minsk: "We will engage in a positive policy toward the White Ruthenians, regardless of what is decided in the future, since it is currently essential for the war effort that we support the White Ruthenian people." At a meeting with the SS, civil administrators defend Dr. E. from criticism: E. has always sought to temper inflated White Ruthenian demands and to inform German authorities about the actual mood in the country.

Dr. E.'s personal relations with General Commissioner Kube

are excellent. On Kube's fifty-fifth birthday, Dr. E. sends heartfelt congratulations on behalf of the entire Self-Help Organization. The general commissioner is touched: "My dear, dear Dr. E.! I thank you as well as the men and women of the White Ruthenian Self-Help Organization for the very friendly birthday wishes. You have all made me very happy, and I ask that you convey my sincere thanks to your coworkers. You can rest assured that in the future I will continue to work together with you in the spirit of our great Führer Adolf Hitler to rebuild White Ruthenia, a country that has endured such difficult trials and tribulations. With the best wishes for you and your work, your Wilhelm Kube."

Dr. E. is appointed Kube's local representative. Later he is supposed to become White Ruthenian minister president.

Encircled

Outside the larger cities, the German occupational presence is limited. In the countryside, numerous Self-Help coworkers are killed by partisans. In Minsk as well there is intrigue and even sabotage. Rumors circulate about corruption and moneymaking in the WSO. Dr. E. attributes these to a Polish or Communist plot. At the end of March 1942, Dr. E.'s coffee is poisoned with arsenic. He barely survives the assassination attempt.

The SS proves to be a more difficult opponent. SS-Obersturmbannführer Eduard Strauch, who regards Dr. E. as the devoted servant of his rival, General Commissioner Kube, directs investigations against the WSO for numerous irregularities, including smuggling gold to Prague and the misappropriation of valuables. Dr. E.'s two sisters-in-law, both employees at the Self-Help Organization, are reported to have furnished their apartment in Minsk entirely with objects from the WSO storeroom. Dr. E. himself is accused of using forty-five pounds of donated flour to acquire a fur coat for his secretary. In the middle of April 1943, the Security Police invite Dr. E. to their offices for a "voluntary" interrogation. Dr. E. is accused of playing the German authorities off against one another and of betraying the White Ruthenian people. The German civil administration, for its part, disputes having been played off against anyone and poses the question: What would the SS prefer, a man who dedicates himself entirely to the German civil administration or a man who engages in anti-German politics in order to make himself popular among his own people?

A week later, Dr. E. is granted temporary leave from prison. Shortly thereafter, he travels to Prague for a convalescent cure for his arsenic poisoning.

On His Own

During Dr. E.'s absence, General Commissar Kube yields to pressure from the SS and agrees to replace him as head of the WSO. Gestapo officers call on Dr. E. in Prague. They inform him that his return to White Ruthenia is no longer desired and confiscate his travel permit.

In Prague, the interrogations regarding irregularities in the White Ruthenian Self-Help Organization continue. Dr. E. is charged, among other things, in the disappearance of 9,000 pounds of salt from the WSO storeroom. In addition to this, the SS in Minsk complain about rumors that Dr. E. was ostensibly subjected to a "rigorous interrogation" by the local Security Police. Dr. E. emphatically denies such charges, designates as false and completely fictitious reports that he was physically mistreated during his arrest and that he grew a full beard in order to conceal facial scars resulting from the interrogation.

Dr. E.'s attempts to reestablish his medical practice in Prague prove difficult. Due to his cooperation with the Germans, he is avoided by his former Czech patients. In desperation, he writes to General Commissioner Kube. He would like to return to Minsk in order to retrieve two automobiles that he placed at the disposal of the WSO. He continues to be available for an administrative post in White Ruthenia.

In the middle of July 1943, Dr. E. is permitted to return to Minsk in order to put his affairs in order. Here, he is received by General Commissioner Kube, who thanks him in the name of the Reich's minister for the eastern territories for his selfless work. As a sign of appreciation, Kube awards Dr. E. the Medal for Eastern Peoples and grants him permission to write a book about his two years of service in White Ruthenia.

The Eastern Ministry decides to continue the payment of Dr. E.'s salary as head of the WSO until January 1, 1944. The commander of the Security Police in the Reich's Protectorate Bohemia and Moravia is instructed not to make any trouble for Dr. E. and to support him in the reestablishment of his medical practice in Prague. Dr. E. is, however, forbidden to engage in any form of political activity and must obtain permission from the SS before leaving the protectorate.

Last Try

In the middle of January 1944, two weeks after the Eastern Ministry has discontinued the payment of his salary, Dr. E. addresses an eleven-page letter to Reich's Minister Alfred Rosenberg. In the letter, he again asserts his innocence and begs for the release of his still imprisoned WSO coworkers, including his two sisters-in-law. He reiterates his desire to resume cooperation with the Germans and places himself one final time at their disposal. The offer is not accepted. SS-Brigadeführer Curt von Gottberg, appointed the new general commissioner of White Ruthenia following Kube's death, has his own collaborators. With the advance of the Red

Army in the spring of 1944, the question of a bilateral cooperation becomes superfluous.

Land of the Free

In January 1948, Dr. E. sails illegally with his wife and two daughters from Bremen to New York. They claim to be refugees, are supported by the anti-Communist organization Church World Service.

Dr. E. adapts quickly to New York City. He calls himself John, finds work as a resident at Gouverneur Hospital in Manhattan. He is trained as a psychiatrist.

In New York, Dr. E. joins up with White Ruthenian exile groups. He is appointed head of the White Ruthenian Relief Committee. On December 2, 1948, he gives a radio interview with Meade Davidson as part of the series *Leaders in Exile*. Excerpt from the interview:

Davidson: But to get back to yourself. You left White Russia to go to Constantinople. What followed your mission there?

E.: After I fulfilled my duty in Constantinople and after White Ruthenia was divided between Russians and Poles, I immigrated, together with other members of our government, to Czechoslovakia, where we were given the right of exile. In Prague, I began my medical studies and obtained the diploma of a medical doctor in 1929. Although I was a student, I never left the work for my country and was a member of many political and cultural organizations whose task it was to create independence of White Ruthenia and rescue it from the terror of Soviet occupation.

Davidson: Doctor, since you have not seen fit to tell our audience, may I interpolate that as a physician you served with the United States Army Medical Corps in the war and that you are now a practicing physician and surgeon here in New York? And what do you feel free to say about the resistance movement in White Ruthenia?

E.: Over a long period of years the Belorussian people have been struggling with arms to protect their liberty and independence from Communist dictatorship. In the moment of general peril the best youth of our nation came forward to side with the democratic nations of America and Europe against the National Socialist dictatorship of Adolf Hitler. It was not Stalin's heroism, or the knowledge of warfare by his marshals, which defeated the German army on the territories of White Ruthenia and Ukraine but to a great degree our White Ruthenian partisans, who in innumerable raids and attacks destroyed communications and rear bases of the German army. Hitler, like Napoleon, was conquered and destroyed by partisanship. And at this very moment, White Ruthenian partisans continue their struggle against another more horrible dictatorship.

In 1949, Dr. E. is offered a position as a resident in psychiatry at the Binghamton State Hospital. In June of that year, he moves with his family to the city of Binghamton. He withdraws from active exile politics, adopts an American last name, and leads a quiet, respectable life in upstate New York.

On May 7, 1956, Dr. E. becomes a United States citizen. As with immigration, naturalization requires that he omit any mention of his cooperation with the Nazis.* On January 1, 1957, Dr. E. is admitted as a practicing psychiatrist to the State of New York. Two years later he becomes an active member of the

---

*It was not possible to reconstruct how or why Dr. E. was allowed to immigrate to the Unites States and then to become an American citizen. The Counter Intelligence Corps, the Central Intelligence Agency, the Federal Bureau of Investigation, and the Justice Department all claim to have no files or information regarding Dr. E. The Immigration and Naturalization Service reported that while its indexes do reflect the existence of a file on Dr. E., its Federal Records Center is, for unexplained reasons, unable to locate it.

Broome County Medical Society. In his application, he claims to have had a general medical practice in Prague between 1929 and 1945, and to have served as a medical officer in the American Army in Germany from 1945 to 1947.

At the age of seventy-two, Dr. E. resigns from his post as supervising psychiatrist at the Binghamton State Hospital and moves to Glen Cove on Long Island, where his elder daughter lives. He dies four years later, on February 25, 1970, at his winter home in Delray Beach, Florida. His obituary states that he was an active member of the Democratic Party on the local and state levels.

GLOSSARY

Aryan   The term was originally used for certain Indo-Germanic languages and then for the Indo-Germanic inhabitants of the Indian subcontinent and Iran. The Nazis used the term Aryan as a synonym for "Nordic" (i.e., members of the "central European race"), in distinction to the term "Jewish."

Aryanized   The term used by the Nazis for the expropriation or compulsory sale of Jewish property either to the German state or private Aryans.

Capos   Concentration camp prisoners who supervised prisoner work crews but did not have to work themselves.

Confessing Church   A German Protestant movement founded by Martin Niemöller in 1933. The Confessing Church was systematically opposed to the Nazi-sponsored German Christian Church. After the arrest of many of its ministers, the church was forced underground.

Einsatzgruppen   Mobile units of the Security Police and Security Service that followed the German army into Poland in 1939 and into the Soviet Union in June 1941. They were charged with eliminating politically undesirable elements—Jews, Communist functionaries, gypsies, etc. They were supported by the German Order Police and often used auxiliary units consisting of Ukrainian, Latvian, Lithuanian, and Estonian volunteers.

Einsatzstab Rosenberg Established in September 1940, the *Einsatzstab Rosenberg* was charged with confiscating art objects relating to or owned by Jews and Free Masons. The organization was first active in occupied France and then later in other occupied territories.

Gottgläubig (literally, "believing in God") The official Nazi term for persons who had formally left the Christian Church.

Government General The Polish territory occupied by German forces after the German invasion of Poland on September 1, 1939. It was declared sovereign German territory, but was not formally incorporated into the German Reich. The capital city of the Government General was Krakow; its districts included Krakow, Radom, Warsaw, and after 1941, Eastern Galicia.

Judenfrei (literally, "free of Jews") The official Nazi term for the removal of Jews from public and private life.

Kleine Festung (or Small Fortress) The concentration camp, established in 1940, located next to Theresienstadt. It was administratively separate from Theresienstadt; most of its inmates were Czech political prisoners. A number of Theresienstadt inmates were transferred to the *Kleine Festung* as a punishment and either killed there or deported to Auschwitz.

Nuremberg Laws The discriminatory laws established on September 15, 1935, in Nuremberg. The Nuremberg Laws included the *Reichsbürgergesetz* or Reich's Citizens' Law, which granted full political rights only to Germans and "like-blooded" persons, thereby establishing the legal basis for the discrimination of German Jews; and the *Blutschutzgesetz* or Law for the Protection of

German Blood, which forbade sexual intercourse between Germans or "like-blooded" persons and Jews, thereby establishing the crime of *Rassenschande* or race defilement.

Organisation Todt   The construction authority established in 1938 by General Inspector Todt. During the war, the *Organisation Todt* was responsible for the construction of fortifications, streets and railway lines. It drew its labor power initially from conscripted German laborers, later from foreign and Jewish slave laborers.

Rassenschande (or race defilement)   Extramarital sexual relations between German or "like-blooded" persons and Jews.

Reich's Association of Jews in Germany   A compulsory organization of German Jews established by order of the SS in July of 1939. The Reich's Association of Jews in Germany was charged with preparing the deportation of German Jews to concentration camps.

Reichskristallnacht   The anti-Jewish pogroms carried out in Germany on November 9, 1938. The pogroms were organized by the Nazis, ostensibly as retribution for Herschel Grynszpan's assassination of the German diplomat Ernst von Rath in Paris. Approximately 30,000 Jews were arrested and 91 Jews were murdered; 250 synagogues and 7,500 businesses and offices were destroyed.

Security Police   In 1936, Himmler ordered that the German Police be divided into two main branches, the *Ordnungspolizei* or Order Police and the *Sicherheitspolizei* or Security Police. The Security Police consisted of Criminal Police and the Political Police (the Gestapo).

Security Service   The intelligence agency responsible for Nazi Party security. The Security Service worked closely with the Security Police.

SS Ranks

SS-Reichsführer	General
SS-Obergruppenführer	Lieutenant General
SS-Gruppenführer	Major General
SS-Brigadeführer	Brigadier General
SS-Oberführer	Colonel
SS-Standartenführer	Lieutenant Colonel
SS-Obersturmbannführer	Major
SS-Sturmbannführer	Captain
SS-Hauptsturmführer	Captain
SS-Obersturmführer	First Lieutenant

Stadtverschönerung (or city beautification)   Program ordered by the SS at the end of 1943 for propaganda purposes. Its goal was to improve the external appearance of Theresienstadt.

Stahlhelm (literally, "steel helmet")   The "Stahlhelm Association of Front Soldiers" was founded in December 1918. It was a paramilitary organization, which, although nominally nonpartisan, was sharply opposed to the Weimar Republic.

Völkischer Beobachter   The official newspaper of the Nazi Party.

Volksgerichtshof   The court of law established in 1934 by Hitler, which was responsible for political crimes such as treason.

Wehrmacht   The designation used from 1935 to 1945 for the German armed forces.

SOURCES

Abbreviations

BT   Beit Theresienstadt (Theresienstadt Martyrs Remembrance Association), Givat Haim-Ihud, Israel

CompB   Compensation Office, Berlin

COSL   Central Office of State Judicial Administration for the Investigation of Nazi Crimes, Ludwigsburg

CSL   Czech State Archive, Litoměřice

GFA-B   German Federal Archive, Berlin-Lichterfelde

GLA/SN   German Literature Archive / Schiller National Museum, Marbach

HC   Heckscher Clinic, Munich

HI   Hoover Institution on War, Revolution, and Peace, Stanford

HSD   Hessian State Archive, Darmstadt

ICH   Institute for Contemporary History, Munich

NSA   Nuremberg State Archive

NWD   Netherlands State Institute for War Documentation, Amsterdam

RestB   Restitution Office, Berlin

White Lies

In September 1933...

Prehistory from Mirjam P.'s case history, File Mirjam P., patient files of the Heckscher Klinik, HC. Mirjam P.'s file is currently located in the

District Archive of Upper Bavaria, Heckscher Clinic Patient File 1757. □ Report by the Tel Aviv Child Welfare Services about Mirjam P. (12/23/1937), File Mirjam P., HC. □ Medical report by the Heckscher Clinic for the Jewish Welfare Office in Munich (3/10/1938), File Mirjam P., HC. □ Report by Dr. V. of the State Public Health Department in Darmstadt (6/1/1938), Files of the criminal proceedings against Mirjam P. on charges of theft and fraud, 2 KM 13/38 (G27, No. 2,252), HSD. □ Information concerning Mirjam P. and the Trüper'sche Home on the Sophien Heights by Jena, letter from the Jena City Archive to the author (12/2/1998).

Promised Land
P. has difficulty adjusting...
"Eine Fahrt an das Tote Meer," essay by Mirjam P., File Mirjam P., HC.
False Start.
Report by the Tel Aviv Child Welfare Services concerning Mirjam P. (12/23/1937), File Mirjam P., HC. □ Prehistory to Mirjam P.'s case history, File Mirjam P., HC.
The specialists...
Medical report by Dr. Ernst K. (9/17/1934) (copy), File Mirjam P., HC. □ Medical report by Dr. H. H. (9/28/1934) (copy), File Mirjam P., HC.
Second Chance.
Report by the Tel Aviv Child Welfare Services concerning Mirjam P. (12/23/1937), File Mirjam P., HC. □ Prehistory to Mirjam P.'s case history, File Mirjam P., HC. □ Medical report by the Heckscher Clinic for the Jewish Welfare Office in Munich (3/10/1938), File Mirjam P., HC.

Alone and On the Move
Homecoming.
Report by Dr. V. of the State Public Health Department for the Darmstadt district (6/1/1938), files of the criminal proceedings against Mirjam P., HSD. □ Medical report by the Heckscher Clinic for the Jewish Welfare Office in Munich (3/10/1938), File Mirjam P., HC.
On the Road.
Prehistory to Mirjam P.'s case history, File Mirjam P., HC. □ Medical report by the Heckscher Clinic for the Jewish Welfare Office in Munich (3/10/1938). □ Résumé by Mirjam P. (5/22/1938), files of the criminal proceedings against Mirjam P., HSD. □ Report by Dr. V. of the State Public Health Department for the Darmstadt district (6/1/1938), files of the criminal proceedings against Mirjam P., HSD.

By Other Means.
Judgment of the Juvenile Court (6/24/1937), Zurich Regional Court, trial
959/1937.

Conflicting Accounts
Judgment of the Regional Court of Rottweil (12/23/1937), Sigmaringen
State Archive. □ Indictment of the district attorney's office in Rottweil
(11/22/1937), Sigmaringen State Archive.

Between Colleagues
Report by the Tel Aviv Child Welfare Services concerning Mirjam P.
(12/23/1937), File Mirjam P., HC. □ Letter from the Welfare Office of the
Association of Bavarian Israelite Communities to the Heckscher Psychi-
atric Hospital and Research Institute (2/17/1938), File Mirjam P., HC. □
"Physical Findings" and "Psychological Behavior," File Mirjam P., HC.
□ "Intelligence Test," File Mirjam P., HC. □ "Psychological Findings"
(Feb. 1938), File Mirjam P., HC.

Case History
Mirjam P.'s case history, File Mirjam P., HC. □ Medical report by the
Heckscher Clinic for the Jewish Welfare Office in Munich (3/10/1938),
File Mirjam P., HC.

On the Run
P.'s *final days in the clinic...*
Letter from Mirjam P. (3/27/1938), File Mirjam P., HC.
After losing the housemaid job...
Statement by Dr. Anne R. (caseworker at the Jewish Welfare Office) to
the State Criminal Police in Munich (3/31/1938), files of the criminal pro-
ceedings against Mirjam P., HSD. □ Statement by the medical student
Hilmy M. to the State Criminal Police in Munich (4/1/1938), files of the
criminal proceedings against Mirjam P., HSD. □ Interrogation of Mirjam
P. by the State Criminal Police in Munich, files of the criminal proceedings against Mirjam P., HSD. □ Judgment of the Regional Court in Darmstadt against Mirjam P. (7/7/1938), files of the criminal proceedings
against Mirjam P., HSD.
That afternoon...
Statement by Dr. Anne R. (caseworker at the Jewish Welfare Office) to
the State Criminal Police in Munich (3/31/1938), files of the criminal

proceedings against Mirjam P., HSD. □ Statement by the medical student Hilmy M. to the State Criminal Police in Munich (4/1/1938), files of the criminal proceedings against Mirjam P., HSD. □ Interrogation of Mirjam P. by the State Criminal Police in Munich, files of the criminal proceedings against Mirjam P., HSD.

In Mannheim, P. initially...
Interrogation of Mirjam P. by the State Criminal Police in Darmstadt, files of the criminal proceedings against Mirjam P., HSD. □ Statement by the hotel owner August B. concerning Mirjam P. to the State Criminal Police in Darmstadt (5/5/1938), files of the criminal proceedings against Mirjam P., HSD. □ Report by the State Criminal Police in Darmstadt (5/6/1938), files of the criminal proceedings against Mirjam P., HSD. □ Judgment of the Regional Court in Darmstadt against Mirjam P. (7/7/1938), files of the criminal proceedings against Mirjam P., HSD.

Deceived

Around 11:30 in the evening... and P. spends a second night...
Interrogation of Mirjam P. by the State Criminal Police in Darmstadt, files of the criminal proceedings against Mirjam P., HSD. □ Interrogation of Gustav H. by the State Criminal Police in Darmstadt, files of the criminal proceedings against Mirjam P., HSD. □ Report of the State Criminal Police in Darmstadt (4/16/1938), files of the criminal proceedings against Mirjam P., HSD. □ Judgment of the Regional Court in Darmstadt against Mirjam P. (7/7/1938), files of the criminal proceedings against Mirjam P., HSD.

At the police station...
Interrogation of Mirjam P. by the State Criminal Police in Darmstadt, files of the criminal proceedings against Mirjam P., HSD.

During his interrogation by the police...
Interrogation of Gustav H. by the State Criminal Police in Darmstadt, files of the criminal proceedings against Mirjam P., HSD.

Convicted

In pretrial detention...
Résumé by Mirjam P. (5/22/1938), files of the criminal proceedings against Mirjam P., HSD.

P.'s lawyer informs the court...
Letter from the lawyer Gustav R. to the senior district attorney at the Regional Court in Darmstadt (6/1/1938), files of the criminal proceedings against Mirjam P., HSD.

The district attorney's office...Psychological results...Physical results... and *Expert opinion...*

Report by Dr. V. of the State Public Health Department for the Darmstadt district (6/1/1938), files of the criminal proceedings against Mirjam P., HSD.

Three days later...

Results of the investigation by the district attorney's office in Darmstadt (6/4/1938), files of the criminal proceedings against Mirjam P., HSD.

On July 7, 1938...

Judgment of the Regional Court in Darmstadt against Mirjam P. (7/7/1938), files of the criminal proceedings against Mirjam P., HSD.

Behind Bars

P. serves the rest of her sentence...

Letter from Mirjam P. to Erich P. (2/5/1939), Personal File Mirjam P., Hessian Regional Court Prison in Mainz, J85 No. 973, Speyer Regional Archive.

Written Contact. and *Human Contact.*

Letter from of the Regional Court Prison in Mainz, Personal File Mirjam P., Hessian Regional Court Prison in Mainz, Speyer Regional Archive.

Conduct.

Personal File Mirjam P., Hessian Regional Court Prison in Mainz, Speyer Regional Archive.

Letter 1.

Letter from Mirjam P. to Erich P. (2/5/1939), Personal File Mirjam P.

Letter 2.

Letter from Erich P. to the senior district attorney at the Regional Court in Darmstadt (4/18/1938), files of the criminal proceedings against Mirjam P., HSD.

In mid-June of 1939...

Note by the senior district attorney at the Regional Court in Darmstadt, judgment of the Regional Court in Darmstadt against Mirjam P. (7/7/1938), files of the criminal proceedings against Mirjam P., HSD.

Last Chance

In the Philippshospital...

Request submitted by Mirjam P. to the senior district attorney's office at the Regional Court in Darmstadt (10/3/1939), files of the criminal proceedings against Mirjam P., HSD.

At the end of October 1939...
Response from Dr. S. to police headquarters in Frankfurt am Main (10/26/1938), files of the criminal proceedings against Mirjam P., HSD.
One year later...
Letter from the Reich's Association of Jews in Germany (District Office in Mainz) to the directorate of the Philippshospital (1/24/1941), Temporary File Mirjam P., Q12 (Transferred Jews), Archive of the Psychiatric Hospital Philippshospital (Archive of the District Welfare Associations in Hessia).
Dr. S.'s response...
Handwritten response by Dr. S., director of the Philippshospital, to the Reichs Association of Jews in Germany (2/3/1941), Temporary File Mirjam P., Archive of the Philippshospital.

Conscious Duplicity
Euthanasia.
See, for example, Götz Aly, *Aktion-T4 1939-1945: Die "Euthanasie"–Zentrale in der Tiergartenstraße 4,* Berlin (1987); Henry Friedlander, *The Origins of Nazi Genocide: From Euthanasia to the Final Solution,* Chapel Hill (1995); Ernst Klee, *Euthanasie im NS-Staat: Die Vernichtung lebensunwerten Lebens,* Frankfurt am Main (1983); Ernst Klee, *Dokumente zur Euthanasie,* Frankfurt am Main (1986); Heidi Schmidt-von Blittersdorf, Dieter Debus, Birgit Klakowsky, "Die Geschichte der Anstalt Hadamar vom 1933 bis 1945 und ihre Funktion im Rahmen von T4," *Psychiatrie im Faschismus: Die Anstalt Hadamar 1933–1945,* ed. Dorothee Roer and Dieter Henkel, Bonn (1986); Isidor J. Kaminer, *Psychiatrie im Nationalsozialismus: Das Philippshospital (Hessen),* Frankfurt am Main (1996).
Jewish Patients.
See Kaminer, *Psychiatrie im Nationalsozialismus,* p. 135ff.; Friedlander, *The Origins of Nazi Genocide,* p. 39.
Hessia.
Note by the senior district attorney at the Regional Court in Darmstadt (1/28/1941), files of the criminal proceedings against Mirjam P., HSD. □
Collective file (transferred Jews), Archive of the Philippshospital. □
Kaminer, *Psychiatrie im Nationalsozialismus,* p.142ff.; Schmidt-von Blittersdorf, *Psychiatrie im Faschismus,* p. 367.
Three months later...
Inquiry by the senior inspector as legal guardian to the director of the District Psychiatric Hospital and Sanatorium Philippshospital (5/3/1941),

Temporary File Mirjam P., Archive of the Philippshospital. □ Letter from
Dr. S., director of the Philippshospital (5/6/1941), Temporary File Mirjam P., Archive of the Philippshospital □ Letter from the Insane Asylum
Cholm to the senior district attorney at the Regional Court in Darmstadt
(6/5/1941), files of the criminal proceedings against Mirjam P., HSD.

Coming to Terms with the Past
Letter from Erich P. to the directorate of the Philippshospital (7/10/1946),
Temporary File Mirjam P., Archive of the Philippshospital □ Letter from
Dr. B. to Erich P. (7/18/1946), Temporary File Mirjam P., Archive of
the Philippshospital □ Kaminer, *Psychiatrie im Nationalsozialismus,* pp.
163–64.

One Life

Wilhelm K. is born...
Hermann Barth, *Wilhelm [K.]* Berlin (n.d.), p. 3ff. Vol. 12 of *Die Reihe
der deutschen Führer.* □ G. Altensteig [Gerhard Rühle], *Wilhelm [K.],*
Leipzig (1933), p. 6f. □ Dr. Siegfried Mauermann, "Wilhelm [K.],"
Totila: Historisches Schauspiel in drei Aufzügen mit einem Vorspiel, ed.
Mauermann, Bielefeld (n.d.), p. 5f. □ Wilhelm K.'s personal file,
GFA-B. □ *Reichenberger Zeitung* (5/15/1933). □ *Der Märkische Adler*
(6/18/1933).
K. embarks on a humanistic...
Baldur von Schirach, *Die Pioniere des Dritten Reiches,* Essen (1933),
p. 140. □ Hermann Barth, p. 3ff. □ Altensteig, p. 6f. □ Wilhelm K.'s *Stu-
dienbuch* (born on 11/13/1887, registration no. 3542, summer 1908),
University Archive, Humboldt University of Berlin.

An Activist by Nature
Knowledge for its own sake...
Altensteig, p. 5ff. □ *German Völkisch University Newspaper,* published on
commission of the German Völkisch Student Alliance in Berlin (1911–14),
Center for Research on Anti-Semitism, Technical University, Berlin.
In 1910, K. is awarded...
"Akta der Köngl. Friedrich-Wilhelms-Universität zu Berlin betreffend der
von dem Geheimen Kommerzienrat F. Mendelssohn gestifteten Moses-
Mendelssohn-Stiftung zu Stipendien für Studierende der Philosophie

(1886)," University Archive, Humboldt University of Berlin. □ Altensteig, p. 9ff., 12f. □ *German Völkisch University Newspaper.*

In 1912, K. is awarded...
Jan Striesow, *Die Deutschnationale Volkspartei und die Völkisch-Radikale 1918–1922,* Frankfurt am Main (1981), vol. 2, p. 538.

Rhetorical Achievements

After eight semesters...
Altensteig, p. 13. □ *German Völkisch University Newspaper,* no. 3/4 (1913), no. 8/9 (1913). □ Wilhelm K.'s personal file, GFA-B. □ Information from the Berlin Regional Archive regarding the K. family (4/18/1997).

Brother-in-Arms.
Altensteig, pp. 7, 14. □ Wilhelm K.'s personal file, GFA-B. □ "Ein Schwindelfreier: Wilhelm K.," *Alarm,* no. 2 (11/15/1929), Wilhelm K.'s personal file, GFA-B. □ Barth, p. 3.

Shaken but Undaunted.
Altensteig, pp. 16, 19.

A Lightning-Fast Tongue and the Voice of a Rhinoceros.
Wilhelm K.'s personal file, GFA-B. □ Altensteig, p. 17f.

Literary Inclinations.
Wilhelm K., *Totila.* □ Altensteig, *Wilhelm K.,* p. 19ff.

A Politically Turbulent Career

Change of Location.
Altensteig, p. 21ff. □ Wilhelm K.'s personal file, GFA-B.

Change of Party.
Wilhelm K.'s personal file, GFA-B. □ "Vermerk der Polizeipräsident, Landeskriminalpolizeiamt, Berlin (3/13/1931) über Wilhelm K.," Wilhelm K.'s personal file, GFA-B.

Völkisch Politics.
Altensteig, p. 25. □ Wilhelm K.'s personal file, GFA-B.

Blows of Fate.
First Blow.
Wilhelm K.'s personal file, GFA-B.
Second Blow.
Wilhelm K.'s personal file, GFA-B. □ "Vermerk der Polizeipräsident," Wilhelm K.'s personal file, GFA-B.
Third Blow.
"Biographische Angaben," Wilhelm K.'s personal file, GFA-B. □ "Herr K.

ruft nach Polizei. Ein Beitrag zum Portrait eines Hakenkreuzführers," *Der Abend*, no. 177 (4/16/1931), Wilhelm K.'s personal file, GFA-B. □ "K.'s 'siebenjähriger Krieg'. Ein höchst seltsames Jubliäum," *Der Alarm*, no. 217 (5/11/1931), Wilhelm K.'s personal file, GFA-B. □ "Bonzokratie im Gau Ostmark der Hitlerpartei," *Die Deutsche Revolution (Kampforgan der Revolutionären Nationalsozialisten)*, no. 23 (6/7/1931), Wilhelm K.'s personal file, GFA-B.

Fourth Blow.

Altensteig, p. 27. □ "Vermerk der Polizeipräsident, " Wilhelm K.'s personal file, GFA-B. □ *Der Märkische Adler*, no. 4 (1927).

Attention!

Der Märkische Adler, no. 4 (1927).

Change of Party.

Der Märkische Adler, no. 3 (1927). □ Altensteig, p. 29. □ "Biographische Angaben," Wilhelm K.'s personal file, GFA-B. □ "Vermerk der Polizeipräsident," Wilhelm K.'s personal file, GFA-B.

Imperialism as the Highest Stage of Finance Capitalism
Der Märkische Adler, no. 1 (1927).

Merger
In 1928, K. joins...
Letter from Wilhelm K. (12/19/1927), rpt. in *Die Deutsche Revolution*, no. 25 (6/21/1931), Wilhelm K.'s personal file, GFA-B.
"Movable Mouthpiece."
"Schaukelstuhl, Dein Name ist K.," *Nationalsozialistische Montagsblatt* (6/22/1931), Wilhelm K.'s personal file, GFA-B. □ "Bonzokratie im Gau Ostmark der Hitlerpartei," *Die Deutsche Revolution (Kampforgan der Revolutionären Nationalsozialisten)*, no. 23 (6/7/1931), Wilhelm K.'s personal file, GFA-B.

Man of the People
May 1928...
"Biographische Angaben," Wilhelm K.'s personal file, GFA-B. □ Hermann Barth, p. 3f. □ Altensteig, pp. 30f., 37ff.
"Prussian Führer."
Altensteig, p. 42.
On the Eve of the National Revolution.
Altensteig, p. 33. □ Barth, p. 3f.

Sieg Heil *and Rich Pickings*
Victor.
Der Märkische Adler, no. 15 (4/9/1933), no. 16 (4/16/1933).
Impediments.
Letter from Wilhelm K. to Kurt Daluege (4/6/1933), Wilhelm K.'s personal file, GFA-B.
Domestic Politics (1933).
Letter from Wilhelm K. to Kurt Daluege (3/25/1933), Wilhelm K.'s personal file, GFA-B. □ Letter from Kurt Daluege to Wilhelm K. (3/28/1933), Wilhelm K.'s personal file, GFA-B.
Stage Politics.
Joseph Wulf, ed., *Theater und Film im Dritten Reich: Eine Dokumentation,* Gütersloh (1964), p. 60.
As an author...
Wilhelm K.'s application form for the "Verband deutscher Bühnenschriftsteller," Wilhelm K.'s personal file, GFA-B. □ Letter from Martin Bormann to Wilhelm K. (10/31/1933), Wilhelm K.'s personal file, GFA-B.
Pedagogical Work.
Westfälische Landeszeitung (5/19/1934), cited in "Aus den Akten des Gauleiters K.," Helmut Heiber, *Vierteljahrshefte für Zeitgeschichte,* vol. 1 (1956), p. 68.

Full Steam Ahead
Peaks and Valleys.
Völkischer Beobachter (6/8–9/1934).
There are more peaks...
Wilhelm K.'s personal file, GFA-B.
On the Road.
Friedrich Zipfel, *Kirchenkampf in Deutschland 1933–1945: Religionsverfolgung und Selbstbehautung der Kirchen in der nationalsozialistischen Zeit,* Berlin (1965), p. 31.
Parade Through the Town of Nauen (1935).
Wilhelm K.'s personal file, GFA-B.
Private Telephone Number (Top Secret!).
"Bericht an den Obersten Richter der Partei betreffend Gau Kurmark" (11/2/1935), Wilhelm K.'s personal file, GFA-B. □ Wilhelm K.'s personal file, GFA-B.
Pinnacle.
Wilhelm K.'s personal file, GFA-B.

"In-Laws."
Information from the Paderborn City Archive concerning the Li. family
(3/19/1998 and 3/24/1998). □ Adolf Li.'s (born 12/29/1877) personal file,
GFA-B. □ Information of the Hamburg State Archive concerning the Li.
family (5/4/1998).

Crossroads.
Judgment of the Fifty-third Civil Court of the Regional Court in Berlin
(11/19/1935), Wilhelm K.'s personal file, GFA-B.

A Dressing-Down
"Shortly before taking office..."
Walter Buch's personal file, GFA-B.

A Moralist. His responsibilities... and *Restraining the Revolution.*
Letter from Walter Buch to Reichsführer-SS Himmler (12/13/1935), Walter Buch's personal file, GFA-B.

Munich, December 10, 1935...
Letter from Walter Buch to Wilhelm K. (12/10/1935), Walter Buch's personal file, GFA-B. □ Letter from Walter Buch to Heinrich Himmler
(12/13/1935), Walter Buch's personal file, GFA-B.

Results: Disappointing.
Letter from Walter Buch to Heinrich Himmler (12/13/1935), Walter
Buch's personal file, GFA-B. □ Letter from Heinrich Himmler to Walter
Buch (12/22/1935), Walter Buch's personal file, GFA-B. □ Letter from
Walter Buch to Heinrich Himmler (1/6/1936), Walter Buch's personal file,
GFA-B.

K., on the contrary...
Letter from Wilhelm K. to Heinrich Himmler (3/11/1936), Wilhelm K.'s
personal file, GFA-B.

Cornered
Letter from Wilhelm K. to Heinrich Himmler (3/11/1936), Wilhelm K.'s
personal file, GFA-B.

K. Strikes Back
K. cannot sit around...
Letter from Wilhelm K. to Heinrich Himmler (3/11/1936), Wilhelm K.'s
personal file, GFA-B. □ Letter from Heinrich Himmler to Wilhelm K.
(3/30/1936), Wilhelm K.'s personal file, GFA-B.

With respect to Supreme Party Judge Walter Buch...
Anonymous letter to Major Buch (4/26/1936), Wilhelm K.'s personal file, GFA-B. Reprinted in Heiber, p. 78.

The Fall

During the course of investigations...
Circular letter no. 99/361 (no date), Wilhelm K.'s personal file, GFA-B. Reprinted in Heiber, p. 77f.

The accusations contained...
Reichssippenamt, Rep. 309, No. 277 (Walter Buch), GFA-B.

Supreme Party Judge Buch would like...
Walter Buch's personal file, GFA-B. □ Letter from Adolf Hitler to Wilhelm K. (10/16/1936), Wilhelm K.'s personal file, GFA-B. See also *Akten der Partei-Kanzlei der NSDAP: Rekonstruktion eines verlorengegangenen Bestandes,* Institut für Zeitgeschichte, Oldenbourg (1983).

Several months later...
Letter from Schneider (head of the Central Office) to the Main Office V (Office for Membership) (4/26/1937), Wilhelm K.'s personal file, GFA-B. □ Letter from Adolf Hitler to Wilhelm K. (10/16/1936), Wilhelm K.'s personal file, GFA-B.

On Ice

In spite of all promises...
Akten der Partei-Kanzlei der NSDAP (1983).

Out of Commission.
Information from the Berlin Regional Archive regarding the K. family (4/18/1997).

Financial Difficulties.
Letter from Wilhelm K. to Reich's Minister Dr. Lammers (4/1/1941), Reichskanzlei R43 4060, GFA-B. □ Letter from Wilhelm K. to Reich's Minister Dr. Lammers (12/22/1940), Reichskanzlei R43 4060, GFA-B.

Hope and Despair.
Letter from Wilhelm K. to Adolf Hitler (1/28/1941), Reichskanzlei R43 4060, GFA-B. □ Letter from Anita K. to Reich's Minister Dr. Lammers (2/24/1941), Reichskanzlei R43 4060, GFA-B.

1939.
Letter from Wilhelm K. to Reich's Minister Dr. Lammers (12/22/1940), Reichskanzlei R43 4060, GFA-B. □ Letter from Anita K. to Reich's Minister Dr. Lammers (2/24/1941), Reichskanzlei R43 4060, GFA-B.

In Dachau.
Letter from Wilhelm K. to Reich's Minister Dr. Lammers (4/17/1941), Reichskanzelei R43 4060, GFA-B. □ Letter from Anita K. to Reich's Minister Dr. Lammers (3/21/1941), Reichskanzelei R43 4060, GFA-B.

In the meantime...
Letter from Dr. Lammers to Wilhelm K. (3/28/1941), Reichskanzelei R43 4060, GFA-B. □ Letter from Wilhelm K. to Reich's Minister Dr. Lammers (4/17/1941), Reichskanzelei R43 4060, GFA-B. □ Remark by Reich's Minister Dr. Lammers (4/16/1941), Reichskanzelei R43 4060, GFA-B. □ Letter from Wilhelm K. to Reich's Minister Dr. Lammers (4/17/1941), Reichskanzelei R43 4060, GFA-B. □ Letter from Reichsleiter Martin Bormann to Reich's Minister Dr. Lammers (5/14/1941), Reichskanzelei R43 4060, GFA-B. □ Letter from Wilhelm K. to Reich's Minister Dr. Lammers (6/4/1941), Reichskanzelei R43 4060, GFA-B. □ Letter from the Reich's Minister for Science, Education, and Culture to Reich's Minister Dr. Lammers (6/7/1941), Reichskanzelei R43 4060, GFA-B. □ Letter from Reichsleiter Martin Bormann to Reich's Minister Dr. Lammers (6/27/1941), Reichskanzelei R43 4060, GFA-B. □ Letter from Wilhelm K. to Reich's Minister Dr. Lammers (7/21/1941), Reichskanzelei R43 4060, GFA-B. □ Memorandum by Martin Bormann (7/16/1941), Nuremberg Document L-221, reprinted in *Der Prozeß gegen die Hauptkriegsverbrecher vor dem Internationalen Militärgerichtshof,* Amtlicher Text, deutsche Ausgabe, Nuremberg 1949 (*IMT*), vol. 28, p. 90.

On Probation
On July 17, 1941...
Official document of appointment (7/17/1941), Nuremberg Document NG-1325, HI. □ "Protokoll über die Tagung der Gebietskommissare, Hauptabteilungsleiter und Abteilungsleiter der Generalkommmissars in Mink vom 8. April bis 10. April 1943," ICH, Fb 85, pp. 38, 127. □ Statement by Karl W. regarding Karl Zenner (2/16/1960), COSL, 202 AR 538/59 IV/V, p. 656ff. □ Interrogation of Joachim R. (1/12/1960), COSL 1a Js 1409/60, VII/VIII, p. 1692ff.

In Ruins.
Interrogation of Joachim R. (1/12/1960), COSL 1a Js 1409/60, VII/VIII, p. 1692ff. □ Letter from Dietrich Sch.'s (on commission of the General Commissionar for White Ruthenia) to the Hamburg Municipal Administration (3/28/1942), Hamburg State Archive. □ Letter from Wilhelm K. to Reich's Minister Dr. Lammers (10/23/1941), GFA-B. □ Diary entry from 9/3/1941,

Erich von dem Bach's war diary, GFA-B, Bestand R 20 (Chef der Ban-
denkampfverbände), 45: Tagebuch des Chef des Bandenkampfverbände
(1941–Ende 1942 Höherer SS- und Polizeiführer Rußland Mitte), p. 11.
Under the prevailing conditions...
Letter from Dietrich Sch.'s (on commission of the general commissioner
for White Ruthenia) to the Hamburg Municipal Administration
(3/28/1942), Hamburg State Archive. □ Letter from Wilhelm K. to
Reich's Minister Dr. Lammers (10/23/1941), GFA-B.
Despite equipment deficiencies...
Remark (3/7/1942), ICH, MA 795, p. 554. See also Christian Gerlach,
*Kalkulierte Morde: Die deutsche Wirtschafts- und Vernichtungspolitik
in Weißrußland 1941–1944,* Hamburg (1999), p. 425. □ Letter from
Wilhelm K. to Reich's Minister Dr. Lammers (10/23/1941), GFA-B. □
Alexander Dallin, *German Rule in Russia, 1941–1945: A Study of Oc-
cupation Policies,* London (1957), p. 204, and Gerlach, p. 100. □ Ein-
satzgruppen Report No. 124, October 1941. Nuremberg Document
R-102; Ereignismeldung UdSSR No. 214 des Chefs des Sipo u. des SD.
Nuremberg Document NO-3160, HI. See also Gerlach, p. 587.

Unresolved Issues
Goals.
Gerlach, p. 94ff. □ Dallin, pp. 217 and 200.
Borders.
Gerlach, p. 156ff.
Sovereignty.
Dallin, p. 203.
According to the Führer's Decree...
Decree concerning the administration of the newly occupied Eastern Ter-
ritories (7/17/1941), *IMT,* vol. 29, p. 234ff. □ Statement by Dr. H. von
R. in the criminal case against Karl Zenner (11/26/1959), COSL, 202 AR
538/59 I, p. 42ff. □ Gerlach, pp. 194f., 627.

Culture Wars
The Minsk Opera...
Statement by Dr. H. von R. (4/15/1960), COSL, 202 AR 538/59.
The battle among...
Letter from Wilhelm K. to Reich's Minister Rosenberg (10/3/1941),
Nuremberg Document PS-1099, HI. □ Memorandum by Himmler
(11/15/1941), Nuremberg Document NO-5329, HI.

"Penal Colony of the East"

Letter from SS-Obersturmbannführer Dr. Eduard Strauch to SS-Obergruppenführer Erich von dem Bach concerning General Commissioner K. (7/25/1943), Nuremberg Document NO-2262. Reprinted in Heiber, p. 80ff.

The Jewish Question I.
End of October 1941.

Report by Territorial Commissioner Heinrich Carl to General Commissioner Wilhelm K. (10/30/1941), Nuremberg Document PS-1104, reprinted in *IMT*, vol. 27, pp. 1–8. See Gerlach, p. 613f.

A day later...

Letter from Wilhelm K. to Hinrich Lohse (11/1/1941), Nuremberg Document PS-1104, HI.

K. has a copy of the petition...

Letter from Bigenwaldt to Dr. Marquart (11/21/1941), Nuremberg Document PS-1104, HI.

Difference of Opinion.

Report by the Security Police and the SD in Minsk, January 1942 ("Burkhardt Report"), ICH, Fb 104/2, p. 5f.

Reich's Commissioner Lohse...

Letter from Reich's Commissioner Lohse to Reich's Minister Lammers (10/14/1941), reprinted in Max Weinreich, *Hitler's Professors*, New York (1946), p. 396f. □ Letter from Dr. Bräutigam to Reich's Commissioner Lohse concerning the Jewish Question (12/18/1941), Nuremberg Document PS-3663, reprinted in IMT, vol. 32, p. 437.

The Jewish Question II.
In Slonim...

Territorial Commissioner Gerhard Erren's situation report (1/25/1942), ICH Fb 104/2, reprinted in Klee, Dreßen, Reiß, *"Schöne Zeiten": Judenmord aus der Sicht der Täter und Gaffer,* Frankfurt am Main (1988), p. 167ff. □ Gerlach, p. 621ff.

Powers of Discernment
In the middle of November 1941...

Gerlach, pp. 747ff., 625. □ Shalom Cholavsky, "The German Jews in the Minsk Ghetto," *Yad Vashem Studies* 17 (1986), p. 219ff.

K., curious about the new arrivals...
Report by the Security Police and the SD in Minsk, January 1942 ("Burkhardt Report"), ICH, Fb 104/2, p. 7f. □ Memorandum, cited in letter from SS-Obersturmbannführer Dr. Eduard Strauch to SS-Obergruppenführer Erich von dem Bach concerning General Commissioner K. (7/25/1943), Nuremberg Document NO-2262, HI. □ Diary entry from 9/3/1941, Erich von dem Bach's war diary, GFA-B.

K. is strangely affected...
Memorandum, cited in letter from SS-Obersturmbannführer Dr. Eduard Strauch to SS-Obergruppenführer Erich von dem Bach concerning General Commissar K. (7/25/1943), Nuremberg Document NO-2262, HI.

In the middle of December 1941...
Letter from Wilhelm K. to Reich's Commissioner Hinrich Lohse (12/16/1941), reprinted in Weinreich, p. 396f.

Preliminary Results.
Report by the Security Police and the SD in Minsk, January 1942 ("Burkhardt Report"), ICH, Fb 104/2, p. 6.

Technical Difficulties

The "Expert on the Jewish Question"...
Report by the Security Police and the SD in Minsk, January 1942 ("Burkhardt Report"), ICH, Fb 104/2, p. 1ff.

Short Circuit.
"Anlage zum Reisebericht," Hänsel to Rosenberg (3/3/1942), cited in Dallin, p. 207.

Special Status I.

Despite the special attention...
Report by the Security Police and the SD in Minsk, January 1942 ("Burkhardt Report"), ICH, Fb 104/2, p. 6ff.

In certain cases...
Secret report about mass executions of Jews carried out by Einsatzgruppe A, Nuremberg Document PS-2273, HI.

Special Status II.

K. employs a number of German Jews... and *There are repeated disputes...*
Excerpt of a letter from Dr. Eduard Strauch to Wilhelm K. (4/25/1942), cited in a letter from SS-Obersturmbannführer Dr. Eduard Strauch to SS-Obergruppenführer Erich von dem Bach concerning General Commis-

sioner K. (7/25/1943), Nuremberg Document NO-2262, HI. □ Report by the Security Police and the SD in Minsk, January 1942 ("Burkhardt Report"), ICH, Fb 104/2, p. 8.

The very fact that Jews...
Judgment of the Koblenz Regional Court 9 Ks 2/62 against Heuser (5/21/1963), *Justiz und NS-Verbrechen: Sammlung deutscher Strafurteile wegen nationalsozialistischer Tötungsverbrechen,* Amsterdam (1978), vol. 19, p. 59ff.

"Stepchildren"

K., who continues to regard himself...
Boguslaw Drewniak, *Das Theater im NS-Staat: Szenarium deutscher Zeitgeschichte,* Düsseldorf (1983), p. 138. See also Vladimir Seduro, *The Belorussian Theater and Drama,* New York (1955), ch. 22.

Weringhard:
Wilhelm K., *Totila,* p. 9, line 15f.

One day...
Letter from SS-Obersturmbannführer Dr. Eduard Strauch to SS-Obergruppenführer Erich von dem Bach concerning General Commissioner K. (7/25/1943), Nuremberg Document NO-2262, HI.

K. would like to found...
Dallin, p. 464f. □ Gerlach, p. 124.

"We offer the White Ruthenians..."
Cited in Gerlach, p. 98.

Major Operation

At the beginning of March 1942..., K., who has been informed of the operation..., and *During the course of the operation...*
Letter from SS-Obersturmbannführer Dr. Eduard Strauch to SS-Obergruppenführer Erich von dem Bach concerning General Commissioner K. (7/25/1943), Nuremberg Document NO-2262, HI. □ Memorandum, cited in the same letter. □ Judgment of the Koblenz Regional Court 9 Ks 2/62 against Heuser (5/21/1963), *Justiz und NS-Verbrechen. Sammlung deutscher Strafurteile wegen natinalsozialistischer Tötungsverbrechen,* vol. 19, pp. 190f. and 59ff.

SS-Hauptsturmführer Stark...
Judgment of the Koblenz Regional Court 9 Ks 2/62 against Heuser (5/21/1963), *Justiz und NS-Verbrechen,* vol. 19. □ "Memorandum by the former Commander of the Sipo and the SD," cited in a letter from

SS-Obersturmbannführer Dr. Eduard Strauch to SS-Obergruppenführer Erich von dem Bach concerning General Commissioner K. (7/25/1943), Nuremberg Document NO-2262, HI.

The next day...
The same letter. □ Meeting between Lohse and K. in Riga (3/21/1941), Nuremberg Document NG-1958, HI.

"A Coarse Letter"
Letter from SS-Obergruppenführer Heydrich to Wilhelm K. (3/21/1942), cited in the letter from Strauch to Bach (7/25/1943), Nuremberg Document NO-2262, HI.

One Life
Letter from Wilhelm K. to Reich's Minister Dr. Lammers concerning Karl Loewenstein (4/12/1942), Reichskanzelei R43 4060, GFA-B. □ See also the letter from Gerlinde B. for Anita K. to the author (8/8/1998).

Final Solution
Gerlach, pp. 694f., 756ff., and 768ff. □ Judgment of the Koblenz Regional Court 9 Ks 2/62 against Heuser (5/21/1963), *Justiz und NS-Verbrechen*, vol. 19, p. 192ff.

Adversary
The extensive organizational preparations...
Judgment, as above, vol. 19.
Dr. Strauch...
Eduard Strauch's personal file, GFA-B.
As a strong supporter...
Hoffmann Report (8/31/1942), GFA-B, NS 6/795, pp. 28–45.
Memorandum by Strauch...
"Memorandum (4/18/1942)," cited in a letter from SS-Obersturmbannführer Dr. Eduard Strauch to SS-Obergruppenführer Erich von dem Bach concerning General Commissioner K. (7/25/1943), Nuremberg Document NO-2262, HI.
Strauch's response...
Excerpt of a letter from Dr. Eduard Strauch to Wilhelm K. (4/25/1942), cited in letter from Stauch to Bach (7/25/1943), Nuremberg Document No-2262, HI.

"Soft-Hearted"
"Report no. 4 White Ruthenia/Minsk (5/26/1942)," Hoffmann Report, GFA-B, NS 6/795, pp. 28–45.

In a Different Tone
Approval.
Letter from Wilhelm K. to his territorial commissioners (7/10/1942), ICH, Fb 104/2.
Altered Logic.
Letter from Wilhelm K. to the Reich's Commissioner for the Occupied Eastern Territories (8/11/1942), ICH, Fb 104/2.
Testimonial.
Letter from Wilhelm K. to SS-Brigadeführer Zenner (7/17/1942), ICH Fa 74. □ Gerlach, pp. 924f., 706. □ Diary entry from 9/3/1941, Erich von dem Bach's war diary, GFA-B.
Cooperation.
Report from General Commissioner K. to Reich's Commissioner Hinrich Lohse (7/13/1942), reprinted in Klee, Dreßen, Reiß, p. 169ff.

K. in Conversation
Forced Assent.
"Memorandum from 12/2/1942," cited in a letter from SS-Obersturmbannführer Dr. Eduard Strauch to SS-Obergruppenführer Erich von dem Bach concerning General Commissioner K. (7/25/1943), Nuremberg Document NO-2262, HI.
Generation Gap (October 1942).
"Memorandum from October 2, 1942," cited in the same letter.

Security Measures
Decree from General Commissioner K. (10/30/1942), cited in the same letter, NO-2262, HI.

"We will clear the way without pangs of conscience, and then…"
Partisan resistance in White Ruthenia…
See Gerlach, p. 860ff.
Albert Hoffmann…
Hoffmann's Report, GFA-B, NS 6/795.

Progress Report.

Report from SS-Unterscharführer Arlt, reprinted in *"Unsere Ehre heißt Treue": Kriegstagebuch des Kommandostabes Reichsführer SS Tätigkeitsberichte der 1. und 2. SS-Inf.-Brigade, der 1. SS-Kav.-Brigade und von Sonderkommandos der SS,"* Vienna (1965), p. 499.

Motto...

Order by the commander of the Security Police and the SD, Operation Staff (11/18/1942), ICH, MA 707/1.

SS-Obergruppenführer Erich von dem Bach...

Guidelines for measures on bandit control from the Reichsführer's plenipotentiary for Bandit Control (2/26/1943), German Federal Archives, Temporary Archive Dahlwitz-Hoppegarten, ZM 1488 A.6. □ Gerlach, p. 996ff.

In the fall of 1942...

Nuremberg Document NO-5437, HI.

Operation Nuremberg (Nov. 1942).

Curt von Gottberg's personal file, GFA-B. Also Nuremberg Documents NO-1732, NO-5156, HI.

Change of Policy (May 1943).

Commander of the Security Police and the SD in White Ruthenia, SS-Obersturmbannführer Strauch (5/11/1943), German Federal Archives, Temporary Archive Dahlwitz-Hoppegarten. □ Gerlach, p. 1004.

Under Way with the Wehrmacht.

Report on the participation on a major operation with the Combat Group of First Lieutnant Kluptsch, Nuremberg Document NO-3028, HI.

At around the same time...

Letters from Territorial Commissioner Langer to the Senior Division Leader I (5/31/1943 and 6/1/1943), Nuremberg Document NO-3028, HI. □ Letter from Wilhelm K. to Reich's Minister Rosenberg through Reich's Commissioner Lohse concerning the Langer Report (6/3/1943), Nuremberg Document NO-3028, HI.

Further Complaints.

Letter from the administrator of prisons in Minsk to Wilhelm K. (5/31/1943), Nuremberg Document R-135, HI. □ Letter from Wilhelm K. to Reich's Commissioner Lohse (6/1/1943), Nuremberg Document R-135, HI. □ Letter from Wilhelm K. to Reich's Minister Rosenberg through Reich's Commissioner Lohse (6/5/1943), Nuremberg Document R-135, HI. □ See the letter from Wilhelm K. to Reich's Minister Rosenberg (6/26/1943), GFA-B, Ordner 217 II, p. 147, and Gerlach, pp. 907ff. and 948ff.

Reich's Commissioner Lohse is indignant...
Letter from Reich's Commissioner Lohse to Reich's Minister Rosenberg (6/18/1943), Nuremberg Document R-135, HI.

End Phase
At the end of June 1943...
Order of the Reichsführer-SS (6/21/1943), Nuremberg Document NO-2403, HI. □ Memorandum (7/10/1943), GFA-B, SS HO 2149.
On July 13, 1943...
Meeting memorandum (8/20/1943), Nuremberg Document NO-1831, HI. □ Memorandum by Gottlob Berger (7/14/1943), Nuremberg Document NO-3370, HI. □ See Gerlach, p. 737f.

"Sentimental Humanitarianism"
Memorandum by SS-Obersturmbannführer Dr. Eduard Strauch (7/20/1943), Nuremberg Document NO-4317, reprinted in Heiber, p. 78f.

Settling Accounts
Letter from SS-Obersturmbannführer Dr. Eduard Strauch to SS-Obergruppenführer Erich von dem Bach concerning General Commissioner K. (7/25/1943), Nuremberg Document NO-2262, HI. □ See also letter from SS-Brigadeführer Curt von Gottberg to SS-Obergruppenführer Erich von dem Bach concerning Wilhelm K., and the memorandum concerning the consultation of Gottberg with K. on Thursday, July 15, 1943, from 11:00 to 11:45 (7/21/1943), Nuremberg Document NO-4316, HI.

Undermined
In Berlin, reports and complaints accumulate...
Letter from Dr. Bräutigam to SS-Obergruppenführer Anton Berger concerning Wilhelm K. (7/10/1943), Nuremberg Document NO-3028, HI. □ Letter from Anton Berger to Dr. Bräutigam (7/13/1943), Nuremberg Document NO-3028, HI. □ Letter from Anton Berger to SS-Obersturmbannführer Dr. Brandt (8/18/1943), Nuremberg Document NO-4315, HI. □ Letter from SS-Brigadeführer Curt von Gottberg to SS-Obergruppenführer Erich von dem Bach concerning Wilhelm K., and the memorandum concerning the consultation of SS-Brigadeführer von Gottberg with District Leader K. on Thursday, July 15, 1943 from 11:00 to 11:45 A.M. (7/21/1943), Nuremberg Document NO-4316,

HI. □ Letter from SS-Obersturmbannführer Dr. Eduard Strauch to SS-Obergruppenführer Erich von dem Bach concerning the General Commissioner K. (7/25/1943), Nuremberg Document NO-2262, HI.

The situation in Minsk...

See Gerlach, p. 704ff.

In spite of everything...

Letter from Wilhelm K. to Hinrich Lohse (9/20/1943), ICH.

> Adolf Hitler, you inspire
> Our belief so profoundly.
> With God's assistance you'll retire
> And defeat the enemy!
>
> —Excerpt from "Our Vow" (8/20/1943, *Minsker Zeitung*)
>   by Wilhelm K.

A day later...

Final report concerning the mine attack on General Commissioner K., on the night of September 21, 1943, German Federal Archives, Temporary Archive Dahlwitz-Hoppegarten, ZstA Potsdam, Film 4121. □ Gerlach, p. 864f.

That same night...

Günther K.'s testimony, Beit Lohamei Haghetoat, H-267. □ Retaliatory executions following the assassination of General Commissioner K. in the fall of 1943, Judgment of the Koblenz Regional Court 9 Ks 2/62 against Heuser (5/21/1963), vol. 19, p. 228.

Among the leading Nazis...

Wilfred von Oven, *Finale Furioso: Mit Goebbels bis zum Ende,* Tübingen (1974), p. 140f. □ Erich von dem Bach's testimony, published in *Aufbau,* New York, 9/6/1946, XII, no. 36. See also Hinrich Lohse's testimony (10/23/1947), COSL, 202 AR 538/59 or ("When K. was murdered in September 1943, Himmler explicitly said to a group of several men, including myself, something like, 'That is the thanks he gets for his kindness to Jews and other races.' ").

A week later...

Reich's Minister Rosenberg's address at the state funeral for Wilhelm K. (9/27/1943), GFA-B, NS 8/71, pp. 171–99.

A Rare Sense of Justice

There is relatively little documentary evidence about Karl L.'s life before 1940. This is not unusual for a private individual, particularly given the destruction of numerous public records in Central Europe as a result the two World Wars. Much of the information available about Karl L.'s life before his deportation to Minsk in 1941 is contained in documents written by Karl L. himself (letters, petitions, resumes, etc.). I was able to verify some of this information either directly or indirectly through other sources. At least one claim made by Karl L.—as a concentration camp prisoner—is demonstrably false: that he was a half-Jew (i.e., that his father was a German Christian). In fact, both of his parents were Jewish. Karl L. also made several claims that could not be verified, but they could not be disproven with certainty either. He reported on numerous occasions that he had been a lieutenant in the Royal German Navy before and during the First World War, and that he had received a doctorate in political economy from the University of Breslau in 1922 (before fleeing with his wife and two small children to Berlin). From at least 1925 onward, Karl L. referred to himself in public as a doctor of political economy. The archive at the University of Wroclaw (formerly the University of Breslau) reported that while university records do exist for this time period, these records are not complete. The archive was unable to find any information about a doctoral dissertation by Karl L., nor could it locate any records indicating that he had been enrolled there either as a student or a doctoral candidate. There is also no listing of a doctoral dissertation by Karl L. at the University of Breslau in the *Jahresverzeichnis der deutschen Hochschulschriften,* an annual journal listing completed dissertations at German universities. In volume 38 of the *Jahresverzeichnis der deutschen Hochschulschriften* (1922), there is a listing for a different Karl L., who completed a dissertation in the department of law at the University of Munich. The Deutsche Dienststelle in Berlin reported that it was unable to find any reference to Karl L. in its records for the Royal German Navy either before or during the First World War. According to the Deutsche Dienststelle, much of the material concerning the Royal German Navy for this time period, including officer's files and complete lists of officers, was destroyed during the Second World War. There are, however, complete lists of officer's promotions in the Royal Navy for this time period. Karl L.'s name does not appear in these lists.

On November 7, 1941...
Karl L., "Meine Verhaftung," unpublished manuscript concerning his imprisonment in Minsk, ICH, p. 1. [Published in slightly abridged form as "Minsk: Im Lager der deutschen Juden," *Aus Politik und Zeitgeschichte,* supplement to the weekly newspaper *Das Parlament* (11/7/1956)]. □ Karl L., "Kurzer Lebenslauf zum Antrag auf Entschädigung," Karl L.'s compensation files, CompB, p. M5. □ Letter from Karl L. to the Compensation Office (2/13/1954), CompB, p. B65.

The housemaid neglects to call L....
Karl L., "Meine Verhaftung," p. 1. □ Statement from Käthe S. (Karl L.'s housemaid) to the Restitution Court, Karl L.'s restitution files, RestB, 83 WGA 2179/51, pp. 59 and 100. □ Karl L., "Kurzer Lebenslauf," CompB, p. M5.

That is what the Gestapo officers think...
Communication from the Jewish Community regarding Karl L. ("Zur Vorlage bei der PrV"), CompB, p. PrV9. □ Communication from Karl L. to the Compensation Office regarding his two sons, CompB, p. D13/15. □ Letter from the Foundation Neue Synagoge Berlin–Centrum Judaicum to the author regarding Marie (Margot) L. (11/25/1997). □ Karl L., "Meine Verhaftung," p. 1.

He has German friends...
Karl L.'s application for compensation to the Central Office for Assets Administration in Bad Nenndorf (11/28/1947), RestB, 83 WGA 4066/51, p. 3. □ Karl L., "Kurzer Lebenslauf," CompB, p. M5. □ Letter from Karl L. to the Restitution Office (10/15/1952), RestB, 83 WGA 2176/51, p. 10. □ Letter from Karl L. to the Restitution Office (11/11/1952), RestB, 83 WGA 2176/51, p. 15. □ Letter from Count Detlef von Moltke to Karl L. (8/16/1935), RestB, 83 WGA 2176/51. □ Letter from Fritz Albrecht to the Restitution Office (1/6/1953), RestB, 83 WGA 2176/51, p. 21. □ Letter from Margot M. to the senior district attorney at the Regional Court of Berlin (2/7/1948), RestB, 83 WGA 2176/51, p. 39. □ Report by Margot M. (11/30/1952), RestB, 83 WGA 2176/51. □ Statement by Margot M. (11/17/1952), RestB, 83 WGA 2176/51. □ Statement by Arno R., RestB, 83 WGA 2176/51, p. 56. □ Statement by Margot M. (1/7/1968), RestB, 83 WGA 2176/51, p. 186. □ Explanation by Karl L. (6/12/1966), RestB, 83 WGA 2176/51, vol. 2, p. 123f. □ "A. Busse & Co. Aktiengesellschaft in Berlin," *Handbuch der Deutschen Aktiengesellschaften,* Berlin (1938).

Detained

At the Gestapo offices...
Karl L., "Meine Verhaftung," p. 2.

When they learn...
Letter from Fritz Albrecht to the Restitution Office (1/6/1953), RestB, 83 WGA 2176/51, p. 21.

For four days...
Karl L., "Meine Verhaftung," p. 2f.

At the detention center...
Karl L., "Meine Verhaftung," p. 3f. □ Statement by Frau B. (custodian at Tasso Strasse No. 5) to the Restitution Court, RestB, 83 WGA 4066/51. □ Testimony by Haim Behrendt, *The Trial of Adolf Eichmann: Record of Proceedings in the District Court of Jerusalem / State of Israel,* Session no. 29 (microfilm), p. 502.

Departure.
Karl L., "Meine Verhaftung," p. 3f. □ Haim Behrendt, p. 502ff.

Arrival

On November 18...
Karl L., "Meine Verhaftung," p. 4f. □ Haim Behrendt, p. 503. □ On the German Jews in Minsk, see:

- Günther K.'s testimony, Beit Lohamai Haghetoat (Ghetto Fighters' House), Israel, H-267.
- Günther H.'s testimony, Beit Lohamai Haghetoat (Ghetto Fighters' House), Israel, H-280.
- Shalom Cholavsky, "The German Jews in the Minsk Ghetto," *Yad Vashem Studies,* p. 219ff.
- Hersch Smolar, *The Minsk Ghetto,* New York (1982).
- *Wegweiser zu ehemaligen jüdischen Leidenstätten der Deportationen von Hamburg nach Minsk,* Deutsch-Jüdische Gesellschaft Hamburg (ed.), Hamburg (1995).
- *Aufzeichnungen aus dem Ghetto Minsk,* Teil I: Berthold Rudner, "Andenken Martha Crohns. Bericht über ihr letztes Jahreswechsel (11/12/1941–1/26/1942)"; Teil II: "Tagebuchblätter, Nov. 1942–Juni 1942 (Verfasser unbekannt)," unpublished diaries, ED 424, ICH.
- The denazification trials against Adolf Rübe (Staatsanwaltschaft Karlsruhe 3a Ks 2/49 and Spruchkammerakte Adolf Rübe, COSL).

Ghetto Police.

Dr. Thomas Mandl in a conversation with the author (10/24/1998). □ Karl L., "Meine Verhaftung," pp. 6 and 16.

Sonderghetto.

Karl L., "Meine Verhaftung," p. 4ff. □ Haim Behrendt's testimony, *The Eichmann Trial Proceedings,* no. 29, p. 503f. □ Günther K.'s testimony, Beit Lohamai Haghetoat (Ghetto Fighters' House). □ Smolar, p. 48ff. □ Cholavsky, p. 220.

Supplementary Rations.

Karl L., "Meine Verhaftung," pp. 13 and 15. □ Günther K.'s testimony, Beit Lohamai Haghetoat (Ghetto Fighters' House).

Decision.

Karl L., "Meine Verhaftung," p. 9ff. □ Haim Behrendt, p. 506f.

Mistaken Identity.

Karl L., "Meine Verhaftung," p. 24f. □ Karl L. (professor of law and political science), in *Dictionary of International Biography,* Part II, G-O, Cambridge (1974), p. 1102. □ Wilhelm Kube's *Studienbuch* (born 11/13/1887, Registration No. 3542, Summer 1908), University Archive, Humboldt University of Berlin. □ Karl L.'s *Studienbuch* (born 11/9/1891, Registration No. 1295, Michaelmas 1912), University Archive, Humboldt University of Berlin.

A Beating.

Karl L., "Meine Verhaftung," p. 18Af. □ Karl L., "Kurzer Lebenslauf," CompB, p. M5. □ Letter from Karl L. to the Compensation Office (8/12/1954), CompB, p. M7. □ Form B (Damages to Body and Health), CompB, p. B1.

Rescued.

Karl L., "Meine Verhaftung," p. 25ff. □ Letter from General Commissioner Wilhelm Kube to Reichsminister Dr. Lammers regarding Karl L. (4/12/1942), Reichskanzelei R43 4060, GFA-B. □ See also Karl L.'s résumé in the Theresienstadt *Prominenten* albums, Czech State Archive, Prague. □ To the author's knowledge, there were only two other Berlin Jews who survived the Minsk ghetto: Haim Behrendt and Margot A. (See the trial against Adolf Rübe, StA Karlsruhe 1 Js 24/48, COSL).

Theresienstadt

After the Munich Accord...

H. G. Adler, *Theresienstadt, 1941–1945: Das Antlitz einer Zwangsgemeinschaft: Geschichte, Soziologie, Psychologie,* 2nd ed. (improved and expanded), Tübingen (1960), pp. 21ff. and 720ff.

The former director...
Adler, p. 74ff. □ Ruth Bondy, *"The Elder of the Jews": Jakob Edelstein of Theresienstadt,* New York (1989).
The head of the Czech gendarmes...
Bondy, p. 352. □ Karl L., "Aus der Hölle Minsk in das 'Paradies' Theresienstadt," unpublished manuscript, ICH, p. 224
The first seven months...
Adler, chapter 3: "Verschickungen nach und aus Theresienstadt," ch. 4: "Geschlossenes Lager November 1941 / Juli 1942," ch. 8: "Verwaltung" and p. 364ff. □ Zdenek Lederer, *Ghetto Theresienstadt,* London (1953).

Special Case
In the camp prison...
Karl L., "Aus der Hölle," p. 56f. □ Statement by Benjamin Murmelstein concerning Karl L., File Karl L., CSA-L. □ Gonda Redlich, *The Terezin Diary of Gonda Redlich,* Saul Friedman (ed.), Kentucky (1991), pp. 73 and 89. □ Lederer, pp. 56–60. □ Bondy, p. 349. □ "An das Ghettogericht: Die Verteidigung des Karl L. stellt Antrag auf Wiederaufnahme des Verfahrens," File Karl L., CSA-L, p. 23.
On September 9, 1942...
Karl L., "Aus der Hölle," p. 58f. □ "An das Ghettogericht," File Karl L., CSA-L, p. 3.
During L.'s four months...
Adler, p. 106ff. □ Miroslav Kárny, "Deutsche Juden in Theresienstadt," *Therestädter Studien und Dokumente 1994,* Kárny, Raimund Kemper, and Margita Kárná (eds.), Prag (1994), pp. 36–53.
In the fall of 1942...
Ruth Bondy, "Prominente auf Widerruf," *Theresienstädter Studien und Dokumente 1995,* Miroslav Kárny, Raimund Kemper, and Margita Kárná (eds.), Prague (1995), pp. 7–32. □ Theresienstadt *Prominenten* albums, Czech State Archive, Prague.

Servant of the Ghetto
L. carries out his duties...
Karl L., "Aus der Hölle," pp. 89 and 128. □ Bondy, *"The Elder,"* p. 350. □ Adler, p. 138ff.
Official regulations...
Dienstordnung des Sicherheitswesens, BT. □ Karl L., "Aus der Hölle," p. 128.

From the beginning...

Karl L., "Aus der Hölle," pp. 60 and 90. See also the letter from Karl L. to H. G. Adler (7/24/1947), Adler Collection (250n), NWD.

"I am loyal to those..."

Karl L., "Aus der Hölle," p. 141f.

A Reliable Organ of Public Safety and Order

On May 14, 1942...

Adler, p. 99ff. □ Karl L., "Aus der Hölle," p. 128ff. "Berufungsbegründung Karl L.'s durch Dr. Sieg. und Dr. Win. an das Ghetto-Strafgericht in Theresienstadt," Adler Collection (250n), NWD.

Responsibilities.

Dienstordnung des Sicherheitswesens (copy), File Karl L., CSA-L. See also Adler, *Theresienstadt*, p. 490.

Role Models.

"Innere und Disziplinarordnung des GW," Karl L., "Aus der Hölle," appendix.

Required Salute.

"Dienstordnung der Gemeinde Wache," Karl L., "Aus der Hölle," appendix. □ Adler, p. 483.

Ranks.

Karl L., "Aus der Hölle," p. 130f.

Accommodations.

Karl L., "Aus der Hölle," p. 130f. □ Letter from Karl L. to Dr. W. through the Jewish community in Prague (3/15/1947) (copy), Adler Collection (250n), NWD.

Privileges

L. convinces...

Karl L., "Aus der Hölle," p. 177f. □ "An das Ghettogericht," File Karl L., CSA-L, p. 10.

As a result of these privileges...

Karl L., "Aus der Hölle," p. 130. □ Adler, p. 496. □ Resi Wegelein, unpublished manuscript, ICH, MS 408.

The privileges enjoyed...

Statement by Benjamin Murmelstein regarding Karl L, File Karl L., CSA-L. □ Karl L., "Aus der Hölle," p. 177.

Clean Hands.

Karl L., "Aus der Hölle," p. 177ff. □ See also Norbert Troller, *Theresienstadt: Hitler's Gift to the Jews.* Chapel Hill (1991), p. 62ff.

A Fanatical Defender of Justice

["Herr L. is feared too greatly because of his sense of justice, for he is a fanatical defender of justice. Herr L. and his organization are feared because of their uncompromising stance, their determination, and their drastic thoroughness." Excerpt from a letter from Paul R. (a Theresienstadt inmate) concerning Karl L. (copy), Adler Collection (250n), NWD.]

After assuming office...

Karl L., "Aus der Hölle," p. 209f. □ Adler, pp. 243ff. and 368ff. □ "An das Ghettogericht," File Karl L., CSA-L, pp. 5ff. and 10ff. □ "Anonymes Protokoll ohne Titel" (1945), cited in Adler, p. 475ff. □ On the subject of theft and corruption in Theresienstadt, see:

- "Heeresbäckerei" (report by the former Theresienstadt inmate Sam B.), Adler Collection (250n), NWD.
- "Betr. Einbrüche im Kartoffelkeller C III/93," Report by Luba G. (Abschrift), Adler Collection (250n), NWD.
- Letter from F. S. to Dr. Fritz Rathenau (10/22/1946) (copy), Adler Collection (250n), NWD.
- Heinrich Klang, "Denkschrift über die Ausübung der Gerichtsbarkeit in Theresienstadt," Adler Collection (250n), NWD.
- Letter from Dr. S. Seg. (excerpts), Adler Collection (250n), NWD.
- Benjamin Murmelstein, *Geschichtlicher Überblick,* unpublished manuscript, BT.
- Gonda Redlich, *The Terezin Diary of Gonda Redlich,* pp. 79, 82, and 84.
- Bondy, pp. 276 and 351; "Jakob Edelstein—der erste Judenälteste von Theresienstadt," *Theresienstadt in der "Endlösung der Judenfrage",* Miroslav Kárny, Vojtêch Blodig, and Margita Kárná (eds.), Prague (1992), p. 83.
- Letter from Dr. Vladimir Weiss to the Jewish Elder Eppstein (8/20/1943), cited in Adler, p. 352.
- "Anonymes Protokoll ohne Titel" (1945), cited in Adler, p. 457ff.

Feeding at the Trough.

Karl L., "Aus der Hölle," p. 108.

Sources of Corruption.

Karl L., "Aus der Hölle," pp. 108f. and 205f.

Further Dens of Corruption.

Letter from Dr. Vladimir Weiss to the Jewish Elder Eppstein (8/20/1943), cited in Adler, p. 348ff. □ Karl L., "Aus der Hölle," pp. 114, 176, 182ff., and 203. □ Adler, pp. 356ff. and 570ff.

"My Battle Against Corruption"
L. decides to act…

Karl L., "Aus der Hölle," chapter 9: "Mein Kampf gegen die Korruption," p. 209ff. □ Adler, pp. 138ff. and 368ff. ("Der aussichtslose Kampf um die gerechte Verteilung der Nahrung.") □ Gonda Redlich's diary entries from 11/3/1942 and 11/7/1942, *Terezin Diary*, p. 82f.

Kitchen Warfare.

Bondy, p. 351. □ Karl L., "Aus der Hölle," p. 200f. □ "An das Ghettogericht," p. 8ff. □ "Rechenschaftsbericht Karl L.'s," cited in Adler, p. 365. □ "Anonymes Protokoll ohne Titel" (1945), cited in Adler, p. 457ff. □ Adler, p. 365.

Reform Measures.

Karl L., "Aus der Hölle," pp. 110, 164f., and 201. □ "Die persönliche Einstellung des Angeklagten," in "Berufungsbegründung Karl L.'s durch Dr. Sieg. und Dr. Win. an das Ghetto-Strafgericht in Theresienstadt," Adler Collection (250n), NWD.

Raid.

Karl L., "Aus der Hölle," pp. 206f. and 212. □ "An das Ghettogericht," File Karl L., CSA-L, p. 9f.

Economic Inspection Authority. and Jurisdiction.

Karl L., "Aus der Hölle," pp. 157ff. and 235. □ Letter from Karl L. to the director of the Central Office (6/1/1943) (copy), Adler Collection (250n), NWD. □ "An das Ghettogericht," File Karl L., CSA-L, p. 4ff. □ Letter from Dr. Vladimir Weiss to the Jewish Elder Eppstein (8/20/1943), cited in Adler, p. 349f.

Further Reform Measures.

"An das Ghettogericht," File Karl L., CSA-L, p. 10.

In the Service of the Common Good
L. puts his heart and soul into his work…

Karl L., "Aus der Hölle," p. 209ff. □ Notes by H. G. Adler on Philipp Manes's unpublished manuscript "Tatsachenbericht," Adler Collection (250n), NWD. □ Statement by Leo Holzer concerning Karl L. (12/6/1946), File Karl L., CSA-L ["I protect…"].

Shortcuts.

Karl L., "Aus der Hölle," p. 184ff. □ See letter from Max F. (Hospital Kitchen EIIIa) to Karl L. regarding the distribution of confiscated foodstuffs (9/15/1943), Adler Collection, and confirmation from Ruth S. (senior nurse of the Tuberculosis Ward EIIIa), Adler Collection (250n), NWD. □ "An das Ghettogericht," File Karl L., CSA-L, p. 10.

Issues of Jurisdiction.
Karl L., "Aus der Hölle," pp. 99ff., 171, and 209. □ Gonda Redlich's diary entry from 2/28/1943, *Terezin Diary*, p. 105.

Presented with the possibility...
Letter from Karl L. to the Jewish Elder Eppstein (2/7/1943), cited in "An das Ghettogericht," File Karl L., CSA-L, p. 12.

Alone and Forsaken

In spite of L.'s interventions...
Statement by Benjamin Murmelstein concerning Karl L, File Karl L., CSA-L. □ Letter from Karl L. to H. G. Adler (4/24/1947), Adler's unpublished papers, GLA/SN. □ Karl L., "Aus der Hölle," pp. 62, 68, and 103. □ Adler, p. 456.

After some initial difficulties...
Adler, pp. 115ff. and 139. □ Bondy, p. 350ff. □ Karl L., "Aus der Hölle," pp. 172, 224, and 227ff. □ Statement by Benjamin Murmelstein, File Karl L., CSA-L. □ Letter from Karl L. to the Jewish Elder Eppstein (5/9/1943), cited in "An das Ghettogericht," File Karl L., CSA-L.

Child of Sorrow.
Karl L., "Aus der Hölle," p. 151f.

Given the lack of support...
Karl L., "Aus der Hölle," p. 215

Decisive Action

From the beginning...
Karl L., "Aus der Hölle," pp. 164ff. and 246. □ Letter from Karl L. to the Jewish Elder Eppstein (9/5/1943) (copy), BT.

All this takes too long...
Karl L., "Aus der Hölle," p. 262ff. □ Spontaneous poem from Uri A., BT. □ Statement by Benjamin Murmelstein. □ "Die persönliche Einstellung des Angeklagten," and "Berufungsbegründung Karl L.'s durch Dr. Sieg. und Dr. Win. an das Ghetto-Strafgericht in Theresienstadt," Adler Collection (250n), NWD. □ "An das Ghettogericht," File Karl L., CSA-L., p. 10f.

The next day...
Letter from the Jewish Elder Eppstein to Karl L. (5/8/1943), photocopy of letter reproduced in Karl L., "Aus der Hölle," p. 264(a).

A Question of Method I.
L.'s relationship with Dr. Erich Munk...
Karl L., "Aus der Hölle," p. 249ff. □ Statement by Benjamin Murmelstein concerning Karl L., File Karl L., CSA-L. □ Adler Collection, p. 501f.

A Question of Method II.
In early May 1943...
Letter from Dr. Munk to the Jewish Elder concerning a suitcase with medications (5/5/1943) (copy), BT. □ Statement by Benjamin Murmelstein concerning Karl L., File Karl L., CSA-L.
The Jewish Elder Dr. Eppstein requests...
Letter from the Jewish Elder Eppstein to Karl L. (5/5/1943) (copy), BT. □ Letter from Karl L. to the Jewish Elder Eppstein (5/14/1943) (copy), BT.
Dr. Reinisch, however, confirms in writing...
Letter from Dr. Reinisch to the Jewish directorate (5/19/1943) (copy), BT. □ Protocol from Dr. Reinisch (6/1/1943) (copy), Adler Collection. □ Letter from the Jewish Elder Eppstein to Karl L. (5/22/1943) (copy), BT.
L. finds this repudiation incomprehensible...
Letter from Karl L. to the Jewish directorate (5/22/1943) (copy), BT.
Dr. Munk, however, is unwilling...
Letter from Dr. Munk to the Jewish directorate (5/25/1943) (copy), BT.
L. cannot endorse...
Letter from Karl L. to the Jewish directorate (6/16/1943) is missing. Reconstructed here from Karl L.'s letter of 6/24/1943 and Erich Munk's letter of 6/18/1943 (see below).
Dr. Munk (June 18, 1943)...
Letter from Dr. Munk to the Jewish directorate (6/18/1943) (copy), BT.
L. sticks to his position (June 24, 1943)...
Letter from Karl L. to the Jewish directorate (6/24/1943) (copy), BT.
This is too much...
Memorandum by Dr. Munk concerning his visit with the Camp Commandant Dr. Seidl (6/24/1943) (copy), BT. □ Letter from Dr. Munk to the Jewish directorate (6/24/1943) (copy), BT. □ Meeting of the Jewish directorate on 6/24/1943 (copy), BT.
Two and a half months later...
Letter from Karl L. to Dr. Munk (9/2/1943) (copy), Adler Collection (250n), NWD.

Before the Fall
Public Relations.
Karl L., "Aus der Hölle," pp. 169ff. and 150. □ Bondy, p. 370. □ Gonda Redlich's diary entry 3/24–25/1943, *Terezin Diary*, p. 109f.
Pinnacle.
Karl L., "Aus der Hölle," pp. 135 and 138ff. □ Gonda Redlich's diary entry from 1/1/1943, *Terezin Diary*, p. 94. □ Program for the performances after the parade, undated commmunication from Karl L. to H. G. Adler, Adler Collection (250n), NWD.
The parade...
Bondy, p. 351. □ H. G. Adler's notes on Philipp Manes's unpublished manuscript "Tatsachenbericht," Adler Collection.

Ouster
On June 3, 1943...
Adler, p. 138. □ Gonda Redlich's diary entry from 6/22/1943, *Terezin Diary*, p. 122. □ See also correspondence from Karl L. to H. G. Adler (2/24/1961), Adler Collection (250n), NWD. □ Karl L., "Aus der Hölle," p. 145ff.
Intrigue.
"Berufungsbegründung Karl L.'s durch Dr. Sieg. und Dr. Win. an das Ghetto-Strafgericht in Theresienstadt," Adler Collection (250n), NWD. □ "An das Ghettogericht." □ Adler, p. 141f. □ Karl L., "Aus der Hölle," File Karl L., CSA-L, p. 270ff. □ Letter from Dr. Vladimir W. to SS-Obersturmführer Karl Bergel (10/30/1943), Adler Collection (250n), NWD.
On September 1, 1943...
Judgment of the Ghetto Court (8/30/1943) (copy), Adler Collection (250n), NWD. □ "An das Ghettogericht," File Karl L., CSA-L. □ "Berufungsbegründung," Adler Collection (250n), NWD.
L. himself does not deny the facts...
"Berufungsbegründung," Adler Collection (250n), NWD. □ "An das Ghettogericht," File Karl L., CSA-L. □ Bianka H. (Karl L.'s former mother-in-law), Central Card Index, BT.
Appeal.
"An das Ghettogericht," File Karl L., CSA-L. □ "Berufungsbegründung,"Adler Collection (250n), NWD. □ Judgment of the Court of Appeals of the Ghetto Court (9/13/1943) (copy), Adler Collection (250n), NWD. □ "Urteil und Strafverfügung: Tagesbefehl des Ältestenrats" (9/17/1943), BT.

L. is particularly outraged…
"An das Ghettogericht," File Karl L., CSA-L. □ See letter from Karl L. to Herr Schliesser (11/3/1942), Adler Collection (250n), NWD. □ Letter from Head Cook F. (8/28/1943), Adler Collection (250n), NWD.
L. plans to petition…
Letter from Dr. Georg S. to Karl L. (9/14/1943), Adler Collection (250n), NWD. □ Letter from Dr. Georg S. to Karl L. (9/25/1943), Adler Collection (250n), NWD. □ "An das Ghettogericht," File Karl L., CSA-L. □ Statement by Benjamin Murmelstein concerning Karl L., File Karl L., CSA-L.
L.'s prison term begins…
"An das Ghettogericht," File Karl L., CSA-L. □ "Strafverfügung" (11/24/1943), Adler Collection (250n), NWD. □ "Beschwerde des Karl L.'s, vertreten durch Dr. Ludwig F., gegen die Strafverfügung vom 11/24/1943," Adler Collection (250n), NWD. □ Statement by Benjamin Murmelstein. □ Gonda Redlich's diary entry from 11/24/1943, *Terezin Diary*, p. 136.
In February 1944…
Karl L., "Aus der Hölle," p. 273f. □ Statement by Josef K. concerning Karl L. (12/10/1945), BT. □ Letter by Karl L. to the Czech investigators (9/2/1946), File Karl L., CSA-L. □ Handwritten memorandum concerning the civilian disciplinary court, Adler Collection (250n), NWD. □ Dr. Otto Stargardt, "Gutachtliches Äußerung zum Prozesse gegen Dr. L. in Theresienstadt" (5/2/1945), Adler Collection (250n), NWD. □ "Gutachten des Oberlandesgerichtsrates Dr. Arthur Goldschmidt" (10/2/1945), Adler Collection (250n), NWD.

Liberation
Following his release…
Statement by Benjamin Murmelstein concerning Karl L., File Karl L., CSA-L. □ Adler, p. 181ff. □ Miroslav Karny, "Die Theresienstädter Herbststransporte 1944," *Theresienstädter Studien und Dokumente 1996*, Prague (1996). □ Karl L., "Aus der Hölle," p. 291ff.
The fall transports…
Adler, pp. 188ff. and 235ff. □ Kárny. □ Karl L., "Meine erneute Festnahme," unpublished manuscript, ICH. □ See also correspondence from Marianne K. to Karl L. (7/7/1945), Adler Collection (250n), NWD.
In late June 1945…
Statement by Robert Prochník concerning Karl L., recorded by the repre-

sentative of the National Committee for Theresienstadt (6/12/1945) (copy), File Karl L., CSA-L. □ Statement by Jiri Vogel concerning Karl L. (10/16/1946), File Karl L., CSA-L. □ Letter from the representative of National Committee for Theresienstadt to the minister of the interior in Prague (7/17/1945), File Karl L., CSA-L. □ Statement by Miroslav K. (copy, excerpts, no date). □ Statement by Alice S., Hanus S., and Desider K. (9/28/1945), File Karl L., CSA-L. □ Statement by Benjamin Murmelstein, File Karl L., CSA-L. □ Statement by Alice S. (10/24/1945), File Karl L., CSA-L. □ Statement by Desider K. (10/30/1945), File Karl L., CSA-L. □ Statement by Hanus S. (11/2/1945). □ Statement by Otto K. (2/21/1946), File Karl L., CSA-L. □ Letter from Rabbi Leo Baeck (8/28/1946), File Karl L., CSA-L. □ Written statement from seven former members of the Ghetto Guard (n.d.), File Karl L., CSA-L. □ Letter from Karl L. to the investigating authorities (9/2/1946), File Karl L., CSA-L. □ Statement by Karl L. concerning his arrest (10/16/1946), File Karl L., CSA-L. □ Statement by Jiri Vogel (10/16/1946), File Karl L., CSA-L. □ Statement by Alice S. (10/18/1946), File Karl L., CSA-L. □ Statement by Hanus S. (10/18/1946), File Karl L., CSA-L. □ Statement by Vilém C. (n.d.), File Karl L., CSA-L. □ Statement by Miroslav K. (11/11/1946), File Karl L., CSA-L. □ Statement by Leo Holzer (12/6/1946), File Karl L., CSA-L. □ See also statement by Josef K. concerning Karl L. (12/10/1945), BT.

During the investigation...
Karl L., "Meine erneute Festnahme," 2ff. □ Letter from Karl L. to the Compensation Office (8/12/1954), CompB, B88. □ Investigators' report to the director of national security in Prague (3/28/1946), File Karl L., CSA-L. □ Statement by Leopold G. concerning Karl L. (12/2/1946), File Karl L., CSA-L. □ Statement by Dr. Richard P. (12/2/1946), File Karl L., CSA-L. □ Statement by Dr. Arnost M. (1/7/1947), File Karl L., CSA-L. □ Statement by Oskar H. (1/8/1947), File Karl L., CSA-L. □ Confirmation of the War Court in Litoměřice (1/13/1947), Karl L.'s compensation files, C3. □ "Decision of the Chamber of the District Court in Litoměřice in Its Secret Sitting in the Criminal Case Against Charles L.," File Karl L., CSA-L.

Homeless
After his release...
Letter from Karl L. to the Restitution Office, RestB, 82 WGA 47/50, p. 16. □ Karl L.'s travel papers ("Movement Authority" from the Ministry of the Interior of the Czechoslovak Republic), CompB, D43. □ Application for emigration and immigration costs (11/30/1954), CompB, D26.

Getting to Australia…
Letter from Karl L. to the Restitution Office, RestB, 82 WGA 47/50, p. 16. □ Application for emigration and immigration costs, CompB, D26.
Melbourne.
Karl L.'s B Form (Damages to Body and Health), CompB, B1. □ Letter from Karl L. to H. G. Adler (6/19/1948), Adler's unpublished papers, GLA/SN.
At seven in the morning…
Letter from Karl L. to H. G. Adler (11/1/1948), Adler's unpublished papers, GLA/SN. □ Letter from Karl L. to Adler (7/18/1949), GLA/SN.
In spite of this…
Letters from Karl L. to H. G. Adler (12/24/1949, 9/16/1950, 1/8/1951, 9/12/1951, and 9/5/1952), GLA/SN. □ Letter from the Victorian Railroad Commissioner's Office to Sir Archie Michaelis (5/6/1952), CompB, M11. □ Karl L., "Kurzer Lebenslauf zum Antrag auf Entschädigung," CompB, M5.

Homecoming

Application for emigration and immigration costs (11/30/1954), CompB, D26. □ Letter from Karl L. to the Compensation Office (10/23/1952), CompB, M25. □ Letter from Karl L. to the Compensation Office (7/30/1953), M58. □ Memorandum by the Compensation Office, CompB, PrV 6.

Compensation

L.'s hopes for prompt compensation…
Letter from Karl L. to the Compensation Office (9/26/1952), CompB, M14. □ Letter from the Berlin Compensation Office to Karl L. (10/1/1952), CompB, M13. □ Letter from the Berlin Compensation Office to Karl L. (10/15/1952), CompB, M20. □ Letter from Karl L. to the Compensation Office (10/29/1952), CompB, M25.
Category B.
Decision (6/11/1953), CompB, B29. □ Letter from Karl L. to the Compensation Office (6/12/1953), CompB, B30. □ Medical report from the surgeon Dr. Sm. (Aug. 1953), CompB, B43. □ Letter from the Compensation Office to Karl L., CompB, B47. □ Letter from Karl L. to the Compensation Office (6/22/1954), CompB, B84. □ Rejection of Karl L.'s petition by the Compensation Office (8/2/1954), CompB, B85. □ Letter from Karl L. to the Compensation Office (8/12/1954), CompB, B88/M7. □ Medical cer-

tificate from Dr. Felix Meyer (8/18/1954), CompB, B92. □ Negative decision (11/4/1954), CompB, B105. □ Letter from Karl L. to the Compensation Office (1/18/1955), CompB, B116. □ Statutory declaration by Dr. H. (12/13/1954), CompB, B123. □ Medical report by Professor V. □ Medical report by Professor R. (1/6/1955), CompB, B118. □ Letter from Karl L. to the Compensation Office (1/18/1955), CompB, B116. □ Alteration of Decision (2/18/1955), CompB, B132. □ Certification from I. F., director of the Accident Department of the United Woolen Mills in Melbourne (10/5/1956), CompB, B209. □ Letter of confirmation from Dr. R. S. (10/15/1956), CompB, B210. □ Report by Dr. H. (10/9/1956). □ Opinion of the Compensation Office (4/10/1970), CompB, B238ff.

Category C.
Karl L.'s C Form, CompB, C1. □ Letter from the Compensation Office to Karl L. (2/18/1953), CompB, C18.

Category D.
Communication from tax officials in Berlin-Weissensee (3/27/1952), CompB, D5. □ Statutory declaration by Marthe W. (10/2/1952), CompB, M22. □ Statutory declaration by Eckart T. (9/25/1952 and 10/13/1952), CompB, M18, M23. □ Statutory declaration by Reverend B. (9/28/1952), CompB, M17. □ Statutory declaration by Charlotte M. (9/24/1952), CompB, PrV8. □ Letter from Rabbi Leo Baeck (5/27/1954), CompB, E21. □ Statutory declaration by Arthur K. (7/15/1954), CompB, E24. □ Declaration by Arno R. (10/10/1954), CompB, M24. □ Declaration by Professor V. and Irmgard V., RestB, 83 WGA 2176/51, vol. 1, p. 39. □ Karl L.'s application for emigration and immigration costs (11/30/1954), CompB, D26. □ Partial decision from 1/10/1954, D35. □ Decision from 11/30/1954, CompB, D44. □ Final decision from 11/19/1959, CompB, D82.

Category E.
Communication from tax officials in Berlin-Weissensee (3/27/1952), CompB, D5. □ Letter from Karl L. to the Compensation Office (10/19/1953), B63. □ Decision (11/19/1957), E36.

Restitution (Material)
Between 1952 and 1960...
Karl L.'s restitution files, RestB.
L.'s chief object of interest...
Karl L., "Kurzer Lebenslauf zum Antrag auf Entschädigung," CompB, M5.

Apartment Buildings.
Karl L.'s restitution files, 3 WGA 78.50, RestB. □ Letter from Karl L. to the Restitution Office in Berlin (11/11/1952), RestB, 83 WGA 2176/51, p. 15.

HBG—Gentlemen's Clothing Company.
Karl L.'s restitution files, 83 WGA 2177/51 (3 vols.), RestB. □ Letter from Karl L. to the Restitution Office in Berlin-Schöneberg (1/6/1953), RestB, 83 WGA 2177/51, vol. 2, p. 28. □ Partial decision of the Restitution Court (1/27/1956), RestB, vol. 1, p. 158. □ Decision of the Third Court of Appeals (4/2/1958), RestB, vol. 1, p. 231. □ Decision of the Highest Restitution Court (12/13/1962), RestB, vol. 2, p. 9. □ Final decision of the Restitution Court (2/10/1966), RestB, vol. 2, p. 75.

Busse & Co.
Karl L.'s restitution files, 83 WGA 2176/51 (2 vols.). □ Communication from Karl L. to the Restitution Office regarding Schliessmann, von Moltke, Albrecht, and Margot M., RestB, p. 77. □ Written declaration by employees at Schmidt's company, vol. 1, p. 120. □ Leonhardt Schliessmann's SS file (born on 9/5/1877), GFA-B. □ Justification of the judgment (11/16/1956), RestB, 83 WGA 2176/51, vol. 1, p. 170. □ Statement by Arno R. (1968), RestB, 83 WGA 2176/51, vol. 2, p. 191. □ Final decision (2/11/1960), vol. 1, p. 236ff. □ Decision (12/14/1960), RestB, 83 WGA 3621/59, p. 21. □ "A. Busse & Co. Aktiengesellschaft in Berlin," *Handbuch der Deutschen Aktiengesellschaften*, 1923–43.

Restitution (Ideal)
Letters from Karl L. to H. G. Adler (7/4/1957, 6/9/1958, 6/16/1958, 3/1/1961, and 3/8/1961), Adler's unpublished papers, GLA/SN.

Working Through the Past
L. continues to intervene...
Letter from Rudolf K. to Karl L. (2/22/1959), Adler Collection (250n), NWD. □ Letter from Karl L. to H. G. Adler (11/25/1963), Adler's unpublished papers, GLA/SN.

In addition to this...
Letters from Karl L. to H.G. Adler (11/1/1948 and 4/3/1953), Adler's unpublished papers, GLA/SN. □ Letter from Karl L. to Grete Salus (11/29/1957) (copy), Adler Collection.

The past, however...
Lederer, *Ghetto Theresienstadt*, pp. 59–60 and 94. □ Letter from Karl L.

to H. G. Adler (4/12/1954), Adler's unpublished papers, GLA/SN. □ Adler, p. 136. □ Letter from Karl L. to Professor Emil U. (6/18/1956), File Karl L., BT.

L. himself writes bluntly...

Karl L., "Aus der Hölle," p. 224ff. □ Letter from Karl L. to Dr. Helmut Krausnick (8/19/1957), File Karl L., ICH. □ Evaluation of L.'s manuscript, commissioned by the Christian-Jewish Society in Berlin (no date), Adler's unpublished papers, GLA/SN. □ Letter from B. (coworker at Yad Vashem) to Karl L. (1/23/1963), Adler's unpublished papers, GLA/SN. □ See also letter from Karl L. to H. G. Adler (4/3/1953), Adler Collection, GLA/SN.

In 1956, L.'s chapter on Minsk...

Karl L., "Minsk: Im Lager der deutschen Juden," *Aus Politik und Zeitgeschichte,* supplement to *Das Parlament* (11/7/1956). □ Karl L., "Aus der Hölle," *Die Mahnung,* 10/1/1957–4/1/1958. □ Karl L., "Meine erneute Festnahme," unpublished manuscript, ICH.

Light and Shadows

Grete Salus, "Eine Frau erzählt," *Aus Politik und Zeitgeschichte* (10/30/1957), p. 700. □ Letter from Karl L. to H. G. Adler (11/9/1957), Adler's unpublished papers, GLA/SN. □ Letter from Grete Salus to Karl L. (11/14/1957) (copy), Adler Collection, GLA/SN. □ Letter from Karl L. to Grete Salus (11/29/1957) (copy), Adler Collection, GLA/SN.

A Question of Honor

Opinion of the Compensation Office (4/10/1970), CompB, B238ff. □ Report by the Compensation Office (2/11/1971), CompB, B249.

"That the just also receive justice..."

(Excerpt from H. G. Adler's character sketch of Karl L., in a letter from Adler to Karl L. for use in his restitution cases [3/12/1954], RestB.)

In February 1960...

Letter from L.s lawyer Dr. M. to the Restitution Court (3/9/1960), RestB, 83 WGA 2176/51. □ Decision of the Third Court of Appeals (11/2/1960), vol. 1, p. 264. □ Letter from Karl L. to the chairman of the 150th Restitution Court of the Regional Court of Berlin (10/2/1963), RestB, 83 WGA 2176/51, vol. 2, p. 24.

First Success.

Decision (1/26/1965), vol. 2, p. 70. □ Immediate appeals, RestB, 83 WGA 2176/51, vol. 2, p. 90f.

Two years later...

Decision of the Third Court of Appeals (1/23/1967), RestB, 83 WGA 2176/51, vol. 2, p. 142.

At roughly the same time...

Decision of the Third Court of Appeals (1/25/1967), RestB, 83 WGA 2177/51, vol. 2, p. 126. □ Memorandum concerning the Hennig estate's share of the proposed settlement (2/14/1968), RestB, 83 WGA 2177/51, vol. 2, p. 200.

At the end of October 1968...

Petition for a written expert's report, RestB, 83 WGA 2177/51, vol. 2, p. 31. □ Decision regarding evidence, vol. 2, p. 213.

Due to a number of unfavorable coincidences...

Correspondence between the Regional Court of Berlin and various auditors (Professor B. and Kurt S., Heinz B., Heinz B., Rudolf G., Professor Heinz L., Dr. Berhard W.), RestB, 83 WGA 2177/51, vol. 2, p. 216ff. □ Expert report by Professor Berhard B. (8/3/1973), RestB, 83 WGA 2176/51, vol. 3, p. 10.

At the beginning of 1974...

Letter from Karl L. to the Regional Court in Berlin (1/28/1974), RestB, 83 WGA 2176/51, vol. 3, p. 38.

In July 1974...

Communication from Karl L.'s lawyer to the Regional Court of Berlin (7/3/1974), RestB, 83 WGA 2176/51, vol. 2, p. 196. □ Memorandum concerning an offer for damage settlement, RestB, 83 WGA 2177/51, vol. 3, p. 54.

Max Schmidt offers...

Communication from Max Schmidt through his lawyer to the Regional Court of Berlin, RestB, 83 WGA 2176/51, vol. 2, p. 205. □ Memorandum concerning the Hennig estate, RestB, 83 WGA 2177/51, vol. 3, p. 58.

On August 9, 1975...

Death certificate for Karl L., Registry Office in Bad Neuenahr-Ahrweiler.

Two years elapse...

Letter from Horst L. to the Regional Court of Berlin (8/23/1977), RestB, 83 WGA 2177/51, vol. 3, p. 72.

On December 11, 1979...

Letter from Judge S. (Regional Court of Berlin) to Karl L.'s heirs (12/11/1979), RestB, 83 WGA 2176/51, vol. 2, p. 274a.

Since the court...
Decision, RestB, 83 WGA 2176/51, vol. 2, p. 260. ☐ Decision (10/23/1981), RestB, 83 WGA 2177/51, vol. 3, p. 75.

Precautionary Measures

Monthy report of the Reichenhall Gendarmerie Station, Berchtesgaden district (12/29/1938), ICH. ☐ Special report of the Reichenhall Gendarmerie Station, Berchtesgaden district (12/15/1938), ICH. Both reports are reproduced in *Bayern in der NS-Zeit: Sozial Lage und politischer Verhalten der Bevölkerung im Spiegel vertraulicher Berichte,* Martin Broszat, Elke Fröhlich, and Falk Wiesemann (eds.), Munich (1977), p. 476. See also Wolfgang Benz, "Bericht über die Barbarei: Bericht über den Pogrom," *Der Judenpogrom 1938: Von der "Reichskristallnacht" zum Völkermord,* Walter Pehle (ed.), Frankfurt am Main (1992), p. 51.

Structural Transformation of the Public Sphere

At the end of August 1942...
Statement by Max R. concerning Wilhelm H. (11/13/1942), file of senior Reich's attorney at the People's Court against Wilhelm H., German Federal Archive, Temporary Archive Dahlwitz-Hoppegarten. ☐ Interrogation of Wilhelm H. (11/13/1942), file of senior Reich's attorney, German Federal Archive, Temporary Archive Dahlwitz-Hoppergarten. ☐ Letter from the chief public prosecutor to the senior Reich's attorney at the People's Court (11/24/1942), file of the criminal proceedings against Wilhelm H., GFA-B. ☐ Judgment of the People's Court (First Court) against Wilhelm H. for conspiracy to commit high treason, etc. (3/8/1943), file of the criminal proceedings against Wilhelm H., GFA-B. ☐ The materials concerning Wilhelm H.'s case are reproduced in part in *Der lautlose Aufstand: Berichte über die Widerstandsbewegung des deutschen Volkes 1933– 1945,* Günther Weisenborn (ed.), Hamburg (1953), p. 333ff. (Appendix: "Ein alter Mann in der Maschinerie der NS-Justiz.")

In Custody
Report of the 107th Police Station (10/28/1942), file of senior Reich's attorney, German Federal Archive, Temporary Archive Dahlwitz-Hoppergarten. ☐ Interrogation of Wilhelm H. (11/13/1942), file of senior Reich's attorney,

German Federal Archive, Temporary Archive Dahlwitz-Hoppergarten. □ "Einlieferungsanzeige" (11/13/1942), file of senior Reich's attorney, German Federal Archive, Temporary Archive Dahlwitz-Hoppergarten. □ Krim.-Oberass. Z.'s final report (11/14/1942), file of senior Reich's attorney, German Federal Archive, Temporary Archive Dahlwitz-Hoppergarten. □ Letter from the chief public prosecutor to the senior Reich's attorney at the People's Court (11/24/1942), file of the criminal proceedings against Wilhelm H., GFA-B.

Investigation
Curriculum Vitae.

Interrogation of Wilhelm H. (11/13/1942), file of senior Reich's attorney, German Federal Archive, Temporary Archive Dahlwitz-Hoppergarten. □ Letter from the chief public prosecutor to the senior Reich's attorney at the People's Court (11/24/1942), file of the criminal proceedings against Wilhelm H., GFA-B. □ "Wesentliches Ergebnis der Ermittlungen," indictment of Wilhelm H. by the senior Reich's attorney at the People's Court (1/25/1943), file of the criminal proceedings against Wilhelm H., GFA-B. □ Judgment of the People's Court (First Court) against Wilhelm H. for conspiracy to commit high treason, etc. (3/8/1943), file of the criminal proceedings against Wilhelm H., GFA-B.

Financial Situation.

Krim.-Oberass. Z.'s final report (11/14/1942), file of senior Reich's attorney, German Federal Archive, Temporary Archive Dahlwitz-Hoppergarten. □ Judgment of the People's Court (First Court) against Wilhelm H.

State of Health.

Interrogation of Wilhelm H. (11/13/1942), file of senior Reich attorney. □ Memorandum by District Attorney S. (1/23/1943), file of the criminal proceedings against Wilhelm H., GFA-B.

Political Views.

Interrogation of Wilhelm H. (11/13/1942), file of senior Reich's attorney, German Federal Archive, Temporary Archive Dahlwitz-Hoppergarten. □ Krim.-Oberass. Z.'s final report.

Interrogation

Interrogation of Wilhelm H. (11/13/1942), file of senior Reich's attorney, German Federal Archive, Temporary Archive Dahlwitz-Hoppergarten. □ Essential results of the investigations, indictment of Wilhelm H. by the senior Reich's attorney at the People's Court (1/25/1943), file of the criminal proceedings against Wilhelm H., GFA-B.

People's Justice

Memorandum by District Attorney S. (1/23/1943), file of the criminal proceedings against Wilhelm H., GFA-B.

Indicted

Indictment of Wilhelm H. by the senior Reich's attorney at the People's Court (1/25/1943), file of the criminal proceedings against Wilhelm H., GFA-B.

Examined

Memorandum by District Attorney S., file of the criminal proceedings against Wilhelm H., GFA-B. □ Medical report (2/23/1943), file of the criminal proceedings against Wilhelm H., GFA-B.

In the Name of the German People (Top Secret!)

Judgment of the People's Court (First Court) against Wilhelm H. (11/13/1942), file of senior Reich's attorney, German Federal Archive, Temporary Archive Dahlwitz-Hoppergarten.

Due Process

Letter from the director of the Plötzensee Prison to the senior Reich's attorney at the People's Court (3/19/1943), file of the criminal proceedings against Wilhelm H., GFA-B. □ Letter from the senior Reich's attorney to the Reich's minister of justice (4/1/1943), file of the criminal proceedings against Wilhelm H., GFA-B. □ "Stellungnahme (Sachbearbeiter: EstA Dr. Fro. 4/13/1943)," file of the criminal proceedings against Wilhelm H., GFA-B. □ Letter from the Reich's minister of justice (represented by Dr. R.) to the senior Reich's attorney at the People's Court (4/30/1943), file of the criminal proceedings against Wilhelm H., GFA-B. □ Letter from Dr. Gerhardt R. to the People's Court (5/2/1943), file of the criminal proceedings against Wilhelm H., GFA-B.

Silence

"Vollstreckung des Todesurteils gegen Wilhelm H. (5/13/1943)," file of the criminal proceedings against Wilhelm H., GFA-B. □ Memorandum by the senior Reich's attorney at the People's Court (5/6/1943), file of the criminal proceedings against Wilhelm H., GFA-B. □ Draft of a press release, file of the criminal proceedings against Wilhelm H., GFA-B.

The Inability to Digest

On June 25, 1941...

Diary entries from 7/25–27/1941, Erich B.'s war diary, GFA-B, Bestand R 20 (Chef der Bandenkampfverbände), 45: Tagebuch des Chef des Bandenkampfverbände (1941–Ende 1942 Höherer SS- und Polizeiführer Rußland Mitte), SS-Obergruppenführer und General der Polizei Erich B.

On August 23, 1951, shortly after his first denazification trial, Erich B. presented to the Denazification Court in Munich a poorly perserved, water-damaged document that he claimed was his war diary and had been buried for six years in the vicinity of Salzburg, Austria. He offered the court the following explanation: "In April 1945, as commanding general of the Oder Corps, I ordered Leopold von S., major of the Tank Troops, who had been transferred to my staff, to bury my private files in a metal canister. He did not know the contents of the canister; but I did give him exact instructions as to where to bury it, in the vicinity of Rielern in the Walser Valley." The Denazification Court in Munich expressed no doubts about the authenticity of the diary, but found it—contrary to B.'s own claims—incriminating rather than exonerating. In 1955, B. turned the diary over the German Federal Archive in the following form: the original of the second part of the diary (May 1943 to Jan. 1945) and a typewritten copy of the entire diary, which B. claimed to have made from the original. According to the Bavarian State Police, it is possible that B. destroyed the first part of the original diary (which disappeared during his denazification trial in Munich) and forged the existing copy. It is likely that B. removed incriminating entries from the diary. The copy, however, is not simply a forgery. The historian Christian Gerlach writes, "Much of the information in the diary can be verified through other sources. It is, without a doubt, authentic in parts. The dating of some events, however, have been displaced one or two days" (*Kalkulierte Morde*, p. 549).

"Go-Getter"

Militarist.

Statement by Erich B. as a prisoner of war in Nuremberg (1946), NSA. *Pauper.*

Statement by Erich B. as a prisoner of war in Nuremberg (1946). □ Statement by Erich B. (5/1/1960), criminal proceedings against Erich B. before the Regional Court in Nuremberg, JS 228/60, KS 3/30, vol. 7, S.1467, NSA.

"A One-Hundred-Percenter."

Erich B.'s SS file, GFA-B. □ Interrogation of Erich Koch (11/30/1949), COSL, 200 AR-Z 52/59, document vol. 7.

Warhorse.

Diary entries from 3/11–12/1937, Erich B.'s diary (1/1/1937–12/31/1937), reprinted in *Acta Universitatis Wratislaviensis*, no. 638 (1982). □ Diary entry from June 27, 1941, Erich B.'s war diary, GFA-B.

Master Race.

Diary entries from 4/15/1937 and 10/19/1937, Erich B.'s diary, reprinted in *Acta*.

Posterity.

Diary entry from 11/25/1941, Erich B.'s war diary, GFA-B. □ Diary entry from 1/6/1937, Erich B.'s diary (1/1/1937–12/31/1937), reprinted in *Acta*.

Power Struggle (1935).

Erich B.'s SS file, GFA-B. □ Diary entry from 6/27/1941, Erich B.'s war diary, GFA-B.

Rehabilitated.

"Niederschrift über die am 8/11/1939 stattgefundene Besprechung beim Generalgouverneur Polen in Krakau" (copy), Erich B.'s SS file., GFA-B, reprinted in *Erich B: SS-Obergruppenführer und General der Polizei, Chef der Bandenkampf-Verbände der Waffen SS: Dokumentensammlung*, Tuviah Friedman (ed.), Haifa (1996). □ Letter from Erich B. to Karl Wolff (9/13/1940), Erich B.'s SS file, reprinted in Friedman.

Combat

July 1941.

Erich B.'s war diary, GFA-B.

Heroic Deeds.

"Bericht über den Verlauf der Pripjet-Aktion vom 7/27–8/11/1941" (Aug. 12,1941, copy of a copy), GFA-B, reprinted in *Unsere Ehre heißt Treue: Kriegstagebuch des Kommandostabes Reichsführer SS Tätigkeitsberichte der 1. und 2. SS-Inf.-Brigade, der 1. SS-Kav.-Brigade und von Sonderkommandos der SS*, p. 227ff. □ Diary entry from 8/3/1941, Erich B.'s war diary, GFA-B. □ Gerlach, *Kalkulierte Morde*, pp. 542ff. and 555ff. □ Ruth Bettina Birn, *Die Höheren SS- und Polizeiführer: Himmlers Vertreter im Reich und in den besetzten Gebieten*, Düsseldorf (1986), pp. 275–90.

During the Same Week.

Situation report from 8/7/1941, cited in diary entry from 8/5/1941, Erich B.'s war diary, GFA-B.

Kulturvolk.

Diary entry from 8/16/1941, Erich B.'s war diary. □ Gerlach, pp. 571ff., 646ff., and 1067ff. □ Raul Hilberg, *The Destruction of the European Jews,* 3rd ed., New Haven (2003), p. 343f.

Rest and Recuperation.

Diary entry from 8/19/1941, Erich B.'s war diary, GFA-B.

Back in Minsk.

Diary entry from 8/20/1941, Erich B.'s war diary, GFA-B. □ Statement by Hans Giese to the district attorney at the Regional Court in Nuremberg-Fürth (6/16/1962), StA Nuremberg-Fürth 1a Js 1409/60, COSL.

An Injustice.

Diary entry from 9/5/1941, Erich B.'s war diary, GFA-B.

The Loving Father.

Diary entry from 9/8/1941, Erich B.'s war diary, GFA-B.

Exemplary.

Diary entry from 9/13/1941, Erich B.'s war diary, GFA-B.

Evening Hours.

Diary entry.

Military Training.

Birn, p. 174.

The Spirit Is Willing

In spite of his successes...

Diary entry from 9/29/1941, Erich B.'s war diary, GFA-B.

Sonderaktion.

Gerlach, p. 587ff.

Bellyache.

Diary entries from 10/5–7 and 13/1941, Erich B.'s war diary, GFA-B.

Back to Work.

Diary entry from 10/14/1941, Erich B.'s war diary, GFA-B.

Civilized.

Letter from Erich B. to his wife October 26, 1941, cited in diary entry from 10/27/1941, Erich B.'s war diary, GFA-B. □ Gerlach, p. 592ff.

On the Battlefield.

Diary entry from 11/5/1941, Erich B.'s war diary.

Promoted.
 Erich B.'s SS file, GFA-B. □ Telegraph from Reichsführer-SS Himmler to Erich B. (11/3/1941), cited in diary entry from 11/5/1941, Erich B.'s war diary. □ Diary entry from 11/7/1941, Erich B.'s war diary.

Revived.
 Diary entries from 11/17, 19, 21, 23, and 25/1941, Erich B.'s war diary, GFA-B.

Iron Will.
 Diary entry from 12/9/1941, Erich B.'s war diary, GFA-B. □ Letter from Erich B. to SS-Gruppenführer Hildebrandt (12/5/1941), Erich B.'s SS file.

Decorated.
 Diary entry from 12/5/1941, Erich B.'s war diary, GFA-B.

Optimist.
 Diary entries from 12/10–11/1941, Erich B.'s war diary, GFA-B.

Reenergized.
 Diary entry from 12/17/1941, Erich B.'s war diary, GFA-B. □ Reichsführer-SS Himmler to Erich B., cited in diary entry from 12/19/1941, Erich B.'s war diary. □ Erich B. to Reichsführer-SS Himmler, cited in diary entry from 12/19/1941, Erich B.'s war diary, GFA-B.

Christmas.
 Diary entries from 12/20, 24, and 26/1941, Erich B.'s war diary, GFA-B.

New Year's.
 Diary entry from 1/18/1942, Erich B.'s war diary. □ See the files of the criminal proceedings against Erich B., StA Nuremberg-Fürth 128KLs 23/61, NSA.

Starvation Diet.
 Diary entry from 1/22/1942, Erich B.'s war diary, GFA-B.

Slacker.
 Diary entry from 1/28/1942, Erich B.'s war diary, GFA-B. □ See also Hans Giese's statement of May 5, 1962, StA Nuremberg-Fürth 1a Js 1409/60, COSL.

Course of Treatment
In February 1942...
 Karl Wolff's statement concerning Erich B. (2/2/1962), StA Munich I Ks 1/64, COSL. □ Letter from Reichsführer-SS Himmler to Reich's Physician SS-Gruppenführer Dr. Grawitz (3/18/1942), Erich B.'s SS file. □ Letter from SS-Brigadeführer Pückler to Reichsführer-SS Himmler (2/11/1942), Erich B.'s SS file, GFA-B.

Three days after Wolff's visit...

Letter from Erich B. to Reichsführer-SS Himmler (3/4/1942), Erich B.'s SS file, GFA-B.

On the same day...

Dr. Grawitz's report to Reichsführer-SS Himmler (3/4/1942), Erich B.'s SS file, GFA-B. □ Dr. Grawitz's interim report to Reichsführer-SS Himmler (3/9/1942), Erich B.'s SS file, GFA-B. □ See also letter from Reichsführer-SS Himmler to Dr. Grawitz (3/18/1942), Erich B.'s SS file, GFA-B.

Five days later...

Letter from Dr. Grawitz to Reichsführer-SS Himmler (3/9/1942), Erich B.'s SS file, GFA-B.

Dr. Grawitz's interim report...

Dr. Grawitz's interim report to Reichsführer-SS Himmler (3/9/1942).

In the third week of March...

Letter from Dr. Grawitz to Reichsführer-SS Himmler (3/21/1942), Erich B.'s SS file, GFA-B. □ Letter from Erich B. to Reichsführer-SS Himmler (3/31/1942), Erich B.'s SS file. □ Telegraph from Reichsführer-SS Himmler to Erich B. (4/6/1942), Erich B.'s SS file, GFA-B.

Restored

Back from his convalescent cure...

Diary entry (date unreadable) from the end of April 1942, Erich B.'s war diary, GFA-B.

Back in Mogilev...

Letter from Erich B. to his wife (5/7/1942), cited in diary entry from 5/7/1942, Erich B.'s war diary, GFA-B.

Return

B. is forced to crack down...

Letter from Erich B. to his wife (5/7/1942).

Back to Business.

Diary entry from 8/11/1942, Erich B.'s war diary.

Tactics.

HSSPF Russland-Mitte (Aug. 1942), GFA-B, NS 19n8, also cited in Birn, p. 45.

Old Ailment.

Diary entry from 8/31/1942, Erich B.'s war diary, GFA-B. □ Letter from Ruth B. to Erich B. (9/6/1942), cited in diary entry from 9/14/1942, Erich

B.'s war diary, GFA-B. □ Diary entry from 10/7/1942, Erich B.'s war diary, GFA-B.

> "At around 9:30 on the fifth, I received a very peculiar telephone call. When I picked up the receiver and said my name, a broken voice from far way said, 'Death is coming, death is coming.'
> —Excerpt from a letter from Ruth B. to Erich B. (9/6/1942), cited in diary entry from 9/14/1941, Erich B.'s war diary, GFA-B.

Selfless Dedication.
Erich B. to Reichsführer-SS Himmler, cited in diary entry from 10/17/1942, Erich B.'s war diary, GFA-B. □ Gerlach, pp. 680 and 1076.

Ambitions
On August 18, 1942...
"Weisung Nr. 46: Richtlinien für die verstärkte Bekämpfung des Bandenunwesens im Osten" (8/18/1942), Nuremberg Document 477-PS/ NO-1666, HI. □ Letter from Erich B. to Reichsführer-SS Himmler (9/5/1942), Nuremberg Document NO-1661, HI. □ Diary entries from 9/10/1942 and 5/22/1943, Erich B.'s war diary, GFA-B. □ Gerlach, p. 922ff.
Enterprising.
Gerlach, p. 898ff. □ Erich B.'s war diary, GFA-B.
Given Germany's increasingly difficult war situation...
"Richtlinien für die Maßnahmen zur Bandenbekämpfung" (2/26/1943), German Federal Archive, Temporary Archive Dahlwitz-Hoppegarten, ZM 1488 A6. □ See Gerlach, pp. 735f., 906ff., 955, and 973.
Further Responsibilities (End of June 1943).
Gerlach, pp. 951f. and 917f.
Pressure to Succeed.
Letter from Eberhard Herf to his cousin Maximilian v. Herff (chief of the SS-Personalhauptamt) (7/19/1943), GFA-B, NS 19 1214. □ Letter from Eberhard Herf to Maximilian v. Herff (7/29/1943). □ Diary entry from 9/28/1943, Erich B.'s war diary, GFA-B. □ See Gerlach, pp. 908 and 952ff.

Relapse

To B.'s dismay...

See Gerlach, pp. 980 and 1100.

Himmler's response (Mar. 12, 1944)...

Letter from Reichsführer-SS Himmler to Erich B. (3/12/1944), cited in diary entry from 3/18/1944, Erich B.'s war diary, GFA-B.

In Karlsbad...

Letter from Dr. Grawitz to Reichsführer-SS Himmler (3/24/1944), Erich B.'s SS file, GFA-B. □ Letter from Dr. Ernst R. (specialist for internal medicine) to Professor Umber (3/22/1944), Erich B.'s SS file, GFA-B. □ Diary entry from 3/18/1944, Erich B.'s war diary, GFA-B.

Impatient.

Diary entries from 4/20 and 24/1944, Erich B.'s war diary, GFA-B.

Temporary "Retirement"

Disappointments.

Diary entries from 5/13 and 7/3/1944, Erich B.'s war diary, GFA-B.

Truest of the True (July 20, 1944).

Letter from Erich B. to Ruth B., cited in diary entry from 7/20/1944, Erich B.'s war diary, GFA-B.

Call to Action.

Diary entry from 8/2/1944, Erich B.'s war diary, GFA-B.

Intensive Deployments

B. is entrusted with suppressing...

Diary entry from 8/15/1944, Erich B.'s war diary, GFA-B.

B.'s diary entry (Aug. 7, 1944)...

Diary entries from 8/7 and 18/1944, Erich B.'s war diary, GFA-B.

On August 23, 1944...

Diary entry from 8/24/1944, Erich B.'s war diary, GFA-B.

Bloody Hand-to-Hand Combat.

Diary entries from 8/24 to 9/28/1944, Erich B.'s war diary, GFA-B.

Feverish Heart.

Janusz Piekalkiewicz, *Kampf um Warschau: Stalins Verrat an der polnischen Heimatarmee 1944*, Munich (1994), p. 246ff. □ Diary entry from 9/29/1944, Erich B.'s war diary, GFA-B.

Supreme Honor.

Diary entry from 10/11/1944, Erich B.'s war diary, GFA-B.

Operation Panzerfaust.
Hilberg, p. 914. □ Admiral Miklós Horthy, *Memoirs,* Historical Text Archive, http://www.msstate.edu/Archives/History/hungary/horthy/21.html, ch. 21. □ Diary entries from 10/15–17/1944, Erich B.'s war diary, GFA-B.
While B. once again travels to Karlsbad...
Diary entries from 10/19 and 26/1944, Erich B.'s war diary, GFA-B. □ Hilberg, p. 915s.
Recovered.
Letter from Dr. Ernst R. to Professor Umber (11/1/1944), Erich B.'s SS file, GFA-B.

Until the Bitter End
Report by Bavarian State Office for the Protection of the Constitution (12/22/1958), NSA, no. 770. □ Statement by Erich B. as a prisoner of war in Nuremberg, NSA. □ Diary entry from 1/22/1945, Erich B.'s war diary, GFA-B.

Tactical Silence
In August 1945...
Report by Bavarian State Office for the Protection of the Constitution (12/22/1958), NSA, no. 770. □ Statement by Erich B. in Nuremberg (11/19/1947, 10:00 A.M.–12:00 P.M.), NSA. See also Gerlach, p. 651. □ Letter from Erich B. to the Denazification Court in Nuremberg (1/5/1949), COSL, AR-Z 52/59, document vol. 7.
Disadvantage...
"Hitler-Mann B. erzählt," *Süddeutsche Zeitung* (1/17/1961).

Denazification
At the end of January 1949...
Report by Bavarian State Office for the Protection of the Constitution. □ Letter from the Ministerialdirektor Camill Sachs to the chief prosecutor of the Denazification Court in Nuremberg (2/5/1949), NSA. □ Letter from Erich B. to the Denazification Court in Nuremberg (5/10/1949), COSL, AR-Z 52/59, document vol. 7.
Illness-Profit.
"Mein Widerstand gegen Auswüschse der nationalsozialistischen Weltanschauung und gegen ihre Befehle" (8/22/1949), COSL, 202 AR-Z52/59, document vol. 7.

At the end of 1949...

Report by Bavarian State Office for the Protection of the Constitution (12/22/1958), NSA, no. 770.

In November 1950...

"Anklageschrift des Generalkläger beim Kassationshof an die Hauptkammer München" (11/27/1950), COSL, 202 AR-Z52/59, document vol. 7.

Two weeks later...

Letter from Erich B. to the Denazification Court in Munich (12/12/1950), COSL, 202 AR-Z52/59, document vol. 7. □ Court records (3/14/1951), Denazification Court in Munich, COSL, 202 AR-Z52/59, document vol. 7. □ See also Gerlach, p. 1051.

At the end of March 1951...

Judgment of of the Denazification Court in Munich (3/30/1951, 3:00 P.M.), COSL, 202 AR-Z52/59, document vol. 7.

After this judgment...

Letter from Erich B. to the Denazification Court in Munich (8/23/1951), COSL, 202 AR-Z52/59, document vol. 7. □ Judgment of the Court of Appeals of the Denazification Court in Munich (Nuremberg, 12/22/1951), 199/51, H/Hi/9374/50, Amtsgericht Munich. □ Letter from Walter H. Rapp to Erich B. (12/19/1951), StA 128 KLs 23/61, NSA. □ "Die Toten stehen auf," *Der Spiegel* (1/7/1959), p. 24.

1954.

Decision of the First Criminal Division of the Regional Court in Nuremberg-Fürth (12/2/1954), StA Nuremberg-Fürth 3 c Js 1917/51, Amtsgericht Munich.

A Matter of Faith

Letter from the state bishop of the Evangelical Lutheran Church in Bavaria to Permanent Secretary Dr. M. (10/6/1954), COSL, 202 AR-Z52/59, document vol. 7. □ Report by Bavarian State Office for the Protection of the Constitution, COSL, 202 AR-Z52/59, document vol. 7. □ "Die Toten stehen auf."

Tried and True

"Ich war immer der typische Kommißkopp," *Frankfurter Allgemeine Zeitung* (1/17/1961).

Memory Gaps
In 1957...

Report by the district attorney's office at the Regional Court in Nuremberg-Fürth (7/30/1960), StA Nuremberg-Fürth 128KLs 23/61, NSA. □ Judgment by the Regional Court in Nuremberg-Fürth from 11/14, 15, and 17/1961, StA Nuremberg-Fürth 128KLs 23/61, NSA.

On August 18, 1960...

Medical report by Regional Medical Director Dr. Bitt. (8/18/1960), StA Nuremberg-Fürth 128KLs 23/61, NSA.

Three months later...

Statements by Dr. F., Dr. K., and Dr. D. concerning Erich B. (11/16/1960), StA Nuremberg-Fürth 128KLs 23/61, NSA.

The court rejects...

Judgment by the Regional Court in Nuremberg-Fürth, StA Nuremberg-Fürth 128KLs 23/61, NSA.

Undigested
In 1958...

Report by the district attorney's office at the Regional Court in Mannheim (7/30/1969), NSA, no. 770.

1959.

Letter from Reinhold G. to the district attorney's office in Nuremberg (2/9/1959), NSA, no. 770. □ Letter from Dr. Otto W. to the district attorney's office in Nuremberg (2/25/1959), StA Nuremberg-Fürth 128KLs 23/61, NSA. □ Letter from Harald K. to the district attorney's office in Nuremberg (5/30/1959).

A Special Commission Erich B....

Report by the district attorney's office in Nuremberg (9/15/1959), NSA, no. 770. □ Memorandum by the Special Commission Erich B. (11/2/1959), NSA, no. 770.

Over the next three years...

Report by the district attorney's office in Nuremberg (3/9/1962), NSA, no. 770.

In August 1962...

Report by the district attorney's office at the Regional Court in Mannheim (7/30/1969), NSA, no. 770. □ Memorandum by the district attorney at the Regional Court in Nuremberg-Fürth (6/10/1963), NSA, no. 770.

For six years...
Report by the district attorney's office at the Regional Court in Mannheim (7/30/1969), NSA, no. 770.

Despite numerous reports...
Memoranda by the district attorney at the Regional Court in Nuremberg-Fürth (4/9/1965 and 6/6/1965), StA Nuremberg-Fürth 128KLs 23/61, NSA. □ Report by the district attorney's office at the Regional Court in Mannheim (7/30/1969), NSA, no. 770. □ Erich B.'s file at the Straubing Penitentiary, StA Nuremberg-Fürth JS 228/60, KS 3/60, NSA.

An Authoritarian Personality

In December 1942...
Judgment of the Regional Court in Düsseldorf (9/3/1965), Criminal Proceedings of the Second Greater Criminal Divison of the Regional Court in Düsseldorf (8 Ks 2/64), central office of the State Nordrhein-Westfalen for the Handling of Nazi Crimes at the district attorney's office in Dortmund. An English translation of the judgment is reproduced in *The Death Camp Treblinka: A Documentary,* Alexander Donat (ed.), New York (1979), pp. 312–14.

Attempt at an Explanation
In 1965...
Judgment of the Regional Court in Düsseldorf (9/3/1965), Criminal Proceedings of the Second Greater Criminal Divison of the Regional Court in Düsseldorf (8 Ks 2/64).

At the end of January 1965...
Summons for Konrad Lorenz to appear before the Second Greater Criminal Division of the Regional Court in Düsseldorf (1/29/1965). □ On May 1, 1938, shortly after the German annexation, or Anschluss, of Austria, Lorenz applied for membership to Nazi Party. He was accepted on June 6, 1938 (membership no. 6170554). See Lorenz's personal file, GFA-B. □ I was unable to find a complete version of Lorenz's testimony. Regional courts in Germany are not required to keep a verbatim protocol of court proceedings. Lorenz presented his report to the Regional Court in Düsseldorf orally, without submitting a written version of it. Court records indicate that his testimony of February 4, 1965 was recorded on audiotape. The tapes of the trial could not be located; according to the district

attorney's office in Düsseldorf, they were probably erased shortly after the trial. The Regional Court in Düsseldorf appears to have recorded Lorenz's report only in summerized form. In the files of the court proceedings, I was able to locate three written summaries: (1) a very brief handwritten protocol of February 2, 1965; (2) a slightly longer, typed summary for the protocol of February 2, 1965; (3) a summary continued in the judgment of the Regional Court. I was also unable to locate any material about the report in archives containing Lorenz's papers. The Konrad Lorenz Institut für Evolutions- und Kognitionsforschung reported that there is no mention of the report in Lorenz's unpublished papers. There was also no information about the report in the archive of the Austrian Academies of Sciences in Vienna or the archive of the Max Planck Society in Berlin.

The Regional Court in Düsseldorf...
Judgment of the Regional Court in Düsseldorf (9/3/1965).

> "The path to understanding human beings proceeds through understanding animals, just as the path which led to the development of human beings itself undoubtedly proceeded through that of animals."
> —Konrad Lorenz in his "Russian Manuscript," written 1944–46 during his internment as a prisoner of war in White Ruthenia.

A New Beginning

In April 1939...
Draft of a letter concerning Dr. E. to the chief of the Security Police and the SD (May 1943), ICH, MA-541. □ Letter from Dr. E. to Alfred Rosenberg (1/17/1944), ICH, MA-541. □ Memorandum concerning the White Ruthenian Self-Help Organization (1/8/1943), ICH, MA-541.

Self-Help
Draft of a letter concerning Dr. E., ICH, MA-541. □ Letter from Dr. E. to Alfred Rosenberg (1/17/1944). □ Gerlach, p. 209ff.

Trials and Tribulations
The country is poor...
Alexander Dallin, *German Rule in Russia,* London (1957), p. 199ff. □
Letter from Dr. E. to Alfred Rosenberg, ICH, MA-541. □ Nicholas P.
Vakar, *Belorussia: The Making of a Nation,* Cambridge (1956).
The SS regards Dr. E mistrustfully...
Memorandum concerning the White Ruthenian Self-Help Organization,
ICH, MA-541. □ Letter from SS-Brigadeführer Curt von Gottberg, ICH,
MA-541.
Dr. E. enjoys active support...
Memorandum concerning the White Ruthenian Self-Help Organization,
ICH, MA-541. □ Memorandum concerning a material guarantee for Dr.
E. in Prague (draft, 7/24/1943), ICH, MA-541.
Dr. E.'s personal relations...
Letter from SS-Obersturmbannführer Dr. Eduard Strauch to SS-
Obergruppenführer Erich von dem Bach concerning General Commis-
sioner K. (7/25/1943), Nuremberg Document NO-2262, HI. □ Letter
from Dr. E. to Alfred Rosenberg (1/17/1944), ICH, MA-541.

Encircled
Outside the larger cities...
Dallin, p. 209ff. □ Letter from Dr. E. to Alfred Rosenberg (1/17/1944),
ICH, MA-541. □ Memorandum by Professor M. concerning Dr. E.,
head of the White Ruthenian Self-Help Organization (7/7/1943), ICH,
MA-541.
The SS proves to be...
Letter from SS-Obersturmbannführer Dr. Eduard Strauch to SS-
Obergruppenführer Erich von dem Bach concerning General Commis-
sioner K. (7/25/1943), Nuremberg Document NO-2262, HI. □ Letter
from Dr. E. to Alfred Rosenberg. □ Letter from Professor M. concerning
Dr. E. (2/11/1944). □ Draft of a letter concerning Dr. E. to the chief of
the Security Police and the SD (May 1943), ICH, MA-541.
A week later...
Letter from Dr. E. to Alfred Rosenberg (1/17/1944), ICH, MA-541.

On His Own
During Dr. E.'s absence...
Letter from SS-Standartenführer Dr. Ehrlich (6/17/1943). □ Memoran-
dum by Professor M. concerning Dr. E. □ Letter from General Commis-

sioner K. to the Reich's minister for the Occupied Eastern Territories (7/20/1943). □ Memorandum concerning a material guarantee for Dr. E. in Prague (draft, 7/24/1943). □ Letter from Dr. E. to Alfred Rosenberg.

In Prague...

Letter from Professor M. concerning Dr. E. □ Letter from Dr. E. to Alfred Rosenberg. □ Memorandum by SS-Hauptsturmführer B. (5/6/1943). □ Memorandum (6/10/1943).

Dr. E.'s attempts to reestablish...

Memorandum by Professor M. concerning Dr. E. □ Memorandum concerning a material guarantee for Dr. E. in Prague (draft, 7/24/1943).

In the middle of July 1943...

Letter from General Commissioner K. □ Letter from SS-Brigadeführer Curt von Gottberg to SS-Obergruppenführer Erich von dem Bach concerning Wilhelm K. (7/21/1943), Nuremberg document NO-4316, HI.

The Eastern Ministry decides...

Memorandum concerning a material guarantee for Dr. E.

Last Try

Letter from Dr. E. to Alfred Rosenberg. □ Dallin, p. 220ff.

Land of the Free

In the middle of January 1948...

Alien Passenger Manifest, *SS Marine Flasher* sailing from Bremen on January 18, 1948, arriving in New York on January 29, 1948, United States National Archives.

Dr. E. adapts quickly to New York City...

Dr. E.'s application to the Broome County Medical Society (Medical Society of the State of New York), 3/5/1959.

In New York...

"The Aspirations of the White Ruthenians (A Radio Interview with Dr. John E.)," *Ukrainian Quarterly* (1948), p. 67ff.

In 1949...

Dr. E.'s application to the Broome County Medical Society. □ See also John Loftus, *The Belarus Secret: The Nazi Connection in America,* (ed. Nathan Miller), New York (1989), pp. 33 and 91. □ "Bylelorussian Political Organization (files 105-15155 and 105-89748)," Federal Bureau of Investigation, Washington DC.

On May 7, 1956...

Letter from Immigration and Naturalization Service (Buffalo, New York) to the author (5/4/1999). □ Dr. E.'s application to the Broome County Medical Society. □ Letter from the Federal Bureau of Investigation to the author (8/12/1999). □ Letters from the Department of the Army, United States Army Intelligence and Security Command to the author (10/2/1998, 11/23/1998, and 7/8/1999). □ Letter from the Central Intelligence Agency to the author (7/23/1999).

At the age of seventy-two...

"Dr. John E.; Rites Saturday" [obituary], *Glen Cove Record* (2/1970).